A HUG A DAY
FOR SINGLE PARENTS

Another book by Patricia Lorenz:

Stuff that Matters for Single Parents

She is also a contributing writer for the following books:

Daily Guideposts Books
1987, 1988, 1989, 1990, 1991
1992, 1995, 1996, 1997, 1998

Guiltless Catholic Parenting from A to Y

A 2nd Helping of Chicken Soup for the Soul

The Key to Contentment and Happiness

A 3rd Serving of Chicken Soup for the Soul

A 4th Course of Chicken Soup for the Soul

Chicken Soup for the Mother's Soul

Healthy Aging ... Inspirational Letters from Americans

Over 400 of her articles have appeared in magazines including
Reader's Digest, Guideposts, Working Mother, Woman's World,
and *Single Parent Family.*

A Hug a Day
for Single Parents

℃

365 Down-to-Earth Daily Devotions

PATRICIA LORENZ

CHARIS

SERVANT PUBLICATIONS
ANN ARBOR, MICHIGAN

Charis Books is an imprint of Servant Publications especially designed to serve
Roman Catholics.

Scripture quotations are taken from *The Living Bible,* copyright 1971. Used by permission of Tyndale House Publishers, Inc. All rights reserved.

Excerpts from *The Psychology of Achievement* audio program by Brian Tracy. © 1984
by Nightingale-Conant Corporation. Reprinted by permission of Nightingale-
Conant Corporation.

Excerpts from this book have been adapted or reprinted from *Daily Guideposts*
books—1987, 1988, 1989, 1990, 1991, 1992, 1995, 1996, and 1997 editions with
permission from Guideposts. Copyrights for all these books are held by
Guideposts, Carmel, NY 10512, registered the year in which the book was released.

Published by Servant Publications
P.O. Box 8617
Ann Arbor, Michigan 48107

97 98 99 00 10 9 8 7 6 5 4 3 2 1

Printed in the United States of America
ISBN 0-89283-993-7

LIBRARY OF CONGRESS CATALOGING-IN-PUBLICATION DATA

Lorenz, Patricia.
A hug a day for single parents : 365 down-to-earth daily devotions / Patricia
Lorenz.
   p.   cm.
ISBN 0-89283-993-7
1. Single parents—Prayer-books and devotions—English.   2. Devotional calendars.
3. Christian life.   I. Title.
BV4596.S48L67   1997
242'.645—dc21   97-7362
                                                                CIP

Dedicated to

All the people I love to hug,

Especially my children:

Jeanne, Julia, Michael, and Andrew,

my daughter-in-law, Amy,

granddaughters, Hailey and Hannah,

and all my friends and relatives

who keep me well supplied with

warm, loving, wonderful, necessary hugs.

A Prayer for January

Thank you, Father,
For a new beginning
Each January first
To take stock
Make repairs
Plan changes
Start anew.

How marvelous
Your grand plan
Of changing seasons
And new years.
It's so good of You
To give us an opportunity
For change.

This year, help me
Mend broken friendships
Break bad habits
Speak more gently
Forgive more quickly
Love harder
And in general, Lord,
Be a better parent to my children.

JANUARY 1

"Accentuate the positive ... eliminate the negative": these six words can change your life if you take them to heart.

So many things are bad for us: pesticides, fat, preservatives, cholesterol, caffeine, and nicotine. The list of no-no's keeps getting longer every year. But one wonderful thing is still risk-free, wholesome, and heartwarming. It makes you feel good all over and doesn't cost a cent. It's fun to give, terrific to get, and stays with you for hours.

What is it? A hug!

Hugs are wonderful, especially for those of us single parents who don't get enough affection. This year, every day, let's give and receive more hugs than we've ever received or given in any single year.

Think about all the people you know who could use a good hug. How about the baby-sitter who takes such good care of your children. A sick friend. Or a working mother. Most of all, don't let your children leave the house in the morning, come home, or go to bed without a big hug.

Let's make a great New Year's resolution! Every day we'll open up those two good arms God us and give someone a hug. Too far away to reach? Give them a long-distance hug by sending a few prayers their way.

Lord, help me to reach out to others ... and squeeze!

So he returned home to his father. And while he was still a long distance away, his father saw him coming, and was filled with loving pity and ran and embraced him and kissed him.   LUKE 15:20

JANUARY 2

While my son, Michael, was a student at the University of Wisconsin and a member of their spectacular 260-member university marching band, I became quite a football fan. For many years, when the team wasn't doing so well, many fans attended the games to watch the band, especially their wild and crazy "fifth quarter" presentation after each game.

But in the fall of 1993, the Wisconsin Badgers made it to the Rose Bowl for the first time in thirty-one years! Michael and his fellow band members were off to Pasadena.

Oh, how I wanted to go, too! I searched my bank accounts, desperately trying to find a way. I entered a newspaper contest to win a trip for two to the game. I warned my out-of-state relatives who were planning to come to my home for New Year's weekend that I might be going.

Well, none of it happened. I stayed home, thirteen relatives came, and we watched Michael perform on television. As he marched down that five-and-a-half-mile Rose Bowl parade route, the camera focused on my son, playing his duos and high-stepping his way through the most exciting day of his life. Surrounded by all my loved ones, I got to see Michael up close. Then we whooped and hollered all afternoon and evening as we watched the Wisconsin Badgers upset UCLA.

I learned something that day. We humans don't always know what's best for us. I was much better off with my big family on New Year's Day in my own home than I would have been in Pasadena, fighting the crowds by myself. Had I been there, I probably wouldn't even have seen my son on his proudest day.

Today, Lord, remind me that your plan for me is always, without a doubt, the best plan, even when it doesn't seem so at the time.

To win the contest you must deny yourselves many things that would keep you from doing your best.
1 CORINTHIANS 9:25

JANUARY 3

For thirty-two years, my dad was a rural mail carrier. Six days a week he traversed fifty miles of blacktop and gravel roads in his little VW bug to deliver mail to five hundred families. Every Christmas at least a hundred of those families gave Dad a gift.

I loved all those homemade cookies and candies stacked up in our kitchen. Dad's cupboards overflowed with neckties, cuff links, and aftershave.

Every January when the Christmas rush was over, Dad, who hated to write letters, sat down at the dining-room table and wrote thank-you letters by hand—over three thousand during his career!

As a child, I often joined Dad and labored over my own letters to family and friends.

It became a tradition. Asking each other how to spell words and nibbling leftover mail-route peanut brittle. But most of all, learning the meaning of the word *gratitude.*

Dad's January project taught me a valuable lesson. Personal thank-you letters were just something you always did when you received a gift.

Today, in my own home, January is still "thank-you letter month." My children and I write thank-yous for every gift we receive. Sometimes we procrastinate, misspell words, and have to be reminded to get the job done. But by the end of the month every letter is in the mail.

Lord, thank you for a dad who, year after year, wrote warm, sincere thank-you letters, even for his tenth bottle of aftershave, and who passed on the tradition of making January "thank-you letter month" at our house.

Oh, give thanks to the Lord, for he is good; his loving-kindness continues forever. PSALMS 136:1

JANUARY 4

When my daughter, Julia, majored in health promotion and wellness at the University of Wisconsin, Stevens Point, I learned that "wellness" is the awareness and practice of healthy behaviors. In order to achieve a healthy mind and body we must be concerned about all seven dimensions of wellness. "Just remember the word species, Mom," Julia said. "Each letter in that word represents one of the seven dimensions: Social, Physical, Emotional, Career, Intellectual, Environmental, and Spiritual. A 'well' person develops each of those seven areas."

During her college years, I watched my daughter develop intellectually as she attended her classes and socially as she expanded her friendship circle. Social workers and teachers boosted her emotional dimension as she balanced her hectic life as a student and as a new mother. Her career goals were enhanced when she worked hard to get hired by the university for her internship program because she knew she eventually wanted to work in a school setting.

Am I a well-rounded species? Not yet. But this year I'm going to work on the "physical" part by taking walks at least three times a week. I've also expanded my recycling efforts for a better "environmental" awareness. And most important, I've joined a Bible-study group to balance the "spiritual" side of my wellness.

Which of the seven dimensions of wellness can you improve upon? This year, why don't we work on *all* of them?

Heavenly Father, this year, help me to become the whole "well" person you intended me to be.

If you do these things, God will shed his own glorious light upon you. He will heal you.   ISAIAH 58:8

JANUARY 5

Imagine that cool, clear, quiet night in Bethlehem, almost two thousand years ago. The black night was pierced by the light of a star so incredibly bright that it guided the wise men on their way to Bethlehem after the birth of the Christ child.

A star, though it seems magical at times, is nothing more than a self-luminous, self-contained mass of gas, visible at night from earth. Yet, if we look closely, we can always find a star twinkling a little faster and shining a little brighter that can light our way, just as the star of Bethlehem did for the wise men.

This coming year I'm going to try harder to appreciate the real "stars" in my life. My older son, when he makes an effort to spend more time with his younger brother. My daughter, when she writes me yet another joyful letter. My neighbor, who offers to drive my child somewhere. My friend, who listens to me and asks nothing in return. My father, who builds beautiful objects for my home. A co-worker who takes the time to explain something with infinite patience. The sales clerk who remembers my name each time I come into the store.

This week, as we celebrate the Epiphany, let's make up a list of the stars in our lives, send them a star-shaped thank-you note, and let them know how much we appreciate the way they light up our lives.

Lord, help me not only to appreciate the "stars" in my life, but to be a "star" myself to all those around me.

The sun has one kind of glory while the moon and stars have another kind. And the stars differ from each other in their beauty and brightness.

1 CORINTHIANS 15:41

JANUARY 6

Each year I was ready to take down the Christmas decorations earlier and earlier. I couldn't wait to get my house "back to normal." By January first, I was tired of the needles falling off the dried-out tree, the stale cookies, and the red and green decorations. Most of all, I was tired of spending those holiday moments alone, when I'd have given anything to be sharing them with an adoring spouse. Quite frankly, by New Year's I'd "had it" with Christmas.

One year when I was putting away the manger scene on January 2, Andrew, age eight, stopped me cold. "Mom, how can you do that? The wise men don't get here until January 6, remember?"

Andrew was right. Even though we celebrate Christmas weeks early by shopping, baking, and attending holiday parties, the twelve days of Christmas don't begin until the day *after* Christmas day, and they officially end on the feast of the Epiphany. From that year on, we started holiday things a little later in December and celebrated the real twelve days by welcoming the three wise men with open arms on January 6.

Even though today marks the official end of the Christmas season, it's a great day to think of ways we can keep Christmas alive. What if, every Sunday during this coming year, each person in our family takes turns choosing a kindness to do for someone outside the family? Then the spirit and true meaning of Christmas will surround us all year long.

Keep the spirit of Christmas in my heart, Lord ... before, during, and after the holidays.

Entering the house where the baby and Mary his mother were, they threw themselves down before him, worshiping. Then they opened their presents and gave him gold, frankincense and myrrh.   MATTHEW 2:11

JANUARY 7

I once read a list of forty-three life events that produce great amounts of stress. Each was given a point value to indicate how stressful the event was. For instance, a spouse's death rated 100 points; divorce, 73; marital separation, 65; change in financial state, 38; and change in living conditions, 25. The study stated that if your score was over 300 your stress potential was severe. Most single parents probably come up with scores well into the "severely stressed" category.

That's why we *must* think about how we can reduce stress that's waiting to engulf us. We must be smarter, more cunning, more determined *not* to let it beat us down.

Regular exercise, making friends with people I trust (and talking to them often), and finding something I enjoy and doing it regularly have worked for me. For years, I combined all three every Saturday morning for a couple of hours. I fast-walked with my dear friend Betsy as we talked about our lives. We also soothed our passion for bargains by hitting lots of rummage and yard sales along the way.

What do *you* need to do to ease the stress in your life? *You*, and *only* you, must take control of it. *You*, after all, are the only person responsible for creating your own happiness. Today is a great day to begin.

Lord, as I inhale deeply every morning and thank you for this day, give me a push to take better care of myself so that I can be a better, happier, less-stressed person for my family.

Since I know it is all for Christ's good, I am quite happy about "the thorn," and about insults and hardships, persecutions and difficulties; for when I am weak, then I am strong—the less I have, the more I depend on him.   2 CORINTHIANS 12:10

JANUARY 8

The temperature was five below zero. The icy wind caught my hat and sent it across the snowdrifts. Now the car wouldn't start. Not a grind or a grumble; the battery was dead. I had left the lights on for the past four hours while I was attending a high school music contest with my son. Praying for a way out of the cold mess, I got out of the car and raised the hood. A few minutes later a man walked out of the high school and right over to my car.

"Battery dead?" he said with a smile.

"Yes, sir. I left the lights on," I said sheepishly.

"No problem, I've got jumper cables. I'll have you up and running in no time."

Within minutes the engine purred to life. I thanked the man and offered him some money. "No, thanks. But, hey, maybe you can help somebody else someday."

The very next day I was at a nearby shopping mall. Over the loudspeaker heard, "If anyone in the store has jumper cables there's a man on the far side of the parking lot who needs help."

I sure didn't want to leave that warm shoe store, walk clear across the parking lot, and stand there in the icy cold while some stranger drained the electricity from my car. But then I remembered my cold, frightening experience the previous day. *Maybe you can help somebody else someday,* the man had said.

When I reached the stranded car, the man's wife and three children were huddled inside, trying to keep warm. The woman jumped out, shook my hand, and asked if they could pay me for the use of my brand-new jumper cables. I smiled, "No, but maybe you can help someone else one of these days."

"It's a deal!" she exclaimed.

Lord, help me to keep the helping chain going. If I'm tempted to become the broken link, give me a boost!

But with the help of God we shall do mighty acts of valor. For he treads down our foes.   PSALMS 108:12

JANUARY 9

It was a few years after my mother died, and my four children and I were having a tough time financially. I mentioned to my dad that I wished I'd inherited my mother's meticulous financial record keeping and budget planning. Dad gave me a box of papers from her desk, which included her down-to-the-penny household statements for each month during my childhood years. Every month she paid eleven bills by check: house payment, taxes, insurance, utilities, groceries, and so on. The rest of the family income was placed in cash in eleven separate envelopes labeled: church, school expenses, clothes, gifts, repair and improvement, dues and licenses, doctor-dentist, Dad's allowance, Mom's allowance, childrens' allowance, and savings.

On June 3, 1960, her ledger states that she wrote $274 worth of checks. The cash in the envelopes totaled $130. Our family of five was living on $404 a month. In spite of the tight budget, Mother and Dad were giving more to the church than they were keeping for themselves. Mom kept $10, Dad kept $10 ... and $24 went to the church.

I'm sure my parents faced many of the same challenges I have. Mortgages. Car repairs. Vacation funds. Life's little emergencies. Yet every month they continued to give, faithfully and generously. As a child I never had the slightest notion how my parents had sacrificed for us to eke out a living. Now that I know how hard it must have been, my childhood memories seem all the richer.

Lord, give me the courage to give more generously, and then to stop worrying and simply trust my budget concerns to you.

The purpose of tithing is to teach you always to put God first in your lives.　　DEUTERONOMY 14:23

JANUARY 10

I've done it often, usually embarrassing myself, especially if I'm at church or in a meeting or listening to a concert. Yawning ... I always thought it was a sign of boredom or restlessness.

But then I learned that yawning is actually *good* for us—and necessary! Yawning, a reflex action caused by too much carbon dioxide in the blood, occurs when the body is tense during prolonged sedentary work. The body says, "Yawn! You're short of oxygen. Stretch yourself! Your body is getting stagnant."

It isn't just our bodies that get stagnant. Our minds, if we don't stretch them with new information every day, grow weary, bored, and out of sorts.

My mind was certainly feeling stagnant until I signed up for a Sunday-morning Bible-study class at a neighboring church. We were a diverse group of men and women, and we learned a lot about ourselves and each other during those sessions. Friendships developed as we grew in our faith.

What about you? Is your life a ho-hum routine these days? Perhaps all you need is a mental yawn. Sign up for a class, organize a study group, research a new topic, or choose a dozen books to read this year. (Try to find at least one on how to be a better single parent.) In other words, stretch yourself!

Lord, thank you for your marvelous creation of body and mind. Help me to stretch both every day of my life.

Use every part of your body to give glory back to God, because he owns it. 1 CORINTHIANS 6:20

JANUARY 11

At the end of a long, exasperating day, I was fixing supper. Andrew, age two, had been watching *Sesame Street* in the family room downstairs but was now in the kitchen underfoot. I decided to give him a special job to do.

"Andrew, please go downstairs, push the button on the TV and turn the TV off." I repeated it three times, emphasizing the words *push*, *TV*, and *off* to help him get the message.

Downstairs he went to do a nice deed for Mommy. A minute later the most awful crash jolted the house. I raced downstairs, praying out loud that my son had not crashed through the patio doors.

Andrew was behind the TV stand, smiling. The TV was face-down on the floor, knobs and green plants scattered about. I scooped up my son and placed him firmly on the sofa.

"Andrew! Why did you do that? You broke the TV!" I ranted until he was near tears.

Later, when I played the scene over in my mind, I remembered how I had emphasized the words *push*, *TV*, and *off*. That was it! Andrew had followed my directions exactly! He had "pushed the TV off."

Until that moment, mentally I'd practically doomed him to a life of juvenile delinquency. Now I realized my own inability to communicate clearly was at fault.

How many times have I started yelling at one of my children before I knew all the facts? How many times have I assumed my communication was crystal clear when it wasn't?

Lord, before I jump to conclusions, help me to listen more carefully, to understand more fully. Get it through my thick head that the best way to handle every situation is to give others the benefit of the doubt.

Come, let us go down and give them different languages, so that they won't understand each other's words!   GENESIS 11:7

JANUARY 12

It wasn't always easy to find the time, but when my three older children were preschoolers, I read aloud to them twice a day, before their afternoon naps and before bedtime. We went through thousands of library books.

When you read aloud, it's like reading twice, because two of you get the benefit. Why don't you try it this year as one of your New Year's resolutions?

Tonight, offer to read a homework chapter aloud to your child. If *you're* taking a class, read a chapter from the textbook aloud to your children so they can understand a little better what it is you're studying.

Read an article to Grandma or an elderly friend with poor eyesight. Or visit a nursing home and read aloud to a dozen people at once.

A friend in the hospital, who may be weary of making "polite" conversation, might enjoy hearing you read an interesting, uplifting article or story.

Perhaps your family could read aloud the entire New Testament this year, a few verses at a time. Or take turns reading your *A Hug a Day* ... devotional book aloud each morning before breakfast.

Lord, help me make this year the year I begin a new habit of sharing the beauty of your world "times two" by reading aloud each day to someone I love.

If you read this prophecy aloud to the church, you will receive a special blessing from the Lord. Those who listen to it being read and do what it says will also be blessed.   REVELATION 1:3

JANUARY 13

When my Aunt Helen was eighty-five years old she sent me something she'd found in her church bulletin, written by Nadine Stair, who was then eighty-five years old as well. I'd like to share her insights.

If I had my life to live over, I'd dare, make more mistakes next time. I'd relax. I'd limber up. I would be sillier than I have been this trip. I would take fewer things seriously. I would take more chances. I would have taken more trips. I would have climbed more mountains.

You see, I've been one of those persons who lived sensibly and sanely hour after hour, day after day. I've never gone anywhere without a thermometer, a hot water bottle, a raincoat, a parachute. If I had to do it over again, I would have traveled lighter.

If I had my life to live over, I would go barefoot earlier in the spring, and later in the fall. I would go to more dances. I would ride more merry-go-rounds. I would pick more daisies.

I would perhaps have had more actual troubles, but I'd have had fewer imaginary ones.

As a single parent, I've developed my own list. If I had my life to live over I'd: Yell at my children less. Hug them more. Praise them every day. Forgive them sooner. Trust them more. Take a mental-health day once a year from school and work and go play with my children. Take more spontaneous trips. Eat healthier food. Ask men to dance when it was "ladies' choice." Exercise more. Get sillier. Never wear high heels or uncomfortable clothes.

What's on your list of things you'd do differently? Hey, guess what? It's not too late to put that list into motion today!

Lord, let me live each day of my life as if it were my last chance to really make a difference in this world.

Hope deferred makes the heart sick; but when dreams come true at last, there is life and joy.   PROVERBS 13:12

JANUARY 14

I was on my way home from work, dead tired, thinking about what I'd fix for my hungry kids, wishing another adult was at home fixing dinner for me. Horrible rush-hour traffic brought me to a dead stop.

Crash! I heard the crunch of plastic and looked in my rearview mirror to see two teenagers on a motorcycle just inches from the back of my car. My blood pressure shot up as I pulled to the side of the road.

Stupid teenagers, I thought, as I slammed my car door shut and stomped toward the two young men. The first thing out of my mouth was, "Do you have insurance?"

When the young driver shook his head no, I looked at the broken plastic that covered my rear brake light. He looked at the ground sheepishly and muttered, "I'll pay for the damage, ma'am."

Sure you will, I thought sarcastically, as we exchanged names and phone numbers. I figured I'd never see him again, but just in case, I also wrote down the make and year of my car and what needed to be replaced.

A week later, the young man called to say that the new plastic taillight cover was in. He and his friend would install it the next day. When they came over, they apologized for the accident.

That day I learned a valuable lesson about trust. I just hope I'm giving my own children the same sense of caring and responsibility that those two boys demonstrated the day they installed my new taillight.

Lord, teach me not to judge others so hastily. Always let me assume that every person I meet is a friend of yours who is made in your image.

Trust in the Lord.... Be kind and good to others; then you will live safely here in the land and prosper, feeding in safety.   PSALMS 37:3

JANUARY 15

When people used to ask me what I did for a living, I liked to say simply, "I'm a writer." I'd hope that they would think I spent long hours at home, laboring over the Great American Novel.

Truthfully, I was embarrassed to admit that I wrote radio commercials for a living. Was spending the bulk of my week writing dozens of thirty- and sixty-second radio ads a "worthy" career?

One day the answer came from an unexpected source. My dad sent me this quote from Dr. Martin Luther King, Jr.: "If a man is called to be a streetsweeper, he should sweep streets even as Michelangelo painted, or Beethoven composed music, or Shakespeare wrote poetry. He should sweep streets so well that all the hosts of heaven and earth will pause to say, 'here lived a great streetsweeper who did his job well.'"

That day I stopped wishing I could be a famous novelist, and started putting more zing into those ads. In seventeen years I wrote over 40,000 commercials. Thanks to the Reverend Martin Luther King, they became music to my ears (and to the listeners' as well, I hope).

Happy birthday, Dr. King.

Today, why don't you type up Dr. King's famous quote and place it prominently where you work? You might also talk about it with your children tonight at supper. They need to know that all jobs are important and noteworthy … if they're done well.

Lord, whether I'm cleaning ashes out of the wood burner, washing windows, or writing a poem, help me to do the job well.

So, my dear brothers, since future victory is sure, be strong and steady, always abounding in the Lord's work, for you know that nothing you do for the Lord is ever wasted as it would be if there were no resurrection.   1 CORINTHIANS 15:58

JANUARY 16

For eight years I worked for a large radio-TV station that employed over three hundred people. Every day I saw the same faces in the halls ... news anchors, radio personalities, reporters, producers, engineers, salespeople, managers, and secretaries. I knew fewer than half of them by name.

At an office Christmas party one year, I got to know one of the news reporters for the AM radio station. After introducing myself, I learned that he and his wife were expecting their first child. We talked about our jobs. Ron learned a little about writing radio commercials from me ... and I learned more about the newsroom from him. After that, whenever we saw each other in the hall we'd often stop and chat for a minute ... or at the very least a "Hi Ron!" "Hi Pat!" was lots more personal and friendly than a cold nod by two people who didn't even know each other's names.

After that office party, I decided to learn the name of one person I worked with every week. Then when I'd see people in the halls, I could address them by name with a comment like, "You sounded great on the air this morning, Bill." Or, "I heard TV sales are up, Sue. Way to go!" Or, "Hi, Ken, what's new in the newsroom?" A new friend every week. Doesn't that sound like a marvelous way to spend a new year?

Why don't you give it a try where you work or at your church or school? Think how full your life will be at the end of this year if you make fifty new friends.

Lord, give me the courage to meet new people ... and then to treasure and nurture that friendship every day.

A true friend is always loyal, and a brother is born to help in time of need. PROVERBS 17:17

JANUARY 17

It had been a terrible week. The washer and the dryer both broke down. The clutch went out on the car. Then the garage door opener's mainspring broke in two, and I couldn't get the car out of the garage. Next, six tiles popped up on the kitchen floor. All that, and my household repair budget was in shambles. The entire chain of events left me bad-tempered and depressed.

Out of sheer desperation, I started skimming through Paul's letters to the Ephesians, mainly because it looked short and easy to read.

Paul told me what a great person I am, that God understands me completely and showers me with his richness. Then he practically gushed about how *we* are the gifts that God delights in! At the end of the fourth chapter he told me to "stop being mean, bad-tempered, and angry." Toward the end he encouraged me to "pray all the time. Ask God for anything in line with the Holy Spirit's wishes."

Paul wrote his letter from *prison,* where he was put for serving the Lord. If he could be that optimistic, I can certainly try harder to solve each household disaster one step at a time.

Next time something goes wrong in your life, take fifteen minutes to read Paul's Letter to the Ephesians. It's a blues buster, for sure.

Lord, when I'm really down and out, remind me to fix a cup of tea and sit down with the Bible for a refreshing look at who I am and where I'm going.

I pray that your hearts will be flooded with light so that you can see something of the future he has called you to share. I want you to realize that God has been made rich because we who are Christ's have been given to him!   EPHESIANS 1:18

JANUARY 18

Do you ever feel as if you've never done anything important in your life?

In 1982, I attended a weeklong writer's workshop in Rye, New York. One of the other participants was a young man named Steven Newman. The next year, when he was only twenty-eight years old, Steven set out from his home town of Bethel, Ohio, and proceeded to walk around the world. It took him four years and over 14,000 miles of walking to do the job, but his is still the only authenticated solo walk around the world.

When all four of my children were still living at home, my days were full of carpools, schedules, squabbles, leftovers, and exhaustion. Nothing amazing or record-breaking ever happened, and I wondered if I'd ever have time to accomplish anything spectacular.

Between May of 1994 and May of 1995, when all three of my older children graduated from college and moved on to start interesting careers, it hit me that I *had* accomplished something. I'd given my children a desire to further their education, and to be responsible for themselves.

As single parents, we may not be able to give our children all the expensive toys, cars, computers, or cash that they want, but we sure can be good examples of what hard work and determination can accomplish.

If you feel wistful because you think you're not accomplishing enough in life, stop thinking that way. As a working single parent who's doing the job of two people, providing stability for your children and a love-filled home, *you* are an amazing person.

Lord, when I get discouraged, help me to see the bright lights of your world in the faces of my children.

Anxious hearts are very heavy, but a word of encouragement does wonders! PROVERBS 12:25

Jeanne, my oldest daughter, looked out the window. "Mom! There are five police cars in front of our house! The policemen have their shotguns out!"

I rushed to the window, where a scene straight out of a TV drama unfolded in our front yard. Had a violent crime been committed in our quiet neighborhood?

As traffic was diverted to a side street, panic set in.

"Julia, Michael, Andrew! Where are you?" I hollered. I found them in their bedrooms doing homework.

"Close your curtains, Julia! Michael, turn off the lights. All of you, come with me."

TV camera crews arrived. Then the special weapons team. More squad cars, more guns.

Finally, I called the police station. "Ma'am, get your children away from the windows," an officer warned. "There's a nineteen-year-old working out his frustrations by shooting out streetlights from his apartment across the street. One stray bullet hit a passing motorist in the shoulder. We're not sure what he'll do next."

The children and I huddled in the center of the house. What if a stray bullet ricocheted and hit one of us or the man escaped and took us hostage?

After an hour, the sniper surrendered peacefully, and I learned that playing the "what if" game during a crisis doesn't accomplish or solve a thing. We'd have been much better off staying calm and saying a few prayers instead.

Lord, when I'm frightened, help me to be strong for my children. Help me to remember that you are always at my side.

With them [wisdom and common sense] on guard you can sleep without fear; you need not be afraid of disaster or the plots of wicked men, for the Lord is with you; he protects you. PROVERBS 3:26

JANUARY 20

The other day I lost my cool with Andrew. I was tired and crabby, and I took it out on him with a sarcastic remark. When he responded in kind, I yelled at him. Later, feeling sad about my lack of patience, I thought about something that happened when Andrew was a baby.

One day I heard a female voice coming out of the small intercom we'd purchased. "Tom, could you bring those diapers up here?" Nobody in our family was named Tom.

The next day a male voice said, "Susie, Cory's crying, and I need to get in the shower. Have you got that bottle ready?"

Now I knew the voices. Susie and Tom were our backyard neighbors, and Cory was their newborn son. They had purchased the same kind of intercom we had, and the signals were getting mixed up.

I phoned Susie and said in my deepest fake voice: "Hurry up with that baby bottle. Tom has to get in the shower!"

When she asked who this was, I said, "This is God speaking," and hung up. After a few days, I finally confessed my prank. They howled with relief and immediately exchanged their intercom for a different model.

God hears every conversation in our homes. Now, whenever I'm tempted to shout or speak unkindly, I remember the intercom and try to give God something pleasant to listen to.

Father in heaven, I know you're listening to my words. Help me make every conversation gentle, loving, and kind.

Listen to me, all of you in far-off lands: The Lord called me before my birth. From within the womb he called me by my name.   ISAIAH 49:1

JANUARY 21

Don't you just hate it when you hear people say that your children come from a "broken home?" Just because we single parents are raising our children with one adult in the house instead of two doesn't mean that our homes are broken! Whenever I hear those words, I remind whoever said them that my home was broken *before* my divorce and I fixed it! Two heads are not always better than one if those two heads are always bumping together over every decision.

There are advantages to single parenting. For one thing, without the tensions our family used to face, it's easier to welcome my children's friends into our home whenever they want to be here.

Perhaps today is the day to get serious about the welcome we offer. How about something like this? "I will welcome my children's friends into my home with open arms. I will speak to them in a warm, loving tone of voice to let them know how welcome they are. I will invite them for meals and to go on family outings with us. I'll provide snacks like popcorn and lemonade. I'll learn all their names and engage them in conversation. I'll get to know their parents. I'll encourage my children to bring their friends to our home and to make it a place where they feel comfortable, welcome, and cherished."

Lord, instead of making ours feel like a broken home, help me to make it feel whole and full of life by welcoming my children's friends. Help me to treat them with respect and to cherish them as individuals, just as if you, Lord, were walking in my front door.

Don't forget to be kind to strangers, for some who have done this have entertained angels without realizing it!   HEBREWS 13:2

JANUARY 22

Cardinal John Henry Newman was a great scholar, writer, and motivator. I have been a fan of his for years.

One of my favorite quotes from him is, "God has created me to do Him some definite service. He has committed some work to me which He has not committed to another. I am a link in a chain, a bond of connection between persons."

What a powerful idea ... that we are links in a chain of humanity. If one link breaks, the whole chain is rendered useless. That makes each link pretty special, eh? Best of all, God has given each of us a job or responsibility or talent that He has not given to another. That's pretty amazing.

Like me, I'm sure you have moments when you think that you have no talent whatsoever and that the mundane jobs you do every day are not that important. But what would happen at work if there was no one to do your job? That link would be broken, and there'd be no way the company could go on until you were replaced.

Same thing would happen at home if you weren't there to parent your children, tie their shoes, wipe their tears, shop, cook, and clean for, listen to, discipline, cuddle with ... need I go on?

If today is one of those gray winter days that leaves you feeling somewhat depressed, or if you're feeling overwhelmed and unimportant, think about what Cardinal Newman said. You are vital. God has given you a unique gift. You have talents and work to do that no other human being *can* do.

Lord, thank you for making me a unique link in the chain of life. Thank you for making me so important to my children.

Thank you for making me so wonderfully complex! It is amazing to think about. Your workmanship is marvelous—and how well I know it.   PSALMS 139:14

JANUARY 23

Today, National Handwriting Day, is the birthday of American patriot and statesman John Hancock.

The phrase "Put your John Hancock on that" simply means to sign something. Because his was the first and most prominent signature on the Declaration of Independence, John Hancock's name became synonymous with any handwritten signature.

So what are you going to put your "John Hancock" on today? Why not write a handwritten note to your child? Place it on her pillow so she can read it before jumping into bed tonight.

Absolutely nothing can touch a child's heart quicker than a love note from Mom or Dad. In a sentence or two tell your child one or two things you especially like about her. Something like, "Dear Jill, I've noticed lately how you start helping with the dishes right after supper each night. I just wanted to tell you how much that means to me and how much I treasure all the help you give me. Love, Dad."

Or, "Dear Rob, Just wanted to say 'thank you' for all the time you spend with your little brother. When you play games with him or read to him, you not only help him, you help me as well. When you help out you make my day. I love you. Mom."

See how easy it is? Believe me, your five-minute effort will last a lifetime in your child's heart.

Lord, thank you for the gift of being able to communicate with others with handwritten notes. Remind me to write little notes to my children every few days.

My heart is overflowing with beautiful thoughts! I will write a lovely poem to the King, for I am as full of words as the speediest writer pouring out his story.

PSALMS 45:1

JANUARY 24

Even though I don't do a *lot* of cooking, I'm in the kitchen a few hours every day, usually at the counter, reading mail, paying bills, writing letters, talking on the phone, or watching the news. Since 1980, when we moved into this house, I've wished that the kitchen ceiling light was brighter. When a new eyeglass prescription loomed, I decided it was time to "light up my life."

I brought home a huge light fixture that held four four-foot-long fluorescent bulbs. After my dad installed the thing, we had our first ceremonial "turn on." The entire kitchen lit up like sunshine. Light bounced off the walls, from window to door, ceiling to floor. There was light everywhere! It made me so happy that I couldn't wait to get up in the morning to turn on that light.

At the same time another area of my life was as dreary as my kitchen before the "great light fixture." My faith. Oh, I went to church every Sunday, said my daily prayers, and even taught catechism. But my faith wasn't growing.

Right around the time the "great light" was installed, our church bulletin announced that Fr. Ron was starting an adult Bible-study class. I decided to go. As we made our way through the book of John, I felt my faith get brighter and stronger as I gained new knowledge of God's Word. Like putting the new light in my kitchen, I only wished I'd done it fifteen years earlier!

We single parents need all the extra light we can put into our lives, so let's get busy and *do* something about it.

Lord, help me to light up my own faith and spirituality by continuing to learn about your Word.

Your words are a flashlight to light the path ahead of me, and keep me from stumbling.   PSALMS 119:105

JANUARY 25

A few years before Harold and I separated, I remember one morning when I was in our bedroom room getting dressed and three-year-old Andrew wandered in. I hadn't made the bed yet. Andrew looked at the rumpled covers and asked, "Is Daddy in there?"

Knowing that Harold had left for work an hour before, I feigned innocence. "I don't know, honey. You better check."

Andrew poked around the covers for a while then hopped off the bed with a serious look, "Mommy, Harold's missing."

I held back a giant laugh and simply said, "Andrew, you don't call your daddy 'Harold.'"

With even more panic and seriousness in his voice, my toddler responded, "I only call him 'Harold' when he's missing!"

How many times do we call on the name of God when something's missing in our lives? So often I call God's name and beseech his help when I'm in trouble, or hurt, or aggravated … when something's not going well in my life.

Today, let's call on God's name at least every hour in praise, thanksgiving, appreciation, joy, or just pure gladness that our lives are filled with blessings that we often forget to acknowledge.

God, thank you for the electrical appliances that make my life so much easier. Thank you for a postal service that delivers letters so quickly to and from my loved ones. Thank you for air that smells so clean and fresh today. Lord, I just want you to know how content and happy I am at this moment.

Let us praise the Lord together, and exalt his name.

PSALMS 34:3

JANUARY 26

George and Helen lived next door to an old man who was practically a recluse. Whenever Helen fixed homemade soup or cookies, she made extra and set it on his porch, then phoned the old man to let him know it was there. "Oh, thank you," was all the old man ever said.

One day the old man died. His son came to clean out his house, and the couple stopped by to introduce themselves. "My name's George. This is my wife, Helen. She's the one who's been fixing the food for your dad all these years."

Stunned, the young man said, "My father never mentioned it."

George noticed a stack of old catalogs on the porch by the back door. "If you're getting rid of these, do you mind if I take them?"

"Help yourself. They're on their way to the dump."

When George finally got around to looking at the old catalogs, he discovered many pages had been glued together on all three sides.

Carefully, he took a razor and slit open the pages. Ten- and twenty-dollar bills started falling out.

"Helen! The old man hid his money in these catalogs! There's a couple thousand dollars here! Do you still have his son's phone number? We'll have to give him the money."

When George reached the son, the young man laughed. "So that's where he kept it. You and Helen keep the money. If you hadn't taken those catalogs they'd have been burned up at the city dump. You fed my dad and watched out for him all those years. The money is your reward. You deserve it."

Sometimes we single parents give and give, and think that we'll never be rewarded. We may not see it on this earth, but believe me, *we will be rewarded.*

Lord, help me give to my children and to others and to keep on giving without thought of reward here on earth. Thank you for the promise of your reward in heaven.

Treat others as you want them to treat you.... Then your reward from heaven will be very great.

LUKE 6:31, 35

JANUARY 27

Happy Birthday, Wolfgang! In Salzburg, Austria, on January 27, 1756, the great composer Wolfgang Amadeus Mozart was born. He began performing at age three and composing minuets at five. At eight he published four sonatas. By age nine he was composing symphonies, and at twelve wrote his first opera.

"What does all this have to do with *my* life?" you ask. Well, if you've ever had one of those days when you think you'll never get all your tasks done, perhaps it's time to slow down, take a deep breath, and decide what's really important.

To reorganize your life, start with a piece of paper. Make three columns: "Things I Like to Do or Want to Do"; "Things I Must Do"; and "Things I Can Do Without." If you enjoy playing the piano or taking aerobics classes, put those down in column one. The things you absolutely must do for your children, like attending their games, checking homework, and spending at least a few minutes talking with each one on a daily basis go in column two.

Most important, in column three, list at least three things you can do without. Talking on the phone too much? Watching too much TV?

You may not create 626 musical pieces, like Mozart, but you can probably accomplish a whole lot more than you thought you could. Mozart died at age thirty-five. What if he'd procrastinated, wasted time, or didn't stay focused on the important things?

Lord, help me to stop feeling sorry for myself because I don't have enough time. Help me to get organized and to stay on track with those things that are truly important.

Be sure that you do all the Lord has told you to.
COLOSSIANS 4:17

Today, January 28, is National Kazoo Day, which recognizes the kazoo as a musical instrument that can be enjoyed by young and old alike. To celebrate this festive holiday, we parents must do something to promote it.

If you don't already have a drawer full of kazoos, call a party-supply store. Run out on your lunch hour and pick up enough for your entire family and a few extras for drop-in kids. During the supper hour place a kazoo on each person's plate and then watch the fun begin.

Or you could tell your children that your family is going to form a "kazoo band" and perform at the local nursing home. Pick out a few standard tunes and practice, practice, practice. Call the nursing home and see if they will provide kazoos for their residents so they can join in.

Your children may think you've suddenly become one rung short of a ladder, one card short of a deck, one slice short of a loaf .... Never mind, that's another game you can play. The point is, since laughter and silliness are the fabric of a happy childhood, we parents must make an effort to create them.

Yes, you are an overworked, underpaid, overstressed, and tired single parent. Too bad. This is your only chance to create wonderful childhood memories. They'll be grown and gone before you know it, so today, right now, is the time to get silly, laugh a lot, and make magic for your little ones.

Lord, help me forget my troubles and to concentrate instead on finding ways to make my children laugh. And thank you Lord, for making laughter infectious. I can use a good laugh myself. Now where's that kazoo?

How we laughed and sang for joy. And the other nations said, "What amazing things the Lord has done for them."   PSALMS 126:2

JANUARY 29

Have you ever written a letter to your own child? Over the years I've written lots of long letters to my children for various reasons. My children need to know what's on my mind and in my heart.

Dear Julia,

The summer you were twelve you changed from a temperamental sixth grader into a lovely, blossoming teenager on her journey toward womanhood. That summer you lost three teeth, grew two inches, started standing up straight, got your hair cut and permed, had your ears pierced, started earning your own money babysitting, lost five pounds, and learned to dive.

Now that you're fourteen, the physical changes are more subtle, but your emotional growth and maturity level are wonderful things to behold. I don't even mind shopping with you anymore. Remember the battles? You wanted the best brand names because they were "in" at school and I, being practical and frugal, refused to give in to the label wars? But now that you're earning most of your own spending money, it's fun to watch you look for bargains and good value.

You are such a good person, Julia. You're much more open with me than I was with my mother.

Thank you for your love. Many girls your age don't kiss their parents good-night. But I'm glad you do and happy you do it with such verve and sincerity. You make *me* feel loved! I love you!

Mom

Lord, give me a nudge every once in a while to share my feelings about my children with them on paper. Thank you for these young lives you have entrusted into my care.

When I was a child I spoke and thought and reasoned as a child does. But ... my thoughts grew far beyond those of my childhood, and now I have put away the childish things.

1 CORINTHIANS 13:11

JANUARY 30

The New York Times once noted that the Lord's Prayer contains 56 words; the Twenty-third Psalm 118 words; the Gettysburg address 226 words; and the Ten Commandments, 297 words ... while the U.S. Department of Agriculture directive on pricing cabbage weighs in at 15,629 words.

The Ag Department directive reminds me of the way I blabber on and on at my children sometimes when they've done something wrong or are even thinking about doing something I don't approve of. First I rant and rave, then I rave and rant, usually repeating what I've said three or four times. Then, when I realize what an idiot I must sound like, I repeat it again for emphasis, only in a quieter, more adult tone. Finally I sum it up with a "do you understand?"

Of *course* they understand. They understood completely the first fifteen seconds of my tirade. Was my fifteen-minute gobbledegook message really necessary? Of course not. One simple, calm directive would have done it ... with a possible silent fifty-six-word "Our Father" tucked on at the end.

Lord, when I'm upset with my children, my friends, or City Hall, help me to be brief and respectful when dealing with my anger or disappointment. Help me to remember that in most cases "less" is "more" ... and then, Lord, help me keep my mouth shut.

If you want a happy, good life, keep control of your tongue, and guard your lips from telling lies.

1 PETER 3:10

JANUARY 31

January 31 is National Popcorn Day, which commemorates the discovery of this single parent's favorite "comfort food." To celebrate, here's a special popcorn-ball recipe. But you must promise to make them *with* your children. Create a memory and then dig in!

Nutty Popcorn Balls

3 qts. of unsalted popped popcorn
(Make sure there are no unpopped kernels)
2 c. salted peanuts
1 c. sugar
1 c. peanut butter
1 tsp. vanilla
1 c. light corn syrup

In a heavy saucepan, combine sugar and syrup. Bring to rolling boil, stirring constantly. Remove from heat, stir in peanut butter and vanilla. Pour over popcorn-peanut mixture and stir. Form into balls and place on waxed paper or press into well-buttered muffin tins or pour into buttered pie pans and form two huge popcorn peanut pies. *Note:* For fun and variety, 1 c. raisins or 1 c. chocolate chips can be added to the popcorn peanut mixture before you pour on the syrup mixture.

Today Lord, give me enough patience and energy to create a happy memory for my children.

"Beware that you don't look down upon a single one of these little children. For I tell you that in heaven their angels have constant access to my Father."
MATTHEW 18:10

A Prayer for February

℘

Heavenly Father, every February,
I marvel at the colors and textures
Of your world.

Crisp-crunch white snow.
Soft, brown groundhog fur.
Star-studded, steel blue sky.
Sweet, seedless oranges, pink grapefruit.
Red velvet Valentine hearts.
Ash Wednesday purple altars.

Colors that blast out
Winter's bleakness.
Textures that touch my heart
And fill my soul with reminders
Of your infinite goodness.

Teach me, Father,
To help my children to
Appreciate February.
To appreciate every color,
Every texture, in your world.

FEBRUARY 1

One day at the radio station where I worked, an advertiser came in to voice one of his commercials. When he was finished, he sat down in the chair next to my desk. Suddenly he slumped to the floor. I jumped up, tried to take his pulse, then put my ear to his mouth. He wasn't breathing!

I'd taken a course in cardiopulmonary resuscitation a few years earlier, but now I was terrified: a man was dying in front of me! Muttering a quick prayer for help, I began a steady rhythm of heart massage and instructed an office worker to hold the man's nose and breathe into his mouth each time I said, "Now!" Before the ambulance arrived, the man started breathing. I was still shaking when I thought about what would have happened to him if I hadn't taken that CPR course years before.

Over the years I've taken plenty of courses: baby-sitting, first aid, swimming, senior lifesaving, home safety, and childbirth classes. Taking them hasn't meant I don't trust God for my future. I know that if we have faith in the Lord, he'll take care of us, but I also believe that he depends on us to master worldly problems by being prepared.

February is American Heart Month. Why don't you and your older children sign up to take a CPR class together? Get your cholesterol tested and start reading those food labels so you can keep the fat grams down to a manageable level. We parents need to teach our children to protect their hearts by being "heart healthy" ourselves.

Lord, protect my heart and the hearts of my loved ones. Let me be a good example to them by learning all I can about how to stay heart-healthy … and then practicing what I preach.

The intelligent man is always open to new ideas. In fact, he looks for them. PROVERBS 18:15

FEBRUARY 2

I'll admit it. I've never looked forward to or enjoyed Groundhog Day. For me, it's a joke. No matter what that groundhog sees when he comes out of his hole, we Wisconsin realists already know that we're going to have at least six more weeks of winter. Probably more like twelve weeks of cold, dreary weather, if the truth be known.

Personally, I like the other holiday that falls on February 2 much better. Candlemas Day. Since the eleventh century, candles have been blessed on Candlemas Day in the Roman Catholic church.

In northern Europe, where Candlemas Day is celebrated with gusto, dark snowy skies on February 2 also offer hope of a quick end to winter, much like Groundhog Day. An old Scottish couplet proclaims: "If Candlemas is fair and clear, There'll be two winters in the year." But if that happens, at least we'll have the warm, bright light from those candles to give us hope for an early spring and warmer weather.

Today, in my home in Oak Creek, Wisconsin, I'm going to light candles on the table at suppertime. My son, Andrew, and I will talk and dream about springtime and warmer weather. Perhaps we'll plan a few weekend vacations for the coming summer months. We'll leave Groundhog Day to those folks around the country who truly do have a chance for less than six more weeks of winter. I'm going to celebrate Candlemas Day instead.

Heavenly Father, as I light these candles on Candlemas Day, help me as a single parent to bring light and warmth and hope into the lives of those around me, especially my children.

You have turned on my light! The Lord my God has made my darkness turn to light.   PSALMS 18:28

FEBRUARY 3

Xvxn though this typxwritxr is an old modxl, it works vxry wxll, xccxpt for onx kxy. You'd think that with all thx othxr kxys working onx kxy would hardly bx noticxd … but just onx kxy out of whack sxxms to ruin thx wholx xffort.

Have you ever said to yourself, "I'm only one person. No one will notice if I don't do my best"? But it *does* make a difference, because to be effective, an organization, business, or family (especially a single-parent family), needs complete participation by each person. Each must also offer his or her best abilities. Somehow, if you don't work together, nothing ever works quite right.

If you're having one of those days when you think you just aren't very important and you're tempted to slack off, remember that old typewriter. You are a key person, and when you don't do your best, nothing else around you works out the way it's supposed to.

Lord, help me do my best whether I'm sharing a special moment with my child, completing a project at work, playing a game with friends, comforting a fatigued parent, or helping out a neighbor. Remind me, Lord, just how important I am in your world.

For you are a holy people, dedicated to the Lord your God. He has chosen you from all the people on the face of the whole earth to be his own chosen ones.

DEUTERONOMY 7:6

FEBRUARY 4

After quitting my radio copywriting job, I decided to try working at home as a freelance writer for magazines. One day when I was feeling very nervous about a job interview with the editor of a small upscale magazine in Milwaukee, I called my friend Sharon.

"This magazine is for rich people! I won't fit in," I lamented.

Sharon confided that she'd had no confidence in herself for the entire four years she'd been in her church choir.

"Can you imagine how I felt last Sunday when we had to sing a cappella? Our accompanist, who is also our best soprano, was home sick and so were four of our eight sopranos! And you know me, softest voice in the choir. For years they've been asking me 'Are you singing, Sharon? We can't hear you!' So last week the choir director kept saying over and over, 'When in doubt, *Belt it out!*'

"Know what happened Sunday?" Sharon continued. "I took a deep breath, and the other three sopranos and I belted it out with gusto. Loudest I've ever sung. And get this, we sounded great! I don't think anybody even noticed half the choir was missing."

I walked into my interview a few days later, dressed in my stylish long black coat, shook hands firmly with the editor, and told him about the other magazines I'd written for and the types of articles I'd done. I "belted out" my assets with great confidence just the way Sharon did. And like Sharon, I got the job done.

Jesus, help me to give glory to the talents you've given me with a sense of confidence and determination to use them ... loud and clear!

I am sure that God who began the good work within
you will keep right on helping you grow in his grace
until his task within you is finally finished.

PHILIPPIANS 1:6

FEBRUARY 5

I am not an autograph collector, but in our home we do have one framed autograph. I got it for my youngest son, Andrew, in 1991 when I was working for a radio station in Milwaukee. One day baseball great Hank Aaron appeared on a talk show to promote his book, *I Had a Hammer, the Hank Aaron Story.*

During a commercial break, I asked Hank for his autograph. He smiled and wrote his name in big letters across one of my radio station notepad sheets.

Of course, Andrew was thrilled. After all, Hank Aaron still holds American major-league baseball's record for the most home runs hit by any player. Though I'm not a diehard fan, I was even more thrilled than Andrew to have this man's autograph. Why?

Hank Aaron is certainly one of baseball's greatest players, but it's more than that. He began his career at a time when few black athletes made it into the big leagues. Because of racism, he had to struggle against the odds. As a single parent I can identify with that.

Do you ever feel you're battling a war against all odds? Do pressures make you feel you're not accomplishing anything worthwhile? Next time you feel that way, think about Hank Aaron. For over twenty years he just "hammered" away, until he beat Babe Ruth's record by forty-one home runs! By the way, today, February 5, is Hammerin' Hank's birthday.

Lord, when I feel as if I'm not accomplishing anything, give me the grace to keep hammerin' away as a parent ... and as a child of God. Give me the strength to know that someday I will have accomplished something great.

"I have come to bring fire to the earth, and, oh, that my task were completed! There is a terrible baptism ahead of me, and how I am pent up until it is accomplished!" LUKE 12:49-50

FEBRUARY 6

My friend, Art, is an origami teacher. He was asked to demonstrate the art at a local mall, and he decided to give away a couple hundred origami paper cranes. As he packed them up, an insistent thought told him to make one special crane out of gold foil paper.

Why am I doing this? Art asked himself. He'd never worked with foil before, but he still felt a nudging. *Make a golden crane, take it to the mall tomorrow, and give it away to a special person.*

Art was getting cranky. *What special person?* he asked.

You'll know which one, he knew inside.

The next day hundreds of people stopped by Art's booth to ask questions about origami. Late in the afternoon an older woman stood in front of Art. He glanced at her face and immediately reached for the delicate gold foil bird and carefully placed it in the woman's hand.

"I don't know why, but I think I'm supposed to give you this golden crane. The crane is an ancient symbol of peace." Art said simply.

The woman slowly cupped her small hand around the fragile bird as if it were alive. When Art looked up he saw tears filling her eyes.

Finally, the woman took a deep breath and formed her words slowly. "My husband died three weeks ago. This is the first time I've been out of the house. Today … today is our golden wedding anniversary. Don't you see? This beautiful crane is a gift from God. It's the most wonderful fiftieth wedding anniversary present I could have received. Now I know my dear husband is at peace. And I'm at peace. Thank you for listening to your heart."

Lord, help me to listen for your voice every day and to teach my children to do the same.

The voice of the Lord echoes from the clouds.

PSALMS 29:3

FEBRUARY 7

This is National Crime Prevention Week. As a parent I'm not only *concerned* about crime, I'm terrified.

I once read in Ann Landers' column that the United States has more guns within its boundaries than any other nation. Our 255 million people possess more than 200 million guns. In 1990 alone, 2,874 boys and girls under the age of nineteen were murdered with guns and 1,474 youngsters committed suicide with guns; four out of ten teenagers know someone who has been shot.

Amazingly this doesn't happen in other countries. In that same column Ann Landers quoted the following statistics: In 1990 handguns murdered ten people in Australia, twenty-two people in Great Britain and sixty-eight in Canada; but in the United States of America handguns murdered 10,567 people.

As parents, it's our responsibility to try to make our neighborhoods safer. What can we do? We can call or write our state senators and congressmen and ask them to get tough on crime. We can join a neighborhood watch group. We can educate our children about avoiding places where crimes are likely to occur. Most important, we must know where our children are at all times.

Keeping our children safe is even more difficult for single parents than for two parents. Part of the answer is spending more time with our children instead of working longer hours just to provide them with "things." It's our job to *protect* our children … up front and in person.

Lord, sometimes I'm afraid to be the only adult in our home at night. Surround my children and me with your loving protection and help us be active in the fight against crime.

Prepare chains for my people, for the land is full of bloody crimes. EZEKIEL 7:23

FEBRUARY 8

Single-parenting three teenagers and one first grader (while trying to hold down three not-so-very-part-time jobs) was almost more than I could handle. After a nine- or ten-hour day of writing radio commercials, I'd be bombarded at the door.

"Mom, is it OK if I spend the night at Heather's? Tomorrow morning we're all going to the art museum. I'll be home by 4:00."

"Huh? OK, sure, honey. Bye."

"Hey Mom, can you drive to cheerleading practice tomorrow? I got a B on my geometry test! Can I make pancakes for supper?"

From child number three, "Bye Mom, don't forget to pick me and the guys up after basketball practice at 8:50. My drum lesson is changed from four to six tomorrow."

And from the blond wee person, "Mommy, we went to the museum on our field trip today! See all the stuff I got on dinosaurs?"

"Mother bombardment" leaves me frustrated and confused. Later, when I ask, "Where's Jeanne?" Julia shakes her head and looks at me as if I'm an Alzheimer's victim.

"Mother, she told you, she's spending the night at Heather's."

I learned that when I get home from work, I *must* really listen to my children. For the first twenty minutes, I must look each of them in the eyes and make a conscious effort to pay attention to what they're saying. When I started doing that, I stopped hearing them saying, "Earth calling Mother, earth calling Mother...."

Lord, help me to say "you're important" to my children by really listening to them and remembering what they say.

Why can't you understand what I am saying? It is because you are prevented from doing so. JOHN 9:43

FEBRUARY 9

"This is your fourth pair of shoes in six months, Andrew!"

Andrew's thirteen-year-old feet had stretched out again, this time into a size thirteen shoe.

Almost six feet tall and just 125 pounds, Andrew looked like a skinny pole on water skis. More often than not, his long flat feet got in the way of a well-executed play. "I'm terrible, Mom! I can't even get up to the basket to make a shot!"

I knew how he felt. As a single parent I often felt awkward, like an ungraceful fish out of water ... the way Andrew felt on the basketball court. On Saturday nights as I sat in my family room alone when the children were off with their friends, I'd wonder what my married friends were doing. My self-pity grew deeper as I pondered the fact that they rarely included me, one of their few "single" friends, in any of their weekend "couples" activities.

A few weeks later I heard Andrew's coach tell him not to think about his awkwardness. He taught him to concentrate on his layup and passing skills instead. I decided to stop thinking about my own awkward "fifth wheel" feelings and to concentrate on making new friends, other "singles" to be exact. I met some interesting women, and we started going out for lunch on weekends or a movie once in a while. I also took on some extra work projects and switched to a parish church closer to my home, where I got to know some other single people. Andrew and I both grew that year.

Lord, help me keep my eyes off my feet and to look up and out, so that I can see what can be changed instead of what can't.

But those doing right come gladly to the Light to let everyone see that they are doing what God wants them to.   JOHN 3:21

With my older children in college and living away from home, Andrew, my youngest, and I were the only occupants of our six-bedroom house. I began to worry that Andrew wouldn't have any male role models, especially since his father died in 1989 and my father, brother, and brother-in-law all live out of state … and that I wouldn't be able to afford to pay the taxes on our home.

I prayed diligently about both problems. Then one day my friend Bruce, a newly hired pilot for a Milwaukee-based commercial airline, called. "Pat, there are a dozen guys in my class, and they're all living in motels for a month during ground school. Why don't you take a couple into your home and put those empty beds to good use?"

I prayed about it, talked it over with Andrew, interviewed the pilots, and within a week we had four houseguests who did their own cooking and laundry and enchanted us with tales of their Air Force and Navy days, as well as the latest antics of their children.

After ground school, three moved their families to Milwaukee, but seven others have joined us over the years and used our home as their Milwaukee "crash pad."

Our houseguests have not only filled our home with interesting conversation and laughter, they've helped pay the taxes as well.

All in all, our unusual lifestyle brought many rewards to both Andrew and me. I learned that if we just open our hearts and minds to change, great things can happen.

Lord, if there is a problem in my life today, help me to be open-minded enough to see whatever unusual solutions you have in mind.

An empty stable stays clean—but there is no income from an empty stable. PROVERBS 14:4

FEBRUARY 11

February eleventh is known as White Shirt Day in Flint, Michigan. On this day in 1937 the unionized workers at General Motors factories settled a forty-four-day sit-down strike. To commemorate that happy event, the blue-collar workers wear white shirts to work on this day, symbolizing the fact that they won their dignity with management when the strike was settled.

We all know that fighting, whether between workers and management or children and parents, is very stressful. Do you ever feel like going out on strike when you and your children can't agree on something?

At times I've wished a strong union backed me up, telling the kids they're being unreasonable, unruly, or disrespectful. But there's rarely another parent around to pinch-hit for single parents, let alone a whole union. We struggle through those unruly times alone.

Or do we? What about calling your mother, father, or grandparent for advice? Or make an appointment with your child's teacher to see if he or she can lend some insight into your child's behavior and attitude. Or call your pastor or a co-worker who's also single-parenting. The list of folks out there who can help single parents through the hard times is enormous.

Next time you're ready to go on strike, ask for help. Before you know it, like the workers in Flint, Michigan, you'll put on a crisp white shirt to symbolize the fact that you solved the disagreement with dignity.

Lord, give me the courage to ask for help when a problem is too big for one parent to handle.

Happy are those who strive for peace—they shall be called the sons of God.　　　　MATTHEW 5:9

Three *s* words that seem to go together are *single-parenting, stress,* and *struggling.* If you're like me, especially if you've experienced divorce, you have days when you think your whole life is one big failure, both financially and socially.

One day, when I was feeling especially glum, I read about a man whose biography did not contain what I'd call stellar material. In fact, it read more like a lesson in failure.

Difficult childhood, less than one year of formal schooling, failed in business in '31. Defeated for legislature in '32. Failed in business in '33. Elected to legislature '34. Fiancée died, '35. Defeated for speaker, '38. Defeated for elector, '40. Married, wife a burden, '42. Only one of four sons lived past age 18. Defeated for Congress, '43. Elected to Congress, '48. Defeated for Senate, '55. Defeated for vice president, '56. Defeated for Senate, '58.

When I read the biography I wondered why the man bothered to continue in politics. Didn't all those failures and defeats teach him anything?

Guess not. That "failure" was Abraham Lincoln, elected president in 1860.

Father, hold my hand through the rough times. Even when it seems my failures are many and my successes few, keep me from giving up. Remind me how willing you are to carry my burdens for me.

Give your burdens to the Lord. He will carry them. He will not permit the godly to slip or fall.

PSALMS 55:22

FEBRUARY 13

Once during a trip to New York City, I visited the Metropolitan Museum of Art. On a self-guided tour, I was struck by a massive painting covering an entire wall—the famous *Washington Crossing the Delaware.*

I stood in awe of the minute detail, lifelike color, feeling of movement, and sheer size. I studied the determined expressions on the faces of Washington and his men as they pushed through the ice with wooden oars that cold Christmas night in 1776.

But what really struck me as I studied the massive twenty-one-foot-wide by twelve-foot-high painting, was the artist's name, Emanuel Gottlieb Leutze. Had a *German* painter created one of America's most treasured historical paintings? Later I learned that Leutze was born in Germany in 1816, immigrated to Philadelphia with his parents when he was nine years old, grew up and studied painting in his adopted homeland. At age thirty-five, he captured this piece of American history on canvas.

Do you suppose George Washington, as he stood in a wobbly wooden boat in that tumultuous river, realized that by continuing his fight for American independence, he would be helping young men and women from countries all over the world realize their dream of freedom of religion, artistic expression, and opportunity in America?

Our lives are a little like our first president's. As we single-handedly raise our children, sometimes with as much difficulty as George Washington experienced that night on the Delaware, we are also helping our children realize their dreams.

We parents have a big job to do with our youngsters. And this week, as we celebrate President's Day, take a few minutes to celebrate the job you're doing as well.

Father, as we remember our founding fathers on Presidents' Day, let me pass on to my children that same spirit of freedom, tolerance, artistic expression, and justice for all.

For he loveth our nation ...   LUKE 7:5

FEBRUARY 14

Valentine's Day generates nearly 25 percent of all seasonal greeting card sales. Something like one billion valentines will be exchanged this year. No wonder the card makers are deliriously happy.

But you know which valentines I've always loved the most? Not the mushy store-bought ones or even the funny tri-folds that cost an arm and a leg. No, it's the handmade ones my children have created over the years. Colored-pencil masterpieces, I call them.

These days I look forward to Valentine's Day. Instead of spending a fortune at the card store, I usually make valentines for my loved ones. A piece of typing paper folded in half twice, a few heart stickers or a paper lace doily glued on the front and a red marker is all I need. I simply write a personal, heartfelt message for each person on my valentine list and *voilà*, I've said "I love you" creatively and very inexpensively.

If you have young children, why don't you sit down together and make fifteen or twenty valentines to take to the local nursing home, hospital, convent, or homeless shelter?

Somehow, doing something nice for someone else just seems to make the day sing. Try it. Make a valentine for someone you don't even know. It'll warm your heart for days.

Today Lord, let me share the love you have for all of us by making a valentine for someone who hasn't experienced the warm caress of love for a long time.

There are three things that remain—faith, hope, and love—and the greatest of these is love.

1 CORINTHIANS 13:13

FEBRUARY 15

The "Day-After-Valentine's-Day" blahs hit me especially hard this year. But instead of giving in and throwing the mother of all pity parties, I quickly decided to do something to beat the overwhelming funk. Then I remembered the sure-fire "depression buster" story Gloria had shared with our weight-loss group.

When her favorite cousin died, Gloria recalls, "I was miserable because I'd never told her I loved her. The guilt was smothering me. Naturally, food seemed to be the answer. But I was in the middle of trying to lose ninety pounds, so I fought the urge to overeat. Instead, I turned on the record player.

"I put the first album I found on the turntable. As I snuggled into the warm, soft comfort of my sofa, the Bickersons, an argumentative, hilarious, couple from the '50s, were bickering their way into my living room.

"Instead of changing the record, I spent the whole afternoon laughing, and before I knew what was happening, I'd laughed my way out of my depression."

Laughter is important when you're sad.Thanks to Gloria, whenever I get the blues, or am feeling particularly lonely, or on the verge of depression, I watch a funny video, visit a funny friend, or read a humorous book. I make myself laugh and the blues disappear.

Lord, thank you for laughter and for the physical changes it creates in our bodies. When I'm "down and out" remind me that I need a good laugh and then push me toward the person, place, or thing that'll give it to me.

There is a right time for everything ... a time to destroy; a time to rebuild; a time to cry; a time to laugh; a time to grieve; a time to dance.

ECCLESIASTES 3:1,3

FEBRUARY 16

I like parties, and I especially like *having them* in my home. This is an amazing statement for a woman who doesn't particularly like to cook, rarely bakes, and hates to clean. But I've learned that single parents can enjoy a rich, full social life if we become the host or hostess, instead of waiting for someone else to invite us to *their* party.

I'm the queen of stress-free parties. Here are my tried, true, and often-used tips.

1. Don't clean your house before a party. Just do a quick dusting of the party room and give the bathroom a quick going-over, but white-glove-inspection clean? Never!

2. When you send out invitations or call your friends on the phone, tell them it's a "Potluck Party." One weekend I had two back-to-back parties. Saturday night I invited five married couples over for dinner. On the typed invitations (cranked out on my computer in less than ten minutes) I asked each couple to bring something from a food category. All I had to do was set the table, prepare a simple casserole, and make lemonade. The next day I had a big football party for all my single friends. The room was full of "potluck" snacks brought by everyone. All I had to buy were the beverages. Say to your guests when you invite them, "Would you please bring a snack to share?"

3. Invite everyone you know. Your guests don't have to know each other. It's more fun if they don't!

Remember, just because you're single doesn't mean you can't have lots of fun with all sorts of wonderful friends. All *you* have to do is get things organized!

Lord, thank you for the gift of friends and for the chance to welcome them into my home. Give me a nudge every once in a while to pick up the phone or send invitations so I can create memories and ease the loneliness of being single.

Sound the trumpet! Come to the joyous celebrations
at full moon, new moon and all the other holidays.
For God has given us these times of joy. PSALMS 81:3-4

FEBRUARY 17

Right after my divorce, I had to work outside the home six hours a day. My job at the local radio station included doing a daily thirty-minute live radio show, during which I "ad-libbed" upcoming community events. I left my three-year-old son Michael at the baby-sitter's, and his boisterous behavior told me he was feeling quite neglected.

The baby-sitter's radio was perched on top of her refrigerator, and, of course, she had me tuned in every day.

The first time Michael heard my voice over the radio he ran up to the refrigerator, looked skyward, and yelled at the top of his lungs, "I love you, Mommy!"

Every morning he waited for my voice to waft down from the ceiling. His behavior and temperament improved each day immediately after he heard me and had made his loud declaration of love. It was as if he knew I was in that room somewhere, and he found my presence comforting. If your children come home after school to an empty house, try to think of some things you can do to help them feel your presence. Leave a message on the answering machine. Tape-record yourself singing a silly song and leave the recorder and a note on the kitchen table. Leave a big sign on the refrigerator, telling them how much you love them. Be creative! There are dozens of ways to let your children feel your presence when they're home and you're not.

Lord, I'd like to be home with my children, but when I can't be, protect them, comfort them, and help them to know I'm there in spirit.

I can never be lost to your Spirit! I can never get away from my God!... If I ride the morning winds to the farthest oceans, even there your hand will guide me, your strength will support me. PSALMS 139:7, 9, 10

Have you ever been mad at God? I have, a number of times. The first time was when I found myself in an abusive marriage with three small children and an alcoholic husband. The second time was during the months I had to watch my mother face death at age fifty-seven. The third time was when my second husband, Harold, died when our child, Andrew, was only nine years old. Then, over a two-year period, the neighbor's dog killed all three of Andrew's beloved pet rabbits. Each tragedy caused me to be mad at God, at least temporarily.

Then I remembered something my mother did during the months before she died. She wrote God a few short letters. One said simply, "God, I have faith that you will help me out of this miserable time. How, I don't know. It's up to you. I love you, God."

Mother's faith was so strong and her relationship with God was as close as that of a best friend. I decided to give it a try, so during the times when I was experiencing bad things I blubbered out my feelings on paper in a private letter to the Almighty himself. The act of writing it all down somehow relieved much of the anguish I was feeling, and before long, it felt as if I were writing to an old friend who really understood what was in my heart.

Every once in a while, whenever my feelings are too intense or my problems too big to handle myself, I still write a letter to God. Instead of being mad at him for the bad things that happen in life, I've learned to go to him for comfort. And somehow, all those letters are answered in time.

Lord, when times are tough, give me strength to come to you in faith, verbally and on paper.

The peace I give isn't fragile like the peace the world gives. So don't be troubled or afraid … now I can go to the Father who is greater than I am.

JOHN 14:27-28

FEBRUARY 19

When I saw my son, Michael, reading the Sunday comics to his little brother, Andrew, another scene flashed into my mind. I remembered my dad reading the Sunday comics to me, thirty-five years earlier, both of us stretched out on the living room floor, in the wintertime by the crackling fireplace and in the summer by the open window.

Another tradition in my family was the super-duper kiss. At night, after toothbrushing, bedtime stories, and prayers, it was always super-duper kiss time. Dad would put his mouth on my neck and blow as hard as he could. If the ridiculous noise, as his lips vibrated on my skin, didn't make me laugh, the tickling feeling and the goose bumps on my arms certainly did. I always fell asleep feeling very loved and delighted by my father's silliness.

I continued the super-duper kiss tradition with my own children. Often they insisted on giving me a super-duper as well, and our days ended with goose bumps and giggles.

What are your family traditions? Making an Advent wreath together? Going to the country to cut down the Christmas tree? Leaving love notes in a lunch box?

What about family prayers? Tonight, why not start a tradition of saying the "Our Father" at bedtime—just before you give out those super-duper kisses?

Lord, help me start traditions that speak of love, gentleness and the joy of being a family.

When we love each other God lives in us and his love within us grows ever stronger.   1 JOHN 4:12

FEBRUARY 20

Five basic communication rules we need to teach our children are: "Stay in your own space. Don't interrupt. No put-downs. No fidgeting. Listen."

They sound simple, but how many adults even understand and practice these basic communication skills? Often, when my child wants to talk about something that's important to him, but I'm tired, irritable, or not interested in the subject, I fidget all over the place. My eyes and thoughts wander. I may even glance at the TV or newspaper while he's talking. Sometimes I even move around from room to room while he or she is talking to me.

Once my son, Michael, came home bursting with good news about his sixth-grade, end-of-the-year field trip. He prattled on about the details of the four-day adventure and the plans his class had for making money to pay for the trip. I nodded my head every couple of minutes and went on with supper preparations, wiping up the stove, and sorting through the mail while Michael chattered on and on.

How could I be so callous? The "stay in your own space" rule means, "Stand or sit still, face the person who's talking, and give that person your undivided attention."

Lord, when I am an unfair listener please remind me to observe basic communication skills. Help me teach my children to communicate better by giving them 100 percent of my attention when they speak to me.

Say only what is good and helpful to those you are talking to, and what will give them a blessing.

EPHESIANS 4:29

As the single parent of trying-hard-to-grow-up teenagers, I often found myself moping around wondering, *Why do they talk to me like that? Why don't they help more without being asked? Why can't they appreciate all the things I do for them?*

I dreamed about having perfectly happy teenagers who agreed with everything I said and did … teenagers who would just naturally think I was "mother of the year." In reality, I had lots of sullenness, guilt, yelling, bitterness, or stony silence.

After visiting our home one weekend, my dad mailed me a poster that said: ATTENTION TEENAGERS: IF YOU ARE TIRED OF BEING HASSLED BY UNREASONABLE PARENTS, NOW IS THE TIME FOR ACTION. LEAVE HOME AND PAY YOUR OWN WAY WHILE YOU STILL KNOW EVERYTHING!

I laughed and quickly attached the poster to the kitchen cupboard. Obviously my dad had a different perspective on parent-teenager crossfire. After all, he'd survived three teens himself. Dad knew conflict between parent and teen actually helps fray those apron strings.

In the meantime, whenever I felt round three was about to begin, I told myself it takes two to create an argument. Since I was the adult, it was up to me to stop adding fuel to their angst and anger by taking more deep breaths and offering more smiles, hugs, and positive statements. It worked. We all survived their teenage years, and we're all still friends.

Lord, when my teens act as if they "know everything," help me to make sure they know how much I love them. And give me patience, Lord, lots of patience.

Have faith and love, and enjoy the companionship of those who love the Lord and have pure hearts. Again I say, don't get involved in foolish arguments which only upset people and make them angry.

2 TIMOTHY 2:22-23

FEBRUARY 22

Today, on George Washington's birthday, I'm reminded of the time I visited Philadelphia and toured Independence Hall. I felt a sense of awe as I gazed at the elaborate silver inkstand that held ink used to sign the Declaration of Independence. Then I felt a sense of wonder, knowing that I was running my hand down the very same stairway banister that George Washington used during his two terms as president.

But what amazed me the most was George Washington's humility. Since the nation's capitol was in Philadelphia during most of Washington's presidency, an elaborate palace was built for him outside the city. Yet George Washington refused to live there. His government, after all, was to be "of the people, by the people, and for the people."

Even though England's monarchs ruled for their lifetimes and Washington would have been easily reelected, he felt that no president should be in power more than eight years. In a precedent-setting act of humility, after just two terms he stepped down and handed the presidency to John Adams.

Today, are there precedent-setting acts of humility we can practice? Perhaps we could quietly make everyone's beds without telling them who did it. Or polish their shoes. We could offer to give our children a manicure or backrub. Or plan a weekend family vacation centered around the interests of the children instead of our own. Perhaps if we humble ourselves by being servants to those we love, we'll be revered in God's eyes the way George Washington was revered by his countrymen.

Today, Lord, help me teach my children about humility by being humble myself. And may the good examples I set for them last for generations.

Better poor and humble than proud and rich.

PROVERBS 16:19

FEBRUARY 23

Years ago whenever I visited the home of some acquaintances, I was shocked by the husband's exploding temper and verbal abuse, usually brought on by bouts of heavy drinking. After a number of visits, I decided I couldn't deal with his abusive personality, so I began to avoid them both.

Years later I received a Christmas card from the man's wife. Tucked inside was her husband's business card with a quote on it. "For every minute you are angry, you lose sixty seconds of happiness." Remembering the man's vicious temper, I tossed the card aside and wondered how anyone could be so two-faced.

Later I learned that he had stopped drinking and his personality had taken a turn for the better. I felt guilty for ignoring them all those years and wondered if I shouldn't have a card printed up that said, "For every minute you hold a grudge or ignore someone, you lose sixty seconds of friendship."

Are you holding a grudge against a family member, friend, co-worker, or your ex-spouse? If you've been feuding with someone, don't waste another sixty seconds of your life. Pick up the phone or write a note to the person. If it's your own child, give him or her a big hug and then start talking. Remember, it takes two to have a fight, but it only takes one to start the healing process.

Lord, when someone offends or hurts me, give me the grace to forgive and the courage to mend broken bridges.

Even if he wrongs you seven times a day and each time turns again and asks forgiveness, forgive him.

LUKE 17:4

It had been one of those days. It all started with a hundred dollar trip to the grocery store. At home, as I juggled three bags of groceries at once, I didn't see the sled on the sidewalk. A jar of grape jelly smashed onto the concrete. Next, the kids tracked melted snow and mud all over the living room. Then, a door-to-door cosmetics saleswoman pointed out my sagging chin and crow's feet before I could get rid of her. Later, a bag of unpopped popcorn split open and tumbled out of the cupboard into the innards of the gas stove.

We've all had days like that, haven't we? I remember those "little children at home" days with indelible clarity. If you're a single mother with young children, I wish I could give you a hug and tell you what a good job you're doing. If you're an older mother whose job is nearly finished, why don't you phone a frazzled mother whose children are pint-sized and invite her over for coffee? You may have forgotten what a treat adult conversation can be for a young mother. Or you could offer to take her kids to the playground for an hour. Or you could write her an encouraging note, pointing out her good mothering qualities. The job of parenting preschoolers, especially when we're doing it alone, requires superhuman patience and kindness. Let's make today "young mothers need a boost" day!

Lord, please hold my hand as I walk, run, skip, stomp, and tiptoe through this job of single-parenting my children. And when my job is over, help me to encourage and support other mothers and fathers who are doing the job alone.

We can rejoice, too, when we run into problems and trials for we know that they are good for us—they help us learn to be patient. ROMANS 5:3

FEBRUARY 25

My dad wrote me long, encouraging letters when I was in college. I always hoped he'd enclose a few extra bucks, but with my parents' tight budget and Dad working two jobs to help put me through school, I never received any surprise cash in the mail.

Once I wrote a complaining letter home about not having enough spending money. Dad answered my letter quite succinctly. "Dear Pat: No mon? No fun? Too bad. So sad. Love Dad."

When my three oldest teens worked their way through college, I would have loved to send them extra cash every now and then. But as it was with Dad and me, my children knew that asking for extra money was futile. I budgeted for part of their school expenses, they earned part, and they made up the rest with scholarships, loans, work-study programs, and government grants. Somehow they all earned degrees.

Even though I wasn't able to send them cash surprises, I did try to keep them entertained and inspired by writing them encouraging letters. I filled them in on the news at home, told them about their little brother's antics, and most important, let them know how proud I was of them.

If you don't have a college student or a child in the military, ask your pastor for the name of a missionary serving abroad or someone who lives in a nursing home who would appreciate an encouraging letter from you. I kept every one of the letters my dad wrote me and still treasure those loving messages—especially the ones about how I could learn to do "without" and still be rich.

Father, help me give my children the gifts they need most: praise, common sense, encouragement, and a sense of humor.

Praise her for the many fine things she does. These good deeds of hers shall bring her honor and recognition from even the leaders of the nations.

PROVERBS 31:31

One of those meant-to-be humorous items was sent sailing from office to office all over the country. At the top it simply said, "The following is excerpted from a 1950s high school home economics textbook."

How to Be a Good Wife

Have dinner ready.... Let him know you have been thinking about him and are concerned about his needs.... Prepare yourself. Clear away the clutter.... Take 15 minutes to rest so that you'll be refreshed when he arrives. Touch up your makeup, put a ribbon in your hair and be fresh looking. He has just been with a lot of work-weary people. Be a little happy and a little more interesting. His boring day may need a lift.... Prepare the children. They are little treasures and he would like to see them playing the part.... Minimize all noise.... Don't greet him with problems or complaints.... Arrange his pillow and offer to take off his shoes. Speak in a low, soft, soothing voice.... Let him talk first.

Are you screaming yet?

Obviously, we single parents of the nineties can hardly relate to any of those wifely suggestions. But as I read that essay I wondered what would happen in our homes today if we tried out just a few of those suggestions.

What if we made our homes havens of peace by keeping the clutter picked up? What if we minimized noise during our most hectic hours? What if we listened harder, talked more softly, and complained less? We might be surprised with what happens.

Lord, you are head of this household. Please help me to make this home a place of peace and comfort.

A cheerful heart does good like medicine, but a broken spirit makes one sick.   PROVERBS 17:22

I remember one of the few times my second husband came to me for advice. As a high school principal, he'd written a letter to send to the students' parents, and he asked me to comment on it. I read the entire two pages, then took a deep breath. As gently as I could, I explained that the sentences were too long and hard to understand, the words were too big, and the tone was too academic. Most of what he was trying to say was in the last two paragraphs—and those were very good.

I asked him to *tell* me what he was trying to say. It was wonderful, interesting, appropriate, and poignant … and I simply wrote it down almost exactly the way he said it. The final version of that letter, shortened to less than one page, was something I'm sure the parents enjoyed reading.

All of us are sometimes guilty of "puffing up" our words on paper. A doctor once wrote on a chart, "negative patient-care outcome." Why didn't he just write that the patient died?

My uncle Ralph told me when he was a young military cadet he was expected to salute his superior officer at the end of each meal and say, "Sir, my gastronomical satiety admonishes me that I have reached that state of deglutition consistent with dietetic integrity." In other words, "I'm full."

Today, Lord, and every day, whether I'm writing a letter to a friend, an office memo, or a simple note to my children, keep me from trying to impress others with my vocabulary and long sentence structure. Instead, help me say what I want to say clearly and stop when I've said it.

My letters have been straightforward and sincere; nothing is written between the lines!

2 CORINTHIANS 1:13

FEBRUARY 28

Are you a nap taker? My father has been taking a daily nap most of his life. When I was a child, I remember seeing Dad stretched out, flat on his back, sound asleep on the floor in front of the fireplace. His day as a rural mail carrier started at 5:00 A.M., and by 1:00 or 2:00 P.M. he was ready for a siesta. Thirty or forty minutes later he'd bounce back up and put in another eight hours of work around the house and yard.

I inherited this refreshing habit from my father. I think naps, even twenty-minute cat naps, should be a daily requirement for single parents. Try it. When you get home from work today, spend twenty minutes with the children, then ask them to leave you alone for twenty minutes. Close your bedroom door, stretch out on the bed, and *voilà*, in twenty minutes when the little ones come bounding in, you'll feel like a new person.

I like to think that Sunday mornings are a sort of "nap time" with which to jump-start the whole week. God gave all of us a commandment to keep holy the Lord's day, to give pause to our hectic weeks. He wanted us to have time to clear our minds and to relax so that we could pray, worship, think about the needs of others, grow in our faith, and enjoy fellowship with our fellow churchgoers.

It's a good plan, the idea of going to church *every* Sunday— just as a refreshing nap is a good idea in the middle of those sixteen-hour days.

Heavenly Father, in this hectic, stress-filled world, let me refresh my soul at your table every week without fail.

Six days a week are for your daily duties and your regular work, but the seventh day is a day of Sabbath rest before the Lord your God.   EXODUS 20:9

FEBRUARY 29

If today is Leap Year Day, rejoice! It's a gift. An extra twenty-four hours to spend as you wish. How many times do we take leap-year days for granted?

We take each other for granted, too. That was made clear to me in a rather unorthodox way early one morning by my son, Andrew, who was then sixteen years old. Out of the blue he asked, "Mom, did my dad have chest hair?"

I almost laughed out loud, but I caught myself in the nick of time when I looked into my son's eyes and saw that he was serious ... very serious. Before me sat a young man whose feet had stretched into a size 14 and whose tall, skinny body was already six feet, three inches tall. His body shape was very similar to his father's. Andrew had been shaving his peach fuzz for over a year, and the hair on his legs was getting thicker and darker. But now he was curious about chest hair. His father died when Andrew was nine, and he just couldn't remember if his father had had hair on his chest.

"Your dad had some, Andrew," I said, "but not much. Let's look in the photo album for pictures of him in swim trunks."

As Andrew paged through the albums, looking at pictures of his Dad, he remarked, "I think I have my Dad's body, but my face and hair color look more like your side of the family, don't you think, Mom?"

"That's right, Andrew," I replied, "You're the perfect combination of both your parents!"

Lord, today on Leap Year Day, let me use this "extra" day, this "gift" of time, to help my children learn more about both sides of their family, and the good qualities they possess, thanks to both of their parents.

Some of us have been given special ability as apostles; to others he has given the gift of being able to preach well; some have special ability in winning people to Christ, helping them to trust him as their Savior; still others have a gift for caring for God's people as a shepherd does his sheep, leading and teaching them in the ways of God.　　　　EPHESIANS 4:11

A Prayer for March

It's windy today, Lord.
I know what you're up to.
You're dusting off the earth
With a cool, refreshing breeze.
Getting rid of winter's residue.
Making way for springtime change.

I'm ready, Lord,
To pack away the children's ice skates,
Snow shovels, winter coats.
I'm ready to move on, change seasons,
Welcome spring.

Change is so good, so uplifting.
Whether I'm moving to a new home,
Making a new friend, starting a new job,
Or just bringing out the spring jackets,
Change is as refreshing
As these March winds, Lord.
And I thank you!

MARCH 1

It's been two weeks since Valentine's Day, and it's more than two weeks until St. Patrick's Day. We need something to celebrate this week, right? Tell your children that today is Red Cross Day! In 1943, March was declared Red Cross Month by presidential proclamation.

The Red Cross is an international humanitarian movement with organizations in seventy-four countries and a membership of over 100 million. That's some organization! Its whole purpose is to help victims of war or natural disasters such as floods, tornadoes, hurricanes, fires, earthquakes, and famines. The Red Cross also maintains blood banks and trains people in first aid and water safety.

If you've ever lived through a natural disaster or volunteered to help the Red Cross during one, you know how important this organization is. When there's a need, thousands upon thousands of Red Cross volunteers rush to that part of the country and often live in primitive conditions while they help feed, house, and care for thousands of people whose lives and homes have been disheveled by disaster. Talk about an army of guardian angels!

Perhaps today is the day you call your local chapter of the American Red Cross and volunteer *your* services. Maybe tonight you and your children could bake cupcakes together and decorate each one with a big red cross on the top. While you're doing that you might tell your children a little bit about the Red Cross.

Lord, thank you for the volunteer Red Cross workers who flock to those in need on a moment's notice. Today Lord, could you see that they get an appreciative hug?

Please, Lord, rescue me! Quick! Come and help me!
PSALMS 40:13

If you ever want to impress a boy or girl of say, ten to fifteen years of age, take him or her to a college football game. The players, the marching band, cheerleaders, mascot, and, of course, the indomitable spirit of thousands of college students provide wild, nonstop excitement. It's also a great food fest: hot dogs, ice cream, soda, and peanuts.

One time at a University of Wisconsin game I bought Andrew a bag of salted, in-the-shell peanuts. When he reached inside, he pulled out a stick the size of a Cuban cigar.

Instead of tossing the stick and the empty bag in the trash I took them both home and the next day sent them and a letter to the president of the company. After praising him for producing such delicious, fresh peanuts, I casually mentioned the stick we'd found in the bag, asking if he had any idea how it got in there. A week later we received a box containing three large packages of their famous salted peanuts and a very nice explanatory letter from the president of the company.

That experience taught me that Grandma was right ... you certainly can catch more flies with honey than vinegar. I also learned how much company leaders appreciate hearing from their customers and how much they enjoy words of praise about their products. Isn't it funny how that same theory works with children as well? Lots of praise brings great behavior.

Lord, when a company, a product, or a child disappoints me, help me to make things better with a positive reaction rather than a negative one.

Timely advice is as lovely as golden apples in a silver basket. It is a badge of honor to accept valid criticism.
PROVERBS 25:11-12

MARCH 3

During the long, cold winter months I used to flip on the TV and find myself sitting there for three or four hours a night, a bowl of microwave popcorn at my elbow. Then one Sunday just before Lent, the following appeared in our church bulletin:

The 23rd Channel (author unknown)

The TV is my shepherd, I shall not want.
It makes me lie down on the sofa.
It leads me away from the faith. It destroys my soul.
It leads me in the path of sex and violence
    for the sponsor's sake.
Yea, though I walk in the shadow of Christian responsibilities
    there will be no interruption, for the TV is with me.
Its cable and remote control, they comfort me.
It prepares a commercial for me in the presence
    of my worldliness.
It anoints my head with humanism and consumerism,
    my coveting runneth over.
Surely, laziness and ignorance shall follow me all the days
    of my life,
and I shall dwell in the house watching TV forever.

After a long conversation with Andrew, we agreed to give up TV during Lent. He pouted the first few nights, but the third night he beat me in Chinese checkers for the first time ever.

During that Lent Andrew and I read, wrote letters, cleaned shelves, worked on his science project, and baked cookies. We also took more time for bedtime prayers and bedside talks.

After that, we often referred to Ash Wednesday as "TV Unplugging Day."

Heavenly Father, inspire me to be creative and energetic as I unplug the TV and plug into life instead.

Don't be fools; be wise: make the most of every opportunity you have for doing good.

EPHESIANS 5:16

MARCH 4

Encourage your children to take music lessons! My oldest daughter, Jeanne, took piano lessons for ten years and played the clarinet in the school band. My second daughter, Julia, wasn't too interested in music, but she did take recorder lessons for a while. Michael asked for a drum from Santa when he was three, and he's now a high-school band director. Andrew, my youngest, has played alto sax since he was in fifth grade, and now plays percussion in the high-school marching band.

Studies have shown that music lessons dramatically improve reasoning skills needed for high-level math and science. Music also strengthens the links between brain neurons and helps build new neural bridges needed for good spatial reasoning. In fact, one study concluded that spatial reasoning was 46 percent higher in young musicians. Tests and studies have also shown that music students score significantly higher on the verbal and math SATs.

From my experience, kids who are in music programs are just plain *good* kids. Music keeps them busy and focused, and they have a great time with the other students.

Musicians can enjoy their skill for a lifetime, whether they're playing professionally, for their own enjoyment, or in church.

Today, Lord, help me encourage my child to want to learn to play a musical instrument and to appreciate the joy music brings to our lives.

Remember what Christ taught and let his words enrich your lives and make you wise; teach them to each other and sing them out in psalms and hymns and spiritual songs, singing to the Lord with thankful hearts.   COLOSSIANS 3:16

MARCH 5

When I was a child, on every Ash Wednesday all the teachers and children at the Catholic grade school I attended received a cross of ashes on our foreheads. It was a sign of humility.

As an adult, I didn't attend early-morning Ash Wednesday services. It embarrassed me to wear my "faith on my sleeve" (or my forehead) in front of my co-workers all day.

But one Ash Wednesday I spotted three or four people at the radio station with ashes on their foreheads. Then I heard one of the Catholic sales reps talking to our Jewish program director.

"They're ashes, Mike. For Ash Wednesday. The cross symbolizes the life Christ gave us by his death on the cross. It's the beginning of Lent, a time to pray, fast, and think of ways to be less selfish and do more for others."

She made it sound so easy. The ashes on her forehead had given her an opportunity to do a little "witnessing for the Lord" without being the least bit pushy or pious.

Lord, whether it's the beginning of Lent, St. Patrick's Day, or any Christian celebration, help me strip away everything that separates me from you, including false pride. Let me witness for you, even at work, Lord. And help me teach my children to share their faith with others gladly.

We are Christ's ambassadors.   2 CORINTHIANS 5:20

MARCH 6

I asked my son to say grace before dinner one night when we had company. He bowed his head and blurted out, "Rub-a-dub-dub. Thanks for the grub. Amen."

We all snickered, then I rattled off our traditional memorized prayer. Later, I started thinking about our formal, memorized family grace. We usually said the words as irreverently as my young son did his "rub-a-dub-dub" version.

From then on I decided to let the children take turns making up their own prayers. Sometimes they were thoughtful, as when Jeanne said, "God bless Grandma and help her to feel better and thank you for this food, our home, and each other." Sometimes a personal plea came from a child tormented by a pending exam. "Lord, bless this food and help me pass my German test."

In 1985, when I became a single parent for the second time, the children and I added another dimension to our evening grace. We took turns reading our daily devotional selection. That inspirational message reminded us of the Lord's goodness and often led to lively dinner conversations.

These days Andrew, my youngest, and I continue the tradition. First the devotional book, then our own heartfelt made-up prayer of thanks, and finally, rub-a-dub-dub, I serve the grub! Perhaps right before supper is the time you and your family could enjoy *this* book together.

Lord, thank you for this food and for my wonderful family. Thank you for giving us this time together each day to draw closer to each other and to you.

Then Jesus took the loaves and gave thanks to God and passed them out to the people. Afterwards he did the same with the fish. And everyone ate until full!   JOHN 6:11

MARCH 7

Sometimes we single parents get so bogged down with our own problems that we forget about others' problems. Today, let's reverse that. Let me tell you a true story.

A number of years ago, when the children in the fourth-grade religion class at our parish church learned that food was being wasted at Milwaukee's sports arena, they went into action. A health regulation demanded that all food cooked or warmed (brats, hot dogs, pizza) or food from packages that had been opened (deli sandwiches, buns, salads, pretzels) had to be thrown out at the end of the night. So the fourth graders wrote letters asking if the leftover food could be given to the four shelters for the homeless located within blocks of the arena.

Within two weeks a response came from an attorney who stated that arrangements had been worked out with the health department so that after each sporting event the unused food could be given to people at the shelters.

What happens to the leftover food at the restaurants, sports arenas, movie houses, and concession stands in your town? Could you be the one to find out and perhaps start the wheels in motion for getting that food to the hungry? Today, why not call your favorite restaurant and ask what they do with their leftover food each night. Could you and your children pick it up and deliver it to a shelter for the homeless one night a week? Could you find half a dozen friends to help you?

Lord, give me the courage to put my faith in action and get out there and find ways to feed your hungry.

What happiness there is for you who are now hungry, for you are going to be satisfied.   LUKE 6:21

MARCH 8

My friend Sharon, a happily married mother of three, has such strong faith that there doesn't seem to be anything she can't handle with God's help. Once when Sharon's husband and her seventeen-year-old son were having one battle after another, I asked how she coped with all the disagreements and hurt feelings that seemed to shroud her family.

"Well," Sharon said with bubbly optimism, "I get up early every morning. I look out the kitchen window and say 'Good morning, God!' If there are dirty dishes from the night before in the sink I'll say, 'God, thank you for these dirty dishes. It means we have enough to eat.' Then I'll start talking to Jesus. Sometimes I ask him why I was so nasty the night before to my husband or to one of the children. I'll pray for more patience. Then I'll ask God to help my husband and son get along better, to respect each other more. Somehow, standing at the kitchen sink, talking to God, just gets my day started off right. It puts me in a good mood so I can help ease my family into their day when they start getting up."

When you pray and talk to God in the early morning the day just seems to begin more softly, quietly, and gently. Somehow those peaceful feelings seem to last throughout the day.

If you're not already a morning prayer person, why not give it a try? Get up five minutes earlier and have a chat with God, heart to heart. Praise him, talk to him, ask him for what you need, thank him for what you already have. Once morning prayer is a habit you might be surprised what happens to the mood in your household.

Good morning, Father! Today and every day I'm going to begin my day with you.

The next morning he was up long before daybreak and went out alone into the wilderness to pray.

MARK 1:35

MARCH 9

When my soon-to-be-ex-husband and I were going through marriage counseling, we learned that we were both proud people. We were both intelligent, with demanding, time-consuming, creative careers. We were both organized, independent, and self-willed.

To help us overcome our natural pride and communicate more openly, our counselor offered a solution: "You two should start praying together. Pray every night aloud, side by side, kneeling by your bed. When you humble yourselves before God, you automatically humble yourselves before each other, and that opens up a whole new way of communicating. If it's difficult to pray aloud, just start with the Lord's Prayer. Soon you'll be making up all sorts of prayers. It'll get easier each time you do it."

Then our counselor drew a triangle on a piece of paper. At the bottom left corner he wrote the word *husband;* at the bottom right corner he wrote the word *wife;* and he wrote *God* at the top corner. If both husband and wife start at the bottom and gradually work their way up to God together, he explained, they also get closer and closer to each other.

This "marriage triangle" can also become the "family triangle" with the children on one corner, the parent on the other, and God at the top. As parent and children get closer to God, they automatically get closer to each other.

Lord, I failed you during my marriage. Now that I'm a single parent, help me put you at the top of the triangle and grow closer to my children as we all get closer to you.

Finally I stood before the Lord in great embarrassment; then I fell to my knees and lifted my hands to the Lord, and cried out, "O my God, I am ashamed; I blush to lift up my face to you, for our sins are piled higher than our heads and our guilt is as boundless as the heavens."   EZRA 9:5-6

MARCH 10

When all my children were still at home, weeks, months, sometimes years went by and my faith life remained static. Isn't it amazing that during those hectic, too-busy years when we don't give as much, or share our faith as much as we should, God still carries us on his shoulders? He doesn't ask for more than we can give, ever. But I've often wondered ... are there ways that even the busiest of us single parents can share our faith and help spread the good news of an all-loving, all-caring God?

Well, here's one idea. Today is the anniversary of the invention of the single parent's best friend, the telephone. We call our friends, family, and neighbors often just to hear another adult's voice. Sometimes we cry, whine, and blabber on and on about how hard it is to be parenting alone. We get support and encouragement on the phone. We organize our hectic lives, arranging car pools, after-school activities, and baby-sitters. We single parents would be lost without the phone. So why don't we use it to help spread the good news of our faith in God?

Today, let's try to say at least one "God bless you," every time we talk on the phone. Or perhaps we could phone a recently singled parent who may be feeling especially lonely or bewildered. Or when we phone our friends and one of their children answers, let's take a few minutes to share a conversation with that child.

Heavenly Father, help all those people I call each week know how important they are to me and to my family. Help me to share my faith over the telephone wires.

And I pray that as you share your faith with others it will grip their lives too, as they see the wealth of good things in you that come from Christ Jesus.

PHILEMON 1:6

MARCH 11

My dear friend and neighbor, Bruce Swezey, is a pilot for a commercial airline as well as the Wisconsin Air National Guard. Bruce is also a Bible scholar who often shares the wonder of God's words with his friends. One day I asked Bruce, "What are the most important words you ever read or learned?"

Of course I expected something profound from the Bible, but without blinking Bruce said, "The thirty-nine-word bold print 'Emergency Action For Spin Recovery.'" Then he rattled off the thirty-nine words in less than twelve seconds: "Throttles: idle. Rudder and ailerons: neutral. Stick: abruptly full aft and hold. Rudder: abruptly apply full rudder opposite spin direction (opposite turn needle) and hold. Stick: full forward one turn after applying rudder. Controls: neutral and recover from dive."

Bruce had learned this life-saving method of getting an airplane out of a downward spin when he was in pilot's training after he graduated from the Air Force Academy in the seventies.

I laughed at Bruce's lightning-fast performance and then shared with him the fifteen most important words I'd ever learned. My fifteen words often help me "recover from a spin" also. They help me get more things accomplished in life; find the answers to many problems; communicate my real feelings to others; get along better with all sorts of people, and show my appreciation for them. My fifteen words?

"I am proud of you."
"What is your opinion?"
"I love you."
"Thank you."
"Yes."

Lord, help me use these fifteen words every day, over and over. Then watch me soar!

Shine out among them like beacon lights, holding out to them the Word of Life.   PHILIPPIANS 2:15-16

MARCH 12

Do you ever let off steam at home by swearing or using inappropriate language in front of your children? We've all done it at one time or another. Trouble is, our children hear enough of it on the playground, on TV, and in the movies. They certainly don't need to hear it from their parents.

I remember when I was writing radio commercials for a Milwaukee radio station, one thing I didn't like about the job was the bad language around the office. Each day I watched the stress level of the sales staff increase as they struggled to make their projected sales. As tensions rose the entire sales staff got into the habit of using bad language to let off steam.

One day, Tom, a radio salesman, mentioned a sermon he'd heard at church about the use of profanity. "You know," he said, "we really abuse it around here. Why don't we give up swearing for Lent? Every time one of us swears or curses let's drop a quarter into a jar."

I typed up the rules of the "clean air fund" and that night cleaned out a peanut butter jar to use for the money.

News of our "swear jar" quickly spread around the building of nearly 300 employees, many of whom dropped in periodically to see how we were doing. Six weeks later a note appeared in our paycheck envelopes. "Congratulations to the AM Radio Sales Staff. Their swearing jar full of 187 swears ($46.75) was delivered to the Rescue Mission this past Friday. AM Sales has decided to continue to 'watch their mouths' and contribute to the jar when necessary."

Lord, if I'm ever tempted to let off steam with bad language, turn my words into a prayer to you instead.

Help me, Lord, to keep my mouth shut and my lips sealed.   PSALMS 141:3

MARCH 13

I've been "single again" since 1985, and over the years I've often thought about whether or not I'll ever remarry. Like many single people, I go through periods when I think I really want to find the perfect mate. Once I even clipped a list of "perfect mate" qualities from a newspaper article and tacked it to my bulletin board. It was quite a list. Things like, "Flexible, adaptable, committed to the relationship. Capacity for warmth and intimacy. Open, honest, ability to share power. Willing to resolve rather than ignore problems. Acknowledges weaknesses and mistakes. Similar needs for autonomy and intimacy. Compatible values and background in education, religion, views on child rearing, and financial management. Willing to share household chores. Some common recreational interests."

I started looking for that man with gusto, but the "perfect mate" never materialized. Then one day a friend suggested I open up my heart and my home to all sorts of people, perfect and not so perfect. She asked if we could use my family room as the monthly meeting place for a woman's group. I agreed and over the years I've met dozens of interesting women in that group.

Since that time I've made an effort to bring other people into my home, both male and female. I have found lots of ways to meet new people: I've joined a few organizations, changed careers, volunteered to teach Sunday School, and started visiting friends and relatives all over the country. Lately, I've been so busy that I've stopped worrying about finding the "perfect mate." And I can't remember being happier than I am right now.

Lord, help me to be the perfect friend to others and to stop worrying about finding the perfect other for me.

You should be like one big happy family, full of sympathy toward each other, loving one another with tender hearts and humble minds.   1 PETER 3:8

MARCH 14

One night Chuck Wall, a professor at Bakersfield College in California, was in his study trying to come up with an assignment to give his human relations class. The radio was on and he heard a newscaster say, "Another random act of senseless violence...."

Professor Wall was struck by how routine and common those words sounded. Within a few minutes, he decided to change one word of that phrase. The next day he told his class, "I want each of you to go out and commit one random act of senseless kindness."

The next week the students reported back. One young man had been shopping at a Salvation Army store when he saw blankets on sale. On impulse, he bought as many as he could afford and gave them to homeless people living under a bridge.

Another student saw a stray dog, rescued it, cleaned it up, placed an ad in a newspaper, and was able to return the dog to its owner.

One woman told her family about the assignment. Later in the week she returned home to find her house sparkling, completely cleaned from front to back.

"No big deal, Mom." Her sons beamed. "We just committed a random act of senseless kindness."

Today, step into the world and commit one random act of senseless kindness. Ask your children to do the same. Repeat assignment tomorrow. And the next day. And the next.

Heavenly Father, help me turn things around in today's world. Help me change the world of senseless violence into a world where senseless kindness isn't so uncommon.

Love each other with brotherly affection and take delight in honoring each other.   ROMANS 12:10

MARCH 15

Today, March 15, is Buzzard Day. Just what is Buzzard Day? Well in Hinckley, Ohio, tradition says that on this day every year the buzzards (which some people call turkey vultures or carrion crows) return to Hinckley from their winter quarters in the Great Smoky Mountains to raise their baby buzzards. As they come swooping back after a long winter, the local townspeople welcome them with celebrations that last through the weekend.

If you really want to turn this day into a chance for a great lesson for your children, tell them about the Hinckley buzzard celebration and then remind them that your home will also always be a place of peace and comfort where they can return any time (for a visit, that is).

You might also remind them that our whole purpose of life on this earth is to prepare ourselves for returning home to our other parent, God the Father, who will also welcome us with open arms in the sanctuary he has prepared for us.

Hey, you might even wish all your friends and co-workers "Happy Buzzard Day" today. And if you're really clever, you could work in that part about "going home" to our real Father and do a little of the Lord's work while you're at it.

Lord, thank you for warm welcomes, both here on earth and in our final home in heaven.

Now we look forward with confidence to our heavenly bodies, realizing that every moment we spend in these earthly bodies is time spent away from our eternal home in heaven with Jesus.   2 CORINTHIANS 5:6

MARCH 16

When my daughter, Julia, sprained her ankle, I felt sorry for her but I couldn't "feel" her pain. Neither could I imagine the clumsiness she felt trying to maneuver the crutches. I quickly grew weary of her daily complaining.

Six months later, I sprained my own ankle. Like Julia, I suffered through two days of "Ace, ice, and elevate." I took crutch-walking lessons at the hospital and gingerly negotiated the steps at home, fearful that I'd fall off every step. I winced in pain and commiserated with Julia, who truly understood my plight.

Until we've actually *been* there, none of us can really "feel" the pain or heartache experienced by another. That's why, during a time of crisis, it's so important to reach out to others who have experienced similar circumstances.

> ... For the alcoholic, to lean on a recovered alcoholic at an AA meeting.
>
> ... For a widow or widower, to mingle with other people who have lost a spouse.
>
> ... For a victim of cancer or any medical illness, to seek people who have suffered through and conquered the same illness.
>
> ... For a divorced person, to reach out to others whose marriages have shattered and who have learned to pick up the pieces.

Thank you, Lord, for the comfort of others who have walked in my shoes and survived!

For a brief moment I abandoned you. But with great compassion I will gather you.   ISAIAH 54:7

MARCH 17

I like celebrating St. Patrick's Day—I'm not sure if it's because I consider St. Patrick my patron saint (I don't think there is a St. Patricia) or if I like celebrating the smidgen of Irish in my Scotch-Irish-English-French-German-Dutch ancestry. It may be because, as a single parent, I identify with St. Patrick as someone who had a mission to do and did it, in spite of great difficulties.

St. Patrick was actually born in England and sold into slavery in Ireland, where he turned to religion. After six years, he escaped back to Britain, but when he was twenty-two years old he returned to Ireland, determined to convert the Irish to Christianity. He eventually became a priest, then a bishop. He succeeded in making many converts even among royal families.

St. Patrick's Day is a great day to celebrate single parenthood. Sometimes our job as single parents is as lonely and fearful and full of struggle as St. Patrick's life was during his years in prison. But he rose above the struggles and did great things.

Like St. Patrick, we have a job to do. We have souls to convert and to care for—the souls of our children.

Heavenly Father, today and every day, remind me that I am doing your work with my children. Be at my side every minute.

But we were as gentle among you as a mother feeding and caring for her own children.
1 THESSALONIANS 2:7

MARCH 18

One morning when I was hard at work in my home office, a friend phoned, obviously wanting to chit-chat for a while. I made it clear by the tone of my voice and by my short, clipped sentences that I was too busy to talk.

That afternoon my son Andrew, age three, interrupted me when I was shampooing the living-room carpet. "Mommy, come quick! To my room! I made my bed and picked up all my toys by myself! Come and see!"

"That's nice, Andrew, thank you. But I'm busy right now, honey."

His little shoulders dropped as he shuffled back to his room, his proud balloon of feelings burst in midair. Guilt pricked my heart as I finished the carpet.

Later I sat down with a cup of tea and tried to figure out why I was feeling so rotten. I thought back to my friend's phone call. She had just wanted to touch base with me and catch up on the news of my family. But I had been too busy to visit with her.

And Andrew had been so proud of cleaning up his room by himself. But I'd brushed him off ... too busy, I said.

Too busy? For a phone call that might have taken fifteen minutes? Or a visit to my son's room that would have taken five? Too busy to write a weekly note to my father, the most beloved man in my life? Too busy to spend five minutes chatting with my elderly neighbor? I think not.

O Lord, help me straighten out my priorities. Help me never be too busy for my children, loved ones or friends. Or you, Lord.

Don't be fools; be wise: make the most of every opportunity you have for doing good.

EPHESIANS 5:16

MARCH 19

I was scrambling to get ready for work. Out of the corner of my eye, I saw my children get on the school bus. Two minutes later I saw Annie from next door running toward the bus stop.

Poor Annie. My heart ached. I'd have to tell her she'd missed the bus. I *should* tell her that I'd take her to school. But the school was three miles in the opposite direction and I was already running late.

My mind reeled. I could afford to be twenty minutes late for work. Or could I? If Annie's dad, who worked second shift and slept late, had to get up and take her to school she'd get a tongue-lashing all the way. I'd heard him yelling at his children many times. But should I interfere in their family problems?

In the end, the selfish chicken in me won out. I let Annie solve her own dilemma and went to work.

That evening, getting ready for a meeting at church, I remembered I was supposed to bring food for the Human Concerns kitchen for the needy. I pulled some canned goods from my overflowing cupboard and tossed them into a bag.

On the way to church I thought, *How much of a sacrifice is it to give up that food? But what about Annie? Taking her to school would have been a real sacrifice. Why can't I be more giving, more considerate of others?*

Have you ever been guilty of giving just the crumbs of your excess? From now on, let's both try harder to give to others until we can actually feel the loss ourselves.

Lord, teach me that giving means giving my time and my talents, as well as my treasure. And when I see a need, Lord, don't let me make excuses.

For if you give, you will get!… Whatever measure you use to give—large or small—will be used to measure what is given back to you.   Luke 6:38

MARCH 20

Do you ever look at your children and wonder where they came from? Do they act different from the way you did as a child? Is one of them the silent, thoughtful type and another a loud, talkative bundle of energy? Do you have to prod one to do his chores and rarely have to remind the others? Is one child built like a brick, short and muscular, while yet another is tall, thin, willowy? How many times have you seen siblings from the same family who look as if they all came from different parents? I have a cousin who has four children: a redhead, a blond, one with brown hair, and one with hair so dark it's almost black.

We parents should count our blessings that our children are so diverse. After all, the world is diverse. It's how God created it. According to *The Practice of Ecological Planning* (New Society Publishers), if one town of 1,000 people were an accurate representation of the cultural diversity of our planet, this is what it would look like: More than half, 584, would be Asian; 124, African; 95, European; 84, Latin American; 52, North American, and 6, Australian and New Zealander. There would be over 200 different languages spoken. Only 329 would be Christians. The rest would be Muslims, Hindus, Buddhists, atheists, Jews, nonreligious, and other, smaller religions. People come in all shapes, sizes, nationalities, colors, religions, and personalities. Our diversity is something to treasure.

Today, March 20, is Earth Day. A day to celebrate all of us on the earth, whether we're different or alike. It's a day to look carefully at our own children and praise God for making each one unique in looks, needs, personality, and behavior.

Thank you Lord, for such a big, multifaceted world. Help me treasure the differences in my world and in my children.

It is God who sits above the circle of the earth.
ISAIAH 40:22

MARCH 21

At age fifty-six, my mother was diagnosed with a terminal illness. There were days she wondered what was waiting for her on the other side of this life. As the disease ravaged her body, she swayed between praying for a miracle and resigning herself to death. Most of the time, Mother's faith in God and her belief in eternal life brought her strength.

I picked up her Bible one day and noticed she had marked John 14:27-28: " ... The peace I give isn't fragile like the peace the world gives. So don't be troubled or afraid.... Now I can go to the Father, who is greater than I am."

Watching Mother's faith grow in spite of her terminal illness inspired me to write and mail her a letter, even though we lived in the same town.

Dear Mom,

Whenever friends or relatives ask me how you are doing, the conversation always seems to end with my saying something about your strong faith. I've been thinking a lot lately about what "faith" means.

Years ago I saw a huge banner inside a church that said "Faith is the bird that knows the dawn and sings while it is still dark." That definition of faith reminds me so much of your beautiful optimism and your faith in God. Even though you are sometimes depressed or filled with despair, I know that you never forget about the dawn even when it is dark. I love you.

Pat

Mother died sixteen months after learning she had the fatal disease. In spite of her discomforts she never lost sight of the knowledge that she was "going to the Father, who is greater than I am."

Lord, I know bad things happen, but because of you and your promise of life eternal I will always be able to sing ... even in the dark. Thank you.

He is given eternal life for believing in me and shall never perish.   JOHN 11:26

MARCH 22

One day my teenage daughter, Jeanne, woke up fifteen minutes before the bus came. I dashed to fix her breakfast for the first time in years. (I taught my children early on how to fix their *own* breakfasts. It's how one survives mornings in a single-parent household.) On her way out the door she grabbed the egg sandwich out of my hands without so much as a "thank you" and raced to catch the bus. I moped around all morning feeling sorry for myself because Jeanne hadn't gushed out profound thank-yous for my early-morning cooking feat.

That afternoon I visited a friend in the hospital, who, as soon as I arrived, started complaining, "I've been in here two days already and my pastor hasn't even stopped by. And my own daughter! She calls, but you'd think she'd come for a visit? And most of the people at work haven't been here, either."

When I left the hospital I thought about the man's self-centeredness. His daughter had two preschoolers and probably felt she could visit with him more easily on the phone than with the children in tow. The co-workers may have thought his rest was more important than a social gathering.

I was complaining about this man when I suddenly remembered my own self-centeredness when Jeanne dashed out the door without thanking me for her breakfast. I, too, had expected too much, considering the circumstances.

Are there people in your life from whom you expect too much? Today, give them a break and try to be happy that you have friends and loved ones. After all, *you* aren't responsible for other people's behavior ... you're only responsible for your own.

Lord, since I'm not perfect, help me not to judge others.

Day by day the Lord observes the good deeds done by godly men, and gives them eternal rewards.
PSALMS 37:18

MARCH 23

When the freezer full of fish for the Friday-night fish fry broke down at St. Catherine's Church, in Milwaukee, it was nothing short of a disaster. But instead of throwing the fish away, the parishioners loaded the 1,200 pounds of raw, frozen fish into a van. They took it to St. Benedict the Moor parish, which serves a free meal to the poor every night of the week.

When the fish arrived at the inner-city church, St. Benedict's freezers were filled to the brim with loaves of bread. Someone called St. Francis parish, another church that served a nightly meal to the city's poor. The freezers there were empty, so half the bread at St. Benedict's was loaded into the van. Then half the fish was put into their freezers … and the remaining fish and loaves were taken to St. Francis Church.

I used to throw away things I was finished with … old clothes, housewares, toys. Then one day a man came to my door asking if he could have the old car battery I'd set out for the garbage pick-up. A woman asked if she could have my raked-up leaves for mulch on her rosebushes. Someone else hauled off a broken teeter-totter the kids had outgrown.

Even if I don't think there's a use for something, instead of throwing it away I either display it in plain sight near the road for the taking or give it to the local help center.

Being the only adult in the household, I can pare down the clutter anytime I feel like it. This week why don't you see if your trash can become somebody's treasure?

Lord, help me not to be wasteful. Help me to share my discards and my treasures with those less fortunate.

And he took the seven loaves and the fish, and gave thanks to God for them, and divided them into pieces, and gave them to the disciples who presented them to the crowd. — MATTHEW 15:36

MARCH 24

The age of computers scared the dickens out of me. But I knew that to be part of the twenty-first century, I would have to buy a computer and learn how to use it.

It took me three months to master the thing, but finally I began to appreciate all it could do that my brain couldn't. Storing volumes of material on little disks and being able to make changes without having to retype entire manuscripts was a dream come true.

But one day my computer ate up three hours worth of work on an article I was writing for a magazine.

I must confess, the fault was mine. In a hurry to finish what I was doing, I'd pushed the wrong button. Instead of saving my manuscript onto a disk, I had erased it from the computer's memory. When I tried to recall the pages, the words "file not found" flashed across the screen. A knot as big as a baseball formed inside my throat. Three hours' work down the drain!

I blubbered, paced, and scolded myself for fifteen minutes, until it dawned on me that the longer I waited to recall my words, the further they would be from my mind. So I started over. An amazing thing happened. An hour and a half later I'd rewritten the entire eight pages almost exactly the way I'd written them in the first place ... only in places the rewrite was even better than the first draft!

Lord, as I use the computerized tools of the twenty-first century don't let me forget your magnificent gift of brain power nestled inside my head.

Commit your work to the Lord, then it will succeed.
PROVERBS 16:3

MARCH 25

There's an old saying that goes: "I hear and I forget. I see and I remember. I do and I understand."

When I was in college, biology lectures were futile for my non-scientific mind. I could never remember what I'd "heard" about DNA or ribonucleic acid. But later in the lab, when I held two white mice and examined them for similar characteristics, the molecular basis of heredity suddenly came alive for me.

Years later, sometime during the late seventies, my son, Michael, ran into the house, out of breath. "Mom! There's a new waterslide at the park! It's really fast and there's a tunnel and everything!"

I'd never seen or heard of a "waterslide" before and what he was trying to describe was as foreign to me as molecular biology. But a few days later Michael and I went to the waterslide together. For a while I stood at the bottom and watched the kids (and a few adults) screaming with delight as they slid down the wet four-story-tall waterslide with its bobsledlike tunnels and hairpin turns.

But it was only when I climbed up the steps, plopped down at the top and experienced the thrill and feel of the heart-stopping speed and the final splash into the pool at the bottom that I really "understood" what Michael had been trying to tell me. And you know what? I couldn't *wait* to do it again!

Lord, help me to understand life by being a "doer" not just an observer. Help me teach my children to experience everything your great world has to offer.

Then he opened their minds to understand at last these many Scriptures!　　　　　LUKE 24:45

I attended practically every T-ball, Little League, baseball, football, basketball, and soccer game my kids ever played. I was in the audience for every piano recital, play, musical, cheerleading competition, band concert, track and swim meet, music contest, and high-school art exhibit. Many times I wished I could have been doing something else, especially when the event of the day included freezing on cold bleachers at a junior-high football game or sweltering for three hours at a high-school swim meet. But I went and I smiled and cheered and chatted with other parents. I learned that it's just a matter of attitude readjustment. If you *act* as if you're having fun, you usually do.

Why did I go to all those events that, for twenty-four years, constituted about 90 percent of my social life? Because it mattered to my children. Because it was my job. Because if they could put in the long hours of practice, rehearsal, and preparation to be in that game, concert, play, or meet, the least I could do was be there to cheer them on and show my pride in their accomplishments.

If you're one of those parents who's "been there" for your children, keep up the good work. But if you've let the "I'm too busy, I'm a single parent" excuse keep you away from your childrens' events, try to reorganize your priorities. The twenty-four years I put in have gone by in the blink of an eye. My reward is that the impact on my children is tremendous and will, I'm sure, last a lifetime. In fact, it's already crept into the next generation. My children are already attending the same kind of events with their children!

Lord, here are the facts: I am a parent, single or not. Help me be there no matter how hard it is to go alone.

And when my heart is right, then you will rejoice in the good that I do. PSALMS 51:19

MARCH 27

A shoe factory in a tiny Wisconsin town burned to the ground shortly after Christmas. The next day the president of the company made arrangements to use an empty schoolhouse as temporary offices. By noon he'd conferred with an architect on plans for another factory on the site. Then he added the hundred displaced workers to the staff of another factory in a town just a few miles up the road.

Later that same day the man told a reporter that it wouldn't do any good for him or his employees to get depressed. "We manufacture the world's finest shoes and we're going to continue to do that. Everything is going to be better than it was."

I wonder how many of us, when faced with disaster, would be so optimistic and energetic so soon after the mishap? Every day in the news we see families torn apart by a tornado, hurricane, earthquake, and more commonly by separation, divorce, or death. After a natural disaster we often see people sitting on the curb with nothing but the shirts on their backs, wringing their hands, crying. How hard it must be to stand up, scoop up the wreckage, and start over to rebuild what may have taken a lifetime to build in the first place.

When a family is torn apart by separation, divorce, or death, it's just as devastating. But it's so important to stand up, take control, and move forward.

Lord, give me courage to be like the factory president who believed that soon everything would be better than before. Help me to buoy up my family and allow us to start over with faith and determination to fix our brokenness and make our lives better than before.

Why then be downcast? Why be discouraged and sad?
Hope in God! I shall yet praise him again.

PSALMS 42:5

MARCH 28

A cliché is a trite, overused phrase. Good writers try to avoid clichés. Me? I collect them! During the eighties, I started collecting clichés and ended up with over 500 examples to use when I teach writing classes. Phrases like: *Apple pie order, Back to the drawing board, Clear as a bell, Do or die, Easy as pie, Few and far between, Green with envy, Head over heals:* that's just *A* through *H*, and believe me, they go clear through *Z*, with dozens for each letter of the alphabet.

Sometimes our lives and relationships feel like clichés. They start out great. Clever, unique, meaningful. But in time, after lots of use, they become trite, mundane, and overused. They lose their zing. And like clichés, relationships can be taken advantage of and taken for granted.

Is there a relationship in your life—perhaps with your children, your ex-spouse, or a friend—that is becoming overused, taken advantage of, or casually taken for granted?

Instead of expecting a friend to always be on time, why don't we compliment him when he shows up at the door at exactly 7:00 P.M.? Instead of yelling at our children when they forget to do the dishes or take out the trash, why don't we praise them when they complete their chores without being reminded? Instead of berating our "ex" for being late with child support, why not thank him or her for being diligent when it *is* on time?

Lord, just as I need to avoid clichés in my writing, talking, and thinking, help me to keep my relationships strong by not abusing or overusing them. Help me to think of fresh ways every day to stay close to those who love me and to those I love.

My heart is overflowing with a beautiful thought!
PSALMS 45:1

MARCH 29

How many times have I said the words, "put your seat belt on" to a teenager who then rolls his or her eyes heavenward and heaves a great exasperated sigh as if I've just asked him or her to rewrite the dictionary in longhand? How many times have I argued with someone I loved about why it's important to wear a seat belt?

Today I'm going to share something with you that I clipped out of *The Milwaukee Journal* years ago.

Do you know what happens in the first seven-tenths of a second after a car going 55 miles an hour hits a solid object? In the first 10th of the second, the front bumper and grille collapse. The second 10th finds the hood crumbling, rising, and hitting the windshield. Although the car's frame has been halted, the rest of the car is still going 55 miles an hour. Instinct causes the driver to stiffen his legs against the crash, and they snap at the knee joint. During the third 10th of the second, the steering column aims for the driver's chest. In the fifth 10th of the second, the driver is impaled on the steering column and blood rushes into his lungs. By the sixth 10th of the second, the driver's feet are ripped out of tightly laced shoes. The brake pedal breaks off. The car frame buckles in the middle. The driver's head smashes into the windshield. In the seventh 10th of the second, hinges rip loose, doors fly open, and the seats break free, striking the driver from behind. The seats striking the driver do not bother him because he is already dead.

Now will you and your children please buckle your seat belts? And make sure your teens read today's devotional.

Thank you.

Lord, help me keep myself safe for my children … and my children safe for me.

God surrounds him with his loving care, and preserves him from every harm.   DEUTERONOMY 33:12

In 1980, Ken, age fifty-five, was on top of the world. As a professional consultant for a big company, he had such a good time working that he said "it didn't even feel like a job."

One night he stepped out of his car, slipped on a patch of ice and broke his ankle and two bones in his right foot. Three days after the cast was removed he fell at the airport, knocked his head on a chair, fractured his skull and ripped a five-inch gash in his face. A piece of his glasses frame went through his eye and into his brain, leaving the left eye hopelessly damaged. Brain damage caused a speech impediment and left him without coordination in his legs.

Two months later, home from the hospital and walking with two canes, Ken tripped down the step into his sunken living room, fell and broke his right wrist. The next day he got out of bed to answer the door, hit the wall in the hallway and fractured his right shoulder in three places, paralyzing it permanently.

In just a few months, Ken's life turned upside down. Years later he lived in constant pain in a one-bedroom apartment for the disabled and needed an aide to bathe him and clean his apartment. Yet Ken smiles and says, "I can do almost anything I want to do."

Does hearing about Ken put your problems in perspective?

Lord, help me not to get discouraged, depressed, or bitter when things don't go my way. Even when I'm "down and out" help me to smile and offer encouragement to others.

But O my soul, don't be discouraged. Don't be upset. Expect God to act! For I know that I shall again have plenty of reason to praise him for all that he will do. He is my help! He is my God!   PSALMS 42:11

MARCH 31

A clever person once suggested that the seven stages of life are made up of spills, drills, thrills, bills, ills, pills, and wills. Spills are for toddlers, drills for young children, thrills for teens and those in their twenties, bills for young couples and home owners, ills for those in midlife, pills for folks in their sixties and up, and wills for the truly aged, right?

Wrong. The older I get the more I realize there are no definite "stages of life." My dad in his seventies and I in my fifties both feel younger than we did in our thirties. I think I'm experiencing more *thrills* now than ever before in my life, thanks to more exciting vacations, outdoor roller-skating, and adventures with humorous new friends.

On a picnic, I watched a woman step onto a grassy, boggy area, take a spill and sink into muddy, sandy goo. I realized that *spills* are for adults as well as children. At a writing workshop I was asked to write something using my five senses and I learned that life's *drills* are never over. And *bills?* I still have them, but I don't worry about them anymore.

Ills and *pills?* They're all around us. Sickness and disease can happen at age two, twenty-two, or one hundred two. I protect my future health with a good diet and weekly exercise. I'll be hiking in the woods when I'm ninety. And *wills?* Mine's all set.

It's quite a ride, this life we've been given. And it's all up for grabs … that's the best part.

Thank you Lord, for the comfort you offer when our lives suddenly move into a new stage. Help me to accept all the ups and downs with grace and dignity.

We can see and understand only a little about God now, as if we were peering at his reflection in a poor mirror; but someday we are going to see him in his completeness, face to face.   1 Corinthians 13:12

A Prayer for April

Lord, it's April,
And your Word seems to be everywhere.

In the front yard
Hidden roots send shoots, then flowers
Through the winter-hard earth.

Baby birds squeak
From the strangest nesting places.
Newborn farm and woodland animals
Accept caresses and nuzzles from their mothers.

Even in the black storm skies
That open into sunshine and rainbows,
It's there, Lord,
Rebirth, again and again.

Just like Easter, year after year.
The celebration of your rebirth
Can become the celebration of my own rebirth.
Yes, Lord.
Help me to become reborn …
To grow up this time more like you.

APRIL 1

At our house, April Fool's Day is lovingly referred to as "Conception Day." That's because my youngest child, Andrew, was conceived on that day in 1979. Even though Andrew's father and I had been married for ten months prior to that great day, we hadn't yet lived together. We certainly weren't planning to have a child together. After all, Harold was fifty years old and already had six children from his previous marriage, and I had three from mine.

Harold was a high-school principal in Wisconsin, and when we met I lived in Illinois with my three children. Jobs, family responsibilities, and the housing market kept us apart during the week. But every single weekend for two and a half years after our wedding, from Friday at 6:00 P.M. until Monday at 4:00 A.M. Harold was with us in our home in Illinois. Because of those "weekend only" visits I was able to pinpoint the exact day of Andrew's conception.

On that particular Sunday morning, April Fool's Day, while Jeanne, Julia, and Michael were downstairs putting sugar in the salt shaker, turning all the kitchen chairs upside down, and hiding the toilet paper, Harold and I were upstairs enjoying each other's company.

Even though I still tease Andrew sometimes and tell him he was God's April Fool's Day joke, I know that Andrew is one of God's finest examples of "God's will, not mine." I can't imagine life without this young man who has blessed our family a hundredfold.

Heavenly Father, when life hands me a surprise, let me know that it's most often a gift from you to be cherished. Thank you so much for Andrew.

Then God did as he had promised, and Sarah became pregnant and gave Abraham a baby son in his old age, at the time God had said. GENESIS 21:1-2

APRIL 2

A spirited octogenarian was shopping in a Milwaukee drugstore. She had quite a few purchases. The man behind her in line only had one item, so she told him to go ahead. When the man started out the door she noticed he'd forgotten the small plant he'd purchased at the last minute.

The elderly woman called out to the man, but the electronic door was already closing behind him. She told the cashier, "That man forgot his plant." The cashier replied, "Oh no, he bought it for you."

When I heard that story I sensed how easy it is for some people to say "thank you" creatively. Why, the opportunities happen every day!

At the grocery store I could buy a candy bar and ask the clerk to give it to the gentleman who showed me the best buy in oranges. I could offer a ride home to the sweet grandmother who read a story to my young son in the doctor's office. At the shoe store I could buy an extra pair of shoelaces for the teenager who helped me reach the shoes on the top shelf.

Today, let's see if we can't find a creative way to say "thank you" to someone unexpectedly.

Lord, teach me to be more generous and to show my appreciation to others by my own tangible deeds of kindness. Let me begin today.

Yes, God will give you much so that you can give away much, and when we take your gifts to those who need them they will break out into thanksgiving and praise to God for your help.　　　2 CORINTHIANS 9:11

APRIL 3

The newspaper picture showed a large group of surly motorcycle riders perched on their "hog" cycles, with an elderly man in front of them, his right arm raised as if to protect himself.

My immediate reaction was, *That poor guy didn't stand a chance! Those wierdos probably mugged him, then laughed as they gunned their engines and raced off.*

Then I read the caption beneath the picture. "About 250 bikers gathered Sunday to picnic with friends while waiting to have their motorcycles blessed by a Lutheran minister."

Next time I saw a group of black-leather-jacketed motorcycle riders whizzing past me on the street, instead of cowering, I smiled and waved. Know what? They smiled, waved back, and went on their way!

I can recall a number of times I misjudged people because of the way they talked, the clothes they wore, or the type of house they lived in. Sometimes we single parents are also misjudged by others. I'm sure you've heard people talk about "children who come from 'broken' homes." I really bristle at that phrase. A few times when I've heard it, I've responded, as politely as possible, "My home was broken before the divorce. I gave my children a happy home with a single parent."

At any rate, whether we're being misjudged by others or doing the misjudging ourselves, we need to work on our critical attitudes.

Lord, help me not to judge people by the way they look, the clothes they wear, mode of transportation, or marital status. Help me strip away all preconceived notions of stereotype and know that underneath all the trappings we are all created by you, plain and simple.

So don't criticize each other any more.

ROMANS 14:13

APRIL 4

Sometimes I don't think my married friends realize how disconcerting it is to be responsible for everything inside and outside the house. One spring day, I surveyed the terrible mess of my yard. Overgrown bushes, weeds all over the place, and grass so tall that it looked as if it were being used for pasture.

I decided to tackle the mowing first, but when I pulled out the mower I discovered the gas can was empty. Then I saw a sign on the mower: "Check oil before starting engine." I couldn't even find the oil gauge!

On the verge of tears, I called a neighbor for help. He and his family were in the midst of a First Communion party for their son. I apologized for interrupting them and quickly hung up the phone.

Feeling very much alone, I plopped down on the cold concrete garage floor and had a good cathartic cry. It made me feel better, but this wasn't getting me anywhere. So I dried my tears and called another neighbor, who gave me a quick lawn-mower-maintenance lesson and loaned me some gas. Two hours later, after mowing the lawn, pulling weeds, and trimming bushes, I was dripping wet from perspiration and totally exhausted. But somehow I felt better than I had in months.

When I'm depressed or having a bad day, if I do something physically exhausting, I end up feeling much better about life in general.

Is today the day you need to cheer up by pulling weeds, washing the car, cleaning gutters, raking the yard, or washing windows?

Lord, when my mind gets bogged down with worries, put my body to work so I can sweat out my problems.

The Lord God placed the man in the Garden of Eden as its gardener, to tend and care for it.

GENESIS 2:15

APRIL 5

One spring, Milwaukee had so much rain for so many days that much of the city and surrounding suburbs became flooded. I drove home from work through flooded streets to discover my carpeted basement family room was underwater.

Desperately, I threw beach towels on the floor and spent the next hour sopping and wringing. Finally I just sat down on the steps, exhausted and feeling somewhat overwhelmed by the task before me. *Is water still coming in?* I wondered. *Should I take a break and start over later?*

I thought about a newspaper article I'd read about a small Wisconsin town that had been hit by a tornado a few years before. The entire town had been destroyed in a matter of seconds. The next day the news coverage showed pictures of people digging in, cleaning out, and starting the long, tedious process of rebuilding.

Those people must have known what the prophets did when the temple had to be rebuilt, that the only way to get over a disaster is to get up, get going, start doing, rebuild ... and to stay with the job until it's finished.

I stood up, threw more beach towels on the mess at my feet, pulled the carpet outside for a good scrubbing, finished mopping the floor, and by the next day, my family room was good as new, probably better, as I'm sure the floor was a whole lot cleaner than before the flood.

Lord, when disaster falls, don't let me give up. Keep my faith strong enough to believe that I'll get through it and that in the end everything will be better than it was before.

> There were prophets in Jerusalem and Judah ... who brought messages from the God of Israel ... encouraging them to begin building again!   EZRA 5:1-2

APRIL 6

Experts say it takes three to five years to become whole again after a loss of a spouse. But someday, when the time is right, if there is nothing preventing you from remarrying, you'll probably want to start dating other adults who share your interests and beliefs.

If, perchance, the good Lord should send someone into your life, the best advice I can give is this: don't rush into the false commitment of premarital sexual intimacy. It's important to wait until you remarry before God and family.

Considering the fact that there are now something like thirty-eight sexually transmitted diseases out there, abstinence during the dating stage of the relationship is important for your physical well-being. In addition, it is God's plan for us: "For God wants You to be holy and pure, and to keep clear of all sexual sin so that each of you will marry in holiness and honor—not in lustful passion as the heathen do, in their ignorance of God and his ways" (1 Thes 4:3-4).

Making a commitment to remain abstinent outside of marriage is good for your heart also. Think of sexual intimacy as a beautiful flower. Each time you sleep with someone new you give away one petal ... one part of yourself, the most intimate part of who you are. If you sleep with several people over the years, the petals disappear quickly and before you know it, you're left with just an ugly old stem and your self-esteem has disappeared. The place for this kind of intimate self-giving is in marriage ... and only in marriage.

Lord, it isn't easy being single in today's world. Guide and strengthen me, and if I should fall in love again, help me to make it a marriage blessed with the beautiful sexual intimacy reserved for marriage.

That is why I say to run from sex sin. No other sin affects the body as this one does. When you sin this sin it is against your own body.   1 CORINTHIANS 6:18

APRIL 7

April dawned with another month of Milwaukee's impetuous cold weather ahead, and I was out of wood for the wood burning stove. My husband had moved out of the house seven months earlier, and the only person around to split logs and use the chain saw was me.

Fear surfaced. *I can't do this. What if I do it all wrong? We do need the wood, but I'm afraid to use the ax and chain saw.* Finally I heaved the heavy ax down over my head and slammed it into one log after another on the chopping block. Most times I missed the log completely. My shoulders ached, my hands shook. Pieces of wood hit me in the face. But two hours later there was a pile of wood ready to be cut to sixteen-inch lengths with the chain saw.

Terrified that I'd cut through the electric cord or amputate a finger I started the saw. Sawdust flew everywhere … on my neck, in my eyes. I worked on, sweating, aching. A blister on my thumb where the chain saw rubbed started bleeding. The pain in my lower back gave way to tears.

O God, why have you forsaken me? I wondered.

Eight hours later, the woodpile was restocked … and I'd learned something more valuable than how to use an ax or work a chain saw. I'd learned that with determination and inspiration we single people can do anything. Anything! Christ on the cross gave us all the inspiration we need.

Isn't there something in your life that you're afraid to do because you don't think you *can*?

Lord, give me courage to try new things. Stick with me when I'm discouraged. And thank you for the inspiration of the cross.

> He went forward a little and fell face downward on the ground and prayed, "My Father, if it is possible let this cup be taken away from me. But I want your will, not mine."   MATTHEW 26:39

"Mommy, let's walk to the park," four-year-old Andrew begged on the first warm day after a long Wisconsin winter. I was in a down mood with a hundred things to do. But Andrew and the sunshine finally convinced me to abandon duty in favor of Mother Nature.

Andrew scampered out the door. I had to jog to keep up with him. "Let's climb that hill!" he squealed when we reached the park.

I stalled. "There are too many tall weeds."

"There's a path!" he shouted.

At the top he turned to run down. Before I could caution him to slow down he fell face down, then rolled the length of the hill. I expected tears and loud wails, but instead I heard him call out, "Hey, Jill! I went up to get a pail of water and I fell down and broke my crown!" His laughter was contagious.

We came to the footbridge that spanned the creek. Andrew scampered down the bank underneath the bridge. "Mommy, walk across the bridge."

I obeyed, wondering what he was up to now. Then a wee voice, trying to sound mean and ornery, shouted, "Who's that tramping on my bridge?"

I followed my cue. "It's just the littlest billy goat gruff. Don't eat me up!"

Walking home, Andrew put his little hand in mine and with an adoring look said, "I love you, Mommy!"

Today, why don't *you* create some one-on-one magic with your children and discover God's beautiful springtime world?

Lord, thank you for little children who can talk us into a walk in the park, even when we think we don't have time. And thanks also, Lord, for the hundreds of library books I've read to my children that gave them such wonderful imaginations.

And a little child shall lead them.   ISAIAH 11:6

APRIL 9

I once read about a woman who described herself as coming from an "intact single parent family." I like that phrase. I don't want my children to think of themselves as products of a "dysfunctional" family or a "broken" home. But with only one parent in the home, it's difficult to do it all alone.

One of the hardest things we single parents have to learn is to ask for help. Over the years, I asked for help many times from various friends and neighbors, first out of desperation and then more easily because I learned that it makes the person asked feel good.

I called my married neighbor, Bob. "Will you come and tell me if I need to hire a plumber to fix the leaking shower faucets?" Bob had me watch him fix the first faucet, then made *me* fix the other one while *he* watched!

I called my married friend, Pat. "Could you or Gail pick Andrew up after his basketball game? I have a meeting at church at 6:30." Pat said, "Sure, no problem!" He got there early enough to watch the second half of Andrew's game, giving my son a great one-man cheering section.

My neighbor, Cary, snowblows my driveway with his big machine every time we have a big snow. Other friends, who know how much I crave adult conversation, drop in for a cold drink or a cup of tea. The point is, you *don't* have to be alone or do it all alone. You just have to make your needs known and ask for help.

Lord, thank you for friends and neighbors who care. Give me courage to ask for help when I need it. Remind me that I don't have to do this monumental job of parenting all by myself.

He does a kindness who lends to his neighbor, and he fulfills the precepts who holds out a helping hand.
SIRACH 29:1

APRIL 10

One morning during breakfast, fourteen-year-old Andrew spilled a huge glass of milk into a neatly organized basket of my favorite recipe cards. I ranted and raved loudly as I desperately tried to get the milk off every card before the milk smeared the words beyond recognition.

Just before he got on the school bus I took a deep breath and apologized. "I know it was an accident," I told him. "If a friend of mine or houseguest had spilled the milk I wouldn't have lost my cool at all. So why did I take it out on you?"

My wise son answered, "Mom, it's OK. You were just mad at the mess, not at me. You needed to yell, to get the anger out."

Andrew was right about one thing. I *was* mad at the mess, not at him. But I still felt terrible about all the yelling I'd done.

That night I asked God to help me control my anger. Now when I get angry at something Andrew does, I take a deep breath, close my eyes, and picture a houseguest doing whatever he's done to upset me. That mental image has saved lots of harsh words from leaving my lips. And Andrew seems to be sailing through his teenage years with mostly happy days instead of deflating ones, thanks to the fact that I've learned (most of the time, anyway) to put my brain in gear before I open my mouth.

Lord, when my anger buttons are pushed, help me keep my cool. Above all, don't let me say hurtful things to anyone, especially my children.

Stop being mean, bad-tempered and angry. Quarreling, harsh words, and dislike of others should have no place in your lives. Instead, be kind to each other, tender-hearted, forgiving one another, just as God has forgiven you because you belong to Christ.

EPHESIANS 4:31-32

APRIL 11

It's not easy, is it, to always refer to our ex-spouses with kindness in our hearts. I've heard some of my divorced friends refer to their "exs" as uncivilized, clumsy, immature, inexperienced braggarts who are incapable of truly understanding another's feelings. It reminds me of some quotes I've read by a few famous foreigners who describe their feelings about America.

America is a large, friendly dog in a very small room. Every time it wags its tail, it knocks over a chair.
ARNOLD TOYNBEE, BRITISH HISTORIAN

America is a land of boys who refuse to grow up.
SALVADOR DE MADARIAGA, SPANISH STATESMAN

In America the young are always ready to give to those who are older than themselves the full benefits of their inexperience.
OSCAR WILDE, IRISH AUTHOR AND PLAYWRIGHT

What the United States does best is to understand itself. What it does worst is understand others. CARLOS FUENTES, MEXICAN NOVELIST

When I read these quotes I wondered what *my* ex-husband Harold would think of me today, if he were still alive. Even though I think I'm a pretty swell person, it's all a matter of perspective. After all, "it takes two to tango" *and* two to tangle.

The next time you're tempted to speak ill of your ex, try to cut him or her as much slack as you would want him or her to give *you.* Today and every day, if possible, think of one good thing to relay to your children about their absent parent.

Lord, help me get over the bitter feelings I have about my ex-spouse and get on with being the best "me" I can be. Help me, also, to build my spouse up in the eyes of my children, instead of tearing him or her down.

When I was a child I spoke and thought and reasoned as a child does. But when I became a man my thoughts grew far beyond those of my childhood, and now I have put away the childish things.
1 CORINTHIANS 13:11

APRIL 12

Today is "Big Wind Day." On the morning of April 12, 1934 in Mount Washington, New Hampshire, three weathermen observed the strongest natural wind ever recorded on the earth's surface. Gusts reached 231 miles per hour!

Speaking of big winds, I heard once that there are basically two kinds of people in the world. Those who "talk to think" and those who "think to talk." I definitely belong to the former, the "big wind" group. I can blabber on and on during a discussion with just about anyone on almost any subject, all the while forming my opinions as I talk. The more I talk, the clearer my ideas become in my own mind. Sometimes, by the end of the discussion my position has changed 180 degrees from the onset.

On the other hand, I know lots of people who "think to talk." These are the strong silent types, the ones who ponder, listen, read, formulate, contemplate, and *then* talk. The "think to talk" types usually have something pretty profound to say when they finally open up.

"Think to talk" types usually drive "talk to think" people crazy. The "thinkers" are often type B personalities, slow to action, calm, collected, while the "talkers" are generally type A, on the go, full of energy, quick problem solvers.

Today, if you're a "talk to think" person try to be more understanding and more sensitive to the needs of the "think to talk" people you know. Likewise, if you're the thinker type, try to converse more with your talkative loved ones.

Heavenly Father, thank you for making each person on earth unique. Help me to be a good listener and not such a "big wind."

They will talk together about the glory of your kingdom and mention examples of your power.

PSALMS 145:11

APRIL 13

Andrew has been interested in a military career since he discovered at the age of three the adventures he could have with those small, plastic, G.I. Joe characters. When Andrew was sixteen, I took him to visit my dear friends Heidi and Floyd in North Carolina for a week.

Floyd is a colonel in the army and at the time was the chief of staff for the Special Forces division. He took Andrew under his wing that week, giving him a tour of Fort Bragg, and talked about the exciting and often dangerous missions in which the Special Forces "A-Team" members find themselves.

Each "A-Team" comprises twelve men. One commander, one executive officer, one operations specialist, one intelligence expert, two communications experts, two medical specialists, two engineers, and two weapons specialists.

Meanwhile, Heidi and I were talking about the tours she leads to the Holy Land. She takes people on pilgrimages through the paths that Christ and his disciples walked.

Suddenly the two conversations seemed to blend into one. I pictured Jesus and his twelve disciples. Weren't these twelve men a sort of "A-Team"? They all had different talents and strengths, and were trained to perform their duties for the Lord with fervor and expertise. With Simon Peter as the commander and John as executive officer, each of the other men brought a special finesse, based on his abilities, to his role as a disciple for the Lord.

Today, Lord, help me to find ways to become a member of your "A-Team." Help m eto become an expert at this parenting job so that I can be called upon at a moment's notice to do the work you would have me do.

Go and announce to them that the kingdom of Heaven is near. Heal the sick, raise the dead, cure the lepers, and cast out demons. Give as freely as you have received!   MATTHEW 10:7-8

APRIL 14

David was one of my son Michael's best friends when both boys were in grade school. I liked David. He saw me at my worst ... in my long flannel nightgown with my green ratty bathrobe and curlers in my hair. But then I saw him when he didn't look so hot, either. One time I even had to insist that he please wash up before eating, for heaven's sake.

With David I could be playful, serious, joking, or downright angry, and he always understood. He came to my house often, always on his bike. Once I insisted that he get a light on that bike if he was going to stay past dark. He agreed.

I fed him so many meals that I stopped counting and even though he never once reciprocated, I figured that's what friends were for.

I really liked David's quiet sense of humor. Even though he was on the shy side, he still managed a funny one-liner once in a while. I liked that.

I felt comfortable around David. He was a person to be trusted, tousled, and teased. He was willing to share his time and his talents with me. A few times he baby-sat Andrew when the older children were busy and I had to run an errand or two. David also hauled firewood down the hill and inside to the family-room fireplace. Once he spent a whole afternoon picking up sticks under the big-top willow tree.

The problem is, I took David for granted. I never told him what a special young man I thought he was. After he moved, we never saw or heard from him again.

Lord, thank you for all my children's friends. Help me to get to know them, make them feel welcome in our home, and most of all, remind me to help build their self-esteem by complimenting them often on their good qualities.

Cheerfully share your home with those who need a meal or a place to stay for the night.   1 PETER 4:9

APRIL 15

Today is a big holiday for the IRS. Income tax payday is the deadline for paying the cost of federal and state government. As you read this, procrastinating taxpayers are rushing to finish filling out those tax forms, write out their checks, and get the packet in the mail before midnight.

Taxpayers bellyache a lot about the high cost of running the government. Sort of reminds me about how my children used to bellyache about doing their chores. Nobody likes to do what must be done to keep a home or a country running smoothly, but in the end we still have to do the work and we still have to pay the price.

Today might be a good time for custodial single parents to say "thank you" to your noncustodial "ex" for helping to support your children. Today might also be a great time to talk to your children about giving a portion of their baby-sitting or allowance money to the church. Children are never too young to learn that we all must contribute to something worthwhile.

If your income has plummeted and you don't feel you can contribute much, just remember that time and talent are as important as money. So get out there and volunteer your time. Help with child care at the church nursery. Use your mathematical skills to help an elderly couple balance their checkbook. Organize activities at a local nursing home. Attend town meetings and get involved in your community. By the way, getting involved as a volunteer is a wonderful way to chase away those single-parenting loneliness blues!

Heavenly Father, I want to do my share to support my church, my community and my government. Please help me do it without complaining.

"Show me a coin. Whose portrait is this on it? And whose name?" They replied, "Caesar's—the Roman emperor's." He said, "Then give the emperor all that is his—and give to God all that is his!" LUKE 20:24-25

APRIL 16

As parents, we've probably all dreamed of the day when our children will be grown up and out of the realm of our responsibility. I know I sure have. Not so long ago I said things like: "I'll be so glad when Jeanne's out of high school and I don't have to do so much carpooling for all those activities." Or, "I can't wait until Andrew starts school. Then I'll have more time to write, to add hours to my part-time job, to redecorate the house, to … "

Like many parents, I was often looking ahead to the next month or the next year. But these days with only one child at home I often long for those hectic days. I wonder, *How could they grow up and leave so quickly?*

I'd like to tell Jeanne to invite her friends over more often. I'd love to walk into the living room and watch Julia go through her cheerleading routine. Instead of yelling at her for jumping around on the new carpet, I'd watch carefully, then applaud. I'd like to hear Michael's animated account of a funny playground incident. Wouldn't it be fun to watch Andrew racing his little matchbox cars, instead of having to teach him how to drive a real car?

Believe me, they *do* grow up and leave home. But I never guessed it would happen in the blink of an eye. Today, promise yourself that you're going to complain less and enjoy them more.

Today, Lord, I'm going to spend some extra time with my youngest. I'm going to laugh out loud at his corny jokes and hug him for no reason at all. I'm going to treasure every mile as I drive him to swim practice. Lord, let me enjoy my child today and every day.

So be careful how you act; these are difficult days. Don't be fools; be wise; make the most of every opportunity you have for doing good.

EPHESIANS 5:15-16

APRIL 17

Every Saturday for six years my mother drove me twenty miles to the next town for my piano lesson. There were teachers in our town, all right, but the *best* teacher was twenty miles away. So off we went, my mother and I, every Saturday for six years.

The lessons took a big chunk out of my parents' meager budget. And of course, every Saturday afternoon of my mother's life was spent driving me to and from my piano lesson and waiting for me during the lesson.

I never did anything with my music background. I simply confined the gift of six years of piano lessons to myself.

It's been nearly forty years since I quit taking those lessons. I wasted that gift, not only by quitting the lessons before I entered high school, but also by begging off when friends asked me to play for them over the years. I simply took the gift and buried it in the ground to be used rarely "for me" when I feel like sitting down at the keyboard and entertaining myself.

What about you? Do you have the ability to play a musical instrument, organize events, make crafts, or counsel others? It's so important that single parents build up their self-esteem, and the easiest way to do that is to simply take the talents God has given us and *use them!* As for me, it's still not too late to start playing the piano for my family and friends … and perhaps, every now and then, for some nursing-home residents.

Lord, give me the courage to use my talents for the good of others and not to bury them for myself.

For the man who uses well what he is given shall be given more, and he shall have abundance.

MATTHEW 25:29

APRIL 18

One day at work I opened the kitchen refrigerator and laughed aloud. It contained seven almost-empty ketchup bottles, eight paper bags containing half-eaten lunches, a gallon of apple juice that looked as if it had been fermenting for a couple of years, a few slimy vegetables, and a gallon jar of pickle relish. That ridiculous collection made me think of my closet clutter at home. In every closet, cupboard, shelf, and cabinet, useless, unneeded "things" were taking up space and invading my sense of orderliness. Toys that my children have long since outgrown. A collection of rags, more than I could possibly use in a lifetime. Empty cardboard boxes. Enough Christmas decorations to deck the halls of every home in Milwaukee.

What about you? Isn't today a good day to start a little spring housecleaning? Get rid of the useless clutter in one closet per week, and you'll have the entire house or apartment done in no time. Gather everything you haven't used in over a year. Put it in a box and put it in the garage or attic. It's almost a given that you won't miss any of the stuff. Six months later you can take the whole box to your local Goodwill or St. Vincent de Paul Society and be done with it forever.

Dear Jesus, You were never burdened in your life by too many "things." Help my children and me come out from under the clutter that a family collects over the years. Help me to give away the things that still have use to someone who needs and will use them. Help me to throw out the rest, never to think about it again, and to concentrate on the people in my life instead of the "things."

The earth has broken down in utter collapse; everything is lost, abandoned and confused.   ISAIAH 24:19

APRIL 19

When a thief broke into Dad's house and stole my mother's jewelry, I felt the grief of her death all over again. Not only was *she* gone, but now I wouldn't have her favorite personal jewelry pieces to treasure and to pass on to my own children as a special memory of their grandmother.

A few days later, I overheard my children talking about their grandmother. Jeanne recalled how Grandma, with hands crippled from the disease that took her life a few months later, had painstakingly taught her how to embroider. Julia remembered the long autumn walks they took along the canal. Grandma always stopped to exclaim over every colorful leaf that Julia retrieved from the water's edge. Michael said Grandma was the only person who could make sweet rolls so good you could eat a hundred! Then they talked about the little jokes Grandma had played on them over the years … the funny valentines, the hide-and-seek games, and the silly outfits she wore on special holidays. Each tale a special memory, a jewel.

My children had taught me a good lesson: I didn't need Mother's jewelry to keep her spirit alive. I would hand down her most important heirlooms … her gentleness, her willingness to always make time for people, and her quiet sense of humor. If I tried to be more like her I would be passing down a legacy of love, certainly more useful and lasting than jewelry.

Lord, help me to be a good parent to my children by passing on to them the jewels of compassion, sensitivity, openness, friendship, loyalty and a warm sense of humor. And thanks, Lord, for your patience with me.

Christian women should be noticed for being kind and good, not for the way they fix their hair or because of their jewels or fancy clothes.

1 TIMOTHY 2:10

APRIL 20

I am a list maker. At the Lorenz household, the dry-erase board near our front door is forever filled with lists of things to do or buy, errands to run, schedules to keep, carpools to drive, and repairs to make.

My children have also become list makers. Years ago when Jeanne desperately wanted a pair of gerbils, she made this list of reasons why she should have them:

Having gerbils will:
1. Teach me to care for other living creatures.
2. Help preserve the gerbil population.
3. Be a learning experience when they have babies.
4. Provide me a speech topic.
5. Make my room the center of fun for family and friends.
6. Help use the oxygen my plants are producing.
7. Be something warm, furry, and lovable to play with.
8. Keep Mom company when Andrew goes to kindergarten.

Jeanne's thoughtful, persuasive list earned her a pair of gerbils. It also reminded me that it's much easier to accomplish our goals when we write them down.

Starting today, let'swrite down some "spiritual goals" and check them off as we accomplish them. How about these:

1. Read one chapter in the Bible each morning or evening.
2. Write an unexpected thank-you letter.
3. Take a neighbor some fresh-baked cookies.
4. Stop by the local nursing home and visit the first patient who's sitting alone.
5. Offer to help another single parent with extra carpooling.
6. Put love notes on your children's pillows.

Heavenly Father, help me to accomplish my spiritual goals each week by becoming a "list maker for the Lord."

So also is my Word. I sent it out and it always produces fruit. It shall accomplish all I want it to, and prosper everywhere I send it.   ISAIAH 55:11

APRIL 21

The court hearing was over. The judge granted the divorce. Darkness eased its way over the city of St. Louis as we began the six-hour drive back to my hometown in northern Illinois. My mother drove as my three preschoolers fell asleep in the backseat, and I sat in the front enjoying the first peaceful moments I'd felt in years. Dad drove the rental truck that was loaded with seven years' worth of furniture and personal belongings.

Two days later, I looked in my mailbox and found my first letter, a love note from my Dad.

> My dearest Patricia, This little communiqué, hopefully, will be the first one arriving at your new home. Welcome home! For a little while Thursday evening while I was wheeling that big U-Haul eastward over the Mississippi I felt like Moses leading his flock out of bondage. A great burden has been lifted from our minds now knowing you are free from further abuse. Thank God that is all past now.
>
> Lovingly, Dad

Changing our lives midstream can be scary. Going through the pain of a divorce is often the most lonely and frightening feeling of all. It was for me. But when I received that letter from my father, I knew I was not alone.

No matter how bleak or frightening our lives become, we need never fear being alone. God is there in the hearts and minds of those closest to us. He is there protecting us, guiding us, and giving us courage to make necessary changes.

> *Heavenly Father, thank you for carrying me across the water into a new life. Help me to look for you when I'm lonely or frightened. Abide in me and in my children and give me strength to make a better life for us all.*

> There is a river of joy flowing through the City of our God—the sacred home of the God above all gods. God himself is living in that City; therefore it stands unmoved despite the turmoil everywhere.
>
> PSALMS 46:4-5

APRIL 22

One Saturday night when I was about seven years old I'd gone to bed at my usual time, 8:00 or 8:30. By 9:00 P.M. I was into a deep, sound sleep.

"Pat, wake up," Dad whispered as he shook my shoulder, "Are you awake? We want you to come out to the kitchen."

"Huh? Why, Daddy?"

"Your Mom and I decided to have root-beer floats, and we don't want you to miss out. Come on, honey, there's a big Brown Cow out there for you."

I padded to the kitchen in my big pink fluffy slippers and plopped down next to Mom at the old wooden table. I watched Dad scoop the vanilla ice cream into the blue, brown, and yellow mugs that had belonged to my mother and her two brothers when she was a girl. The foam from the root beer tickled my nose as I chatted with my folks about school and then listened excitedly as Mom and Dad discussed plans for our family vacation.

I never felt more loved than I did that night in the kitchen as I groggily slurped root beer and ice cream with my parents. Why? Because Mom and Dad wanted my company enough to wake me up so I could be there. That one simple act did more for my self-esteem than anything I can remember before or since.

Today, Lord, as my children and I work to make our single-parent family a complete family, help me think of many ways to build their self-esteem.

Children are a gift from God; they are his reward.
PSALMS 127:3

APRIL 23

When I was a young girl, my mother developed a painful case of arthritis in her wrist and had to have an injection of cortisone directly into her wrist joint. In my forties my mother's experience became my own. My ankle had hurt for nine months after a bad sprain. I finally went to a specialist, who recommended a shot of cortisone directly into the joint. Suddenly, after thirty years, the memories of what I'd imagined my mother's pain to be surfaced, and terror struck.

As injection time grew closer, my heart beat faster, my fingers and toes turned to ice, and my head throbbed. In the hospital waiting room I stood up twice to walk out, thinking, *I've lived with this pain for nine months. It can't be any worse than the injection.* My conscience answered, *You're being foolish, sit down.*

A nurse scrubbed my ankle and talked about the coming election. I tried to listen but my mind was terrorized. Then the doctor appeared. In five seconds it was over and the sting was no worse than getting a shot in the arm.

For a while I felt foolish for wasting all that time being fearful. I learned that the anticipation of pain is often worse than the pain itself.

Next time your child, parent, or friend comes to you anticipating the worst, be patient. Let that person talk about the fears. Hold his or her hand and listen carefully. Finally, lots of hugs can do wonders to calm a frightened mind.

Lord, thank you for the strength to endure pain. Give me generous doses of compassion so I can help my loved ones deal with it as well. Help me to be understanding, Lord.

Fear grips the waiting people; their faces grow pale with fright.　　　　　　　　　　　　　　　　JOEL 2:6

APRIL 24

"Oh, him? He's been cheating on his wife for years!"

"Those two? Druggies. I know somebody who went to a party at their house once and they were actually selling cocaine."

"Did you see what she had on at work? I'm surprised her husband lets her out of the house in clothes like that."

Gossip. Mean and ugly? You bet. But few of us haven't gotten caught up in it at one time or another.

One time at work I overheard the receptionist talking on the phone about a woman who was living with one man, dating another, and trying to break up her sister's marriage at the same time. It sounded like a soap opera, and I was tempted to find out who she was talking about. But my mother's words, "If you can't say something nice about someone, don't say anything at all," flashed through my mind, and I walked out the door.

How many times had I repeated Mother's words to my own children, especially when they reached the junior-high gossip stage when raking a friend over the coals seemed to be the "in" thing to do?

Reputations are made and destroyed in school hallways, on the telephone, by passed notes, a raised eyebrow, or a questioning look. It's easy to talk about someone who has done wrong. But remember what Jesus said to the crowd who was about to stone the young woman suspected of adultery, "Only he who never sinned may throw the first stone."

Lord, when I'm tempted to harm someone's reputation or hurt their feelings by an unkind or untrue statement, or even an exaggeration of the truth, help me to think of a positive, helpful statement about that person and to say it aloud instead. Help me build others up, not tear them down.

Don't tell your secrets to a gossip unless you want them broadcast to the world.　　PROVERBS 20:19

APRIL 25

The word *please* itself is a great thing to remember when raising children. Say it often and teach them to say it. Politeness goes a long way in this hurry-up world of ours.

You can also use the word "please" to help you remember six important parenting tips:

P = **Positive statements.** Tell your child what he *can* do rather than constantly focusing on what he *can't.*

L = **Limits.** Set clear, fair limits. Explain those limits and the consequences frequently, then stick to them.

E = **Express Emotions.** Tell your children what and how you're feeling, and encourage them to do the same. "You sound angry and hurt. Would you like to talk about it?"

A = **Acceptance.** Your children are not perfect. Neither are you. It's OK for them to know that. Accept your children's weaknesses and concentrate on their strengths.

S = **Sense of Humor.** Nothing breaks tension better than humor. Keep funny movies and a slew of jokes on hand. Be silly! Laughter in the home is an absolute necessity.

E = **Encouragement.** Encourage your child to accept realistic challenges and then to stick with them. Build them up when they become discouraged, praise them when they're successful.

Lord, please, please, please help me to be a better parent. Help me to be loving and patient and to have the courage and energy to do the job well.

And now a word to you parents. Don't keep on scolding and nagging your children, making them angry and resentful. Rather, bring them up with the loving discipline the Lord himself approves, with suggestions and godly advice. EPHESIANS 6:4

APRIL 26

This is the time of year when much of the country sets its clocks ahead for daylight savings time. I remember a few years ago when I arrived at church an hour late for the 9:30 service ... and an hour early for the 11:30 service, because I'd forgotten to set my clock. I felt rather sheepish as Fr. Joe, who was waiting to greet people at the end of the 9:30 service, sent me on my way with a hearty "go home, set your clocks, have an extra cup of coffee, and I'll see you in an hour!"

On my way home I thought, "Wow, I do have a whole extra hour to myself!" Besides setting the clocks and fixing a cup of tea, I had time to read the Sunday paper and put the roast in the oven.

Then it dawned on me that I'd been given the gift of an extra hour of daylight every day until October. I wondered if I'd fritter it away each night in front of the TV or treasure the light by using it wisely?

I decided to take a walk or a bike ride every evening. Or at least work outside in the yard, pulling weeds or watering flowers. Some nights I brought my newspaper out to the patio to enjoy the spring or summer air during my "extra" hour each day.

Starting today, why don't we find something creative to do with our "extra" hour of daylight? Walk with an elderly neighbor. Cheer on a youngster at his or her Little League game. Escape to a secluded spot in the backyard with a Bible—the psalms make lovely reading in the springtime outdoors.

Lord, thank you for this extra hour of daylight after my workday is over. Help me think of ways to use it wisely and lovingly.

There are twelve hours of daylight every day, and during every hour of it a man can walk safely and not stumble.   JOHN 11:9

I like contemporary greeting cards for every occasion, the wilder and funnier the better. One year for Valentine's Day, I gave my husband a card with a photograph of two bananas on the front. Inside, the card simply said, "You're driving me bananas, but I love you anyway."

He gave me one of those gloppy, flower-filled, serious cards with a mushy verse that went on and on. I honestly didn't even bother to read all the words.

On our second wedding anniversary, he sent me his typical mushy card. My card to him that year was homemade with a funny picture on the front and a goofy verse inside.

As the years went on I continued to howl at the funny, pun-filled, slapstick, silly cards I sent him. And Harold continued to say, "Did you read the words?" after I opened his sentimental cards and barely skimmed the verse.

Then one year I was thanking my mother for some beautiful dinner napkins she'd given me for my birthday. "It's the perfect gift! How did you know I wanted napkins?"

"Simple," she said. "You've been giving cloth napkins to everyone lately, and people often give what they themselves want."

Mom was right. I did give what I really wanted. I thought about all those silly cards I'd given my husband. He obviously liked sentimental cards better, because he had a need to read those soft, romantic words. He had been giving to me what he actually needed for himself.

When I look back at our separation and divorce, I wonder if that was just one of the many things about relationships that I learned too late.

Lord, help me look more carefully into the hearts of my loved ones, especially my children, and to see their needs, their longings. Teach me to give with the receiver's needs in mind, not mine.

Be delighted with the Lord. Then he will give you all your heart's desires.   PSALMS 37:4

APRIL 28

When I was growing up, as well as when my four children were growing up, my godmother, Aunt Bernadine, had three words of advice for us. "Just say no." It was as if her mission in life was to tattoo those words to the brains of all her nieces and nephews. Aunt B didn't go into great detail about it, but we all knew we were to say no to drugs, drinking, and premarital sex.

As a single parent raising children in the nineties, I've tried to adapt and expand on Aunt Bernadine's simple philosophy.

In addition to saying "no" to the big three, I've added a few others in my discussions with my children.

"Just say no" to stereotypes. Don't be afraid to be your own person. Find out who *you* are and then *be* that person.

"Just say no" to brutality, emotional and physical abuse, violence, and cruelty. No one should *ever* tolerate these.

"Just say no" to ethnic jokes and racial slurs. Choose your friends based on what you have in common, rather than on the color of their skin.

"Just say no" to doing half the job. Don't quit the team once you've made the commitment. Read the entire book.

"Just say no" to going too fast, whether it's in a relationship or in a car. Speed kills.

"Just say no" to wasting time. There are too many things to do, places to go, adventures to have, and people to meet to waste time doing unnecessary things.

Lord, help me to follow my conscience and "just say no" and to teach my children not to be afraid to do the same.

Assign me Godliness and Integrity as my bodyguards,
for I expect you to protect me. PSALMS 25:21

APRIL 29

I'll never forget what happened when a fire killed five of the nine children of a Mennonite family in rural Wisconsin. According to the extensive media coverage, the fire also destroyed the family's home. As news of the tragedy spread across the country, donations poured in to help pay for a new home.

However, the other forty families that lived in the rural Mennonite community went the extra mile. In little over a month they actually built a new two-story, four-bedroom house right next to the foundation of the old one.

There were even some Mennonites from the Pennsylvania area who came to Wisconsin to help rebuild their house, people who left their farms, jobs, and families and interrupted their lives to help out.

Giving money to someone in need is indeed praiseworthy. But I wonder, if a friend of mine lost everything in a fire, would I offer to interrupt my life and help build a new home, working day and night until the job was finished? I doubt it. Oh, I might invite them for dinner, offer to care for the children, or donate household goods and clothes ... but I doubt if my "giving" would go much further.

Perhaps we need to try to pattern our lives after those in the Mennonite community when it comes to giving. It's true, especially for single parents, that a five-dollar donation can be a big sacrifice, but let's not forget the value of giving time and talent as well. Sometimes, giving time and talent is an even bigger sacrifice ... and much more helpful.

Lord, help me to be a better, more complete giver by putting my own needs behind those of others. Help me to teach my children how to give their time, talent and treasure by being a threefold giver myself.

Be sure that you feed and shepherd God's flock.
ACTS 20:28

APRIL 30

As the car winds down the steep road, I anticipate the first glance of Lake Michigan. There it is: a picture-postcard-perfect scene. Steel-blue lake water. Rhythmic white-capped waves. Hundreds of gray-white seagulls foraging for their breakfast in the fine, crinkly beige sand. An early morning soft-blue sky, flecked with pink and white horizontal streaks. A gentle wind across my face seems to revive my frazzled emotions.

Last night's heated argument with my fourteen-year-old daughter comes to mind. I wince at the many sharp words we've exchanged lately over the messy condition of her room. Why can't she keep her space orderly?

I notice this exquisite scene before me, strewn with bits of paper, aluminum cans, picnic trash, broken bottles. It's hard for many people to keep their special places in order. Do the people who left the litter have bedrooms that look like my daughter's?

I smile, knowing my daughter would never leave litter along this beach. She loves this place as much as I do.

In spite of the rubble, the lake is still breathtakingly beautiful … just like my daughter. I think about her beauty as a person and her remarkable artistic and musical talent and decide to quit nagging her. I toss cans and trash into a bin, knowing someone will clean up the whole beach area with a front-end loader, just as I know that on Saturday my daughter will clean up her room.

Lord, thank you for this lake and for allowing me to use it to put my life in proper perspective. Help me become a better, more patient, more appreciative single parent. And please, Lord, let the children notice.

Are you going to condemn me just because I impulsively cried out in desperation?   JOB 6:26

A Prayer for May

It's May? Already, Lord?
Oh no! The busy month!
Yardwork to do, flowers and garden.
End of school, children's programs.
Backyard parties, graduations.
Hurry, hurry.
Spring luncheons, buy new clothes.
Piano recital, weekend guests.
Exams to take, deadlines to meet.
Shop for gifts, showers, weddings.
Hurry, faster, we're going to be late!

Lord, grab hold of me.
Stop me. Settle me down.
Help me to find time for you.
In the hammock, under the trees,
With the Book of Psalms.
Help me to collect my thoughts,
Ponder my riches (my family and this hammock)
And to praise your glory and your calm.

In many parts of the country, the first week in May is observed as National Family Week. Single parents may have to work a little harder to create the love, warmth, loyalty, spirit, and devotion that may be more obvious in a traditional two-parent family. When Michael was a teenager and I'd tell him he couldn't do something because we had "family" plans, he'd grumble, "We aren't a family, not a *real* one." His words stung, but I knew in time he'd understand that we *were* and *are* a real family. Now that he's a husband, father, and high-school teacher, Michael is very proud of the "family" he grew up in.

There are many ways to create a "family" attitude. Plan to have family dinners where you sit down together to dine, discuss, and dream. Let the children know that at least three times a week, nothing short of a tornado will interrupt your family dinnertime. Plan family vacations at least once or twice a year, even if it's just a three-hour drive to visit grandparents or other relatives. Have a family meeting at least once a week to discuss coming events and family problems. Attend church as a family, every Sunday. Your faith is the glue that holds your family together. Weekly church attendance and Sunday school classes for everyone will help bond you together as a family.

Lord, help us to cherish each other so much that there's no doubt in anyone's mind that we are a real family … a growing, loving tribute to your goodness.

Your strength must come from the Lord's mighty power within you.   EPHESIANS 6:10

MAY 2

Oh, the things our children say. How many times have you said, "I wish I could remember all those funny things Johnny said when he was little"?

Children can come up with the most amazing philosophical, hilarious, nonsensical, whimsical, wise, and downright inspirational one-liners. Our childrens' verbal gems need to be written down so they can be preserved for all time.

If you still have young children at home, or even grandchildren, buy a notebook that you can keep in a convenient place so you can grab it in a hurry. Then, whenever your child comes up with one of those "I don't believe you said that!" gems, write it down. Be sure to put the child's name and the date on the entry.

When your children are grown you'll have the makings for a best-seller ... or at the very least a treasure to share at family gatherings.

Here are a few examples from my own children.

Jeanne, at age seven: "Daddy's kisses are always wet. So I wipe 'em off on my teddy bear and save 'em!"

Julia, age eight: "I love your Christmas gift best, Mommy! What was it again?"

Michael, age ten: "We better cut it out. Dad's about to say 'Jeepers crimeney!'"

Andrew, age three: "Deedle deedle dumpling, mice on John."

Thank you, God, for my children and for the wise, witty, and wonderful things they say. Help me to always speak from my heart the way they do.

Out of the mouths of babes ...   PSALMS 8:2, KJV

The most wonderful greeting card I ever received was the hand-made, beautifully painted Father's Day card my daughter, Jeanne, sent me a few years after I became a single parent. Her sweet note said that I'd been both mother and father to her, and she just wanted me to know how much she appreciated it.

Ever since I became a single parent, my Mother's Days have varied considerably. Some were wonderful, others not so great.

The fact is, Mother's Day is generally orchestrated by fathers. In two-parent families, the dads take the kids shopping and help them buy gifts for Mom. Some husbands give their wives gifts. But when there's no dad around, a mom is lucky if a thoughtful teacher has organized the making of a Mother's Day card during art class.

For many single parents, Mother's Day (or Father's Day) is the most important day of the year. That's because parenting is our most important job. For just this one day, we truly *do* want to be cherished.

So this year why don't you find another single parent and offer to "orchestrate" this celebration for each other? Trade kids for a few hours. Take the children shopping for Mother's Day surprises. Help wrap the gifts, if necessary. Plan a festive brunch with both families. The children will be excited about the whole idea … and believe me, *you* will have a day to remember.

Jesus, you so loved and honored your mother. Please help me make this coming Mother's Day truly special for a mother whose children may not have the ways and means to do it for her.

I will comfort you as a little one is comforted by its mother.   ISAIAH 66:13

I never owned a dog and, until a few years ago, didn't even know how much care they needed. My friend Betsy taught me one Saturday morning when, during one of our weekly five-mile "fast walks," a well-groomed, stocky, pointy-eared puppy appeared at our heels. Of course Betsy had to break stride and bend down to pet him. I agreed he was cute, but secretly wished he'd go home so I wouldn't be tripping over him.

The puppy followed us six blocks to a service station where Betsy insisted we stop to get him some water. Our next stop was the police station, where we reported the "found" dog. When we left the station the puppy was right on our heels. A half-mile later Betsy scooped up the little tail wagger because she said he was getting tired.

By mile four I reached for His Little Majesty to give Betsy a break. It was like carrying a squirming twenty-pound bag of flour. I could feel the puppy's heart beating wildly against my chest. I'd never carried a dog before in my life, but I could tell he was glad he didn't have to race to keep up with us anymore.

No one claimed the puppy, so Betsy's family welcomed "Bandit" into their lives, justly named because he "stole" their hearts.

The day I watched Betsy treat that little pup with respect, dignity, and kindness and I saw him respond likewise, was the day I learned what it means to "be kind to animals." And even though I will probably never be a dog owner myself, I am always amazed at the vast amount of affection and loyalty my friends' pets have for them ... and vice versa.

Lord, since this is Be Kind to Animals Week, keep me mindful that basic kindness to animals always returns itself a hundredfold. Keep me mindful that it works the same way with humans as well.

> May the Lord be loyal to you in return, and reward you with many demonstrations of his love! And I too will be kind to you because of what you have done.
>
> 2 SAMUEL 2:6

MAY 5

Eight-year-old Andrew and I were out to buy sneakers. There was only one other person in the shoe store with the sales clerk … a teenage boy, wearing trendy clothes, loafers, and no socks. He was paying for a pair of athletic shoes when we walked in. He received his change and walked over to a rack of sport socks.

The clerk went to the back room to find Andrew's blue size fives. I glanced up to see the young man shove a pair of fluffy white socks into his bag as he walked toward the front door.

When the clerk returned I whispered, "Did he buy a pair of socks?"

"No, why?"

"Well, I just saw him stuff a pair of socks into his bag."

The clerk ran after the young shoplifter. I felt smug. Perhaps he'd learn his lesson and avoid a life of petty crime.

Suddenly the clerk returned, a bit red-faced. "Those were socks he brought into the store to try on his sneakers with."

"Oh, I'm sorry," was all I could say.

Did you ever misjudge or accuse someone wrongly? After that day I tried to gather *all* the facts before I opened my mouth … especially when I was dealing with fragile teenage egos.

Today Lord, help me make a list of my own faults and to look at it periodically, so I won't be so quick to criticize or accuse others.

Never criticize or condemn—or it will all come back on you. Go easy on others; then they will do the same for you. LUKE 6:37

MAY 6

Today is National Nurses Day. The official declaration states that its purpose is "to pay tribute to all those in the nursing profession for their vital contribution to mankind in providing health-care services to people of all ages."

We all know how vital nurses are. All of us probably know at least one nurse personally. I am close to seven of them: my daughter-in-law, Amy; my godmother, Aunt Bernadine; my daughter's boyfriend; and four of my dearest friends.

From what I've gathered, nursing is a profession for the saintly. It involves life-and-death details coupled with never knowing what to expect from one minute to the next. Nursing is for the person who is so magnanimous that he or she can empty a bedpan one minute, fill out tons of paperwork the next, and comfort a hurting soul while administering treatment and easing pain.

Why don't we do something nice for the nurses we know? A big bear hug in appreciation for their tough job would be a great starter. A kind letter or small plant delivered to a hospital, clinic, nursing home, or school where your nurse friend or relative works would be nice. Ask your children for suggestions!

Lord, when I'm sick and in need of physical and emotional comforting, thank you for nurses who care about me. Thank you for my loved ones who are nurses. Today, let me be the one to comfort them.

Are they my children? Am I their father? Is that why you have given me the job of nursing them along like babies until we get to the land you promised their ancestors?   NUMBERS 11:12

MAY 7

One spring morning, I rolled out of bed at 6:30 to say a few cheery words to my sixteen-year-old daughter, Jeanne, who was auditioning for the high-school musical that day.

I started, "Your hair sure looks nice, honey. I like it pulled up in a twist."

She grunted. "I hate it. It looks dorky. I'm going to take it down."

Undaunted, I proceeded. "Well, your singing sounds good. I'm sure you'll do fine at the audition today."

She scooted the piano bench under the piano and scowled, "I sound terrible. My voice stinks."

Determinedly, I went on. "You know, I really like your new sweater. It's a good color for you."

"It's too big," she growled.

If there's such a thing as getting up on the wrong side of the bed, she must have done it twice that day.

Those early-morning "wrong side of the bed" encounters with my teenagers could have left me in tears … or in the midst of a no-win shouting match. But I'd learned not to let them get to me. Why? Because by the time those teenagers walked back into our kitchen eight hours later, things were *always* much different.

That afternoon Jeanne danced in the door. She was gleeful, "I got the part!" And then we hugged.

Lord, I don't always understand my teenagers. Help me to remember that they just need to blow off steam and I just need to be there to listen. Help me to remember that the exasperating times with my teens make the sweet times even sweeter.

Keep silence and I will teach you wisdom!   JOB 33:33

Self-esteem gurus, psychiatrists, sociologists, and health-care workers know how important it is for us to have specific goals and to work toward them.

Goal setting is especially important for single parents. We often get so caught up in life's rat race that we feel as if we're on a treadmill. Today, take a few minutes to decide what you want that you don't already have. It can be anything ... a better job, more time for your children, more time for yourself, or a closer relationship with God. Make a plan and back it up with plenty of determination and persistence, and you'll get what you want ... guaranteed.

Here are a few ideas for helping you get more out of life: Believe you can achieve your goal and repeat it aloud in a positive way every day. For instance, say, "I make enough money to support my family." Or, "I am a happy, healthy person." Write down what you want. List the benefits of achieving it. Make a deadline for when you expect to accomplish it. Figure out what must be done to get it. Write down your detailed, step-by-step plan. Find people who can help you make it work. Every day picture yourself after you've achieved your goal. How will you look, what will you be doing, where will you be? Make a list of the pitfalls you need to avoid ... for example, arguing with the boss, or buying junk food. Never give up. Winners never quit. Quitters never win.

Lord, help me to get where I need to be in life by reaching for specific goals. Be with me every inch of the way.

So I run straight to the goal with purpose in every step. I fight to win. I'm not just shadow-boxing or playing around.   1 CORINTHIANS 9:26

MAY 9

Somehow the month of May brings all sorts of reminders that we are single in a world geared to couples. Besides Mother's Day and Father's Day, springtime brings couples out of the woodwork, walking blissfully hand in hand. Bridal showers, weddings, and numerous family events seem to pop up this time of year.

So let's make today a new holiday. Let's call it "Singlehood Day." Why don't we make a list of the things we like about being single? Here is part of my list.

1. You don't have to pick up after another adult.
2. You can sleep in the middle of the bed if you want.
3. There's only one alarm clock in your bedroom to irritate you in the wee hours.
4. Toothpaste is always rolled up the way you like.
5. Your favorite *healthy* cereal doesn't disappear after two days.
6. You can spend time with your friends and relatives any time you want for as long as you want.
7. You get to make all the decisions without long discussions or arguments.
8. You don't have to feel guilty for being in control of the checkbook.
9. The car seat is always in the right position.
10. Best of all, you get to be "head of household" without any arguments.

Heavenly Father, be with me as I live my life as a single adult in a "couples" world. Help me to cherish my freedom and to use my energy to be a great parent and a great person.

I have learned the secret of contentment in every situation.   PHILIPPIANS 4:12

MAY 10

As a radio copywriter, I learned that anything said well can best be said with as few words as possible. Over the years I wrote nearly fifty thousand radio commercials, and I learned you can say a lot in sixty or thirty seconds. Sometimes you can get your message across in ten seconds.

George Washington knew the value of a *few* well-chosen words. His inaugural address took less than ninety seconds to deliver. When I heard that, I started to wonder if I could get my point across to my children in fewer words, especially when I was correcting them.

Next time I was angry with fourteen-year-old Andrew about leaving his room a mess, I wanted to bombard him with my usual lengthy maternal wisdom about why he should keep his room clean. If I hadn't stopped myself, I'd have delivered my usual five-minute "messy room" tirade. But instead I delivered my message in ten seconds flat. Andrew got the point.

Later that evening, Andrew beamed as I inspected his room. "So Mom, how do you like my room now?"

I smiled, knowing *now* was the right time to blabber on and on. I congratulated him, praised him, and pointed out how nice it was that he'd finally found an organized home for some of his latest acquisitions. Andrew didn't seem to mind my "wordiness" a bit during my praise fest.

I learned that when you're correcting a child, fewer words work best. Less is definitely more. But when it's time for some positive strokes, the more the merrier.

Lord, when I'm upset, help me to keep my words brief—and let me save my wordiness for praising.

The man who uses well what he is given shall be given more.　　　　　　　　　　　　　　MATTHEW 25:29

It's a beautiful May morning, seventy degrees outside, and I'm sitting in a very comfortable yellow rocker on my deck with a large mug of Irish breakfast tea. Two squirrels are dining on the ear of corn attached to the "squirrel diner" at the end of the deck, and a dozen birds are singing their way through breakfast, also provided by the management.

This deck at 7:00 A.M. is my piece of heaven ... and my place and time for prayer. No newspapers, books, people, or phone calls. Just me, the birds, squirrels, and God.

Morning prayers were part of my life as a child. From first through twelfth grades the Sisters of Loretto orchestrated morning prayers at school. But in the course of college, marriage, and motherhood, my morning prayers fell by the wayside.

Then one summer, as a busy single parent, I discovered how quiet and peaceful it was on my deck in the early morning. Those moments filled me with such calm that I began to pray, mostly from sheer joy. I thanked God for this place of beauty and this hour of quiet. I praised him for the trees ... and asked him for many favors.

Do you have a specific place and a definite time for morning prayer? No matter where you pray, it's an amazing way to begin your day. It starts each day on a positive, happy note.

Promise yourself twenty or thirty minutes alone in your favorite spot every morning. Bring a cup of tea or coffee and perhaps the Book of Psalms to get you started.

Today Lord, bless this place and time that I've set aside to be with you. And bless all those I pray for.

Each morning I will look to you in heaven and lay my requests before you, praying earnestly.   PSALMS 5:3

MAY 12

Research tells us that between the ages of two and four, 95 percent of all children are highly creative. But by age seven only 4 percent of all children are highly creative. What destroys their natural creativity? Adults constantly tell children, "Don't do this, don't do that, color between the lines, stand here, sit there, play with these toys, don't spill." Is it any wonder they lose their natural sense of creativity?

One year I decided to try an experiment. I sent my four favorite little people (nieces, nephew, and granddaughter) a dollar each with this note:

Dear Sarah, Jacob, Anna, and Hailey:

The enclosed dollar is for you to buy a bag of cherry red "Pull 'n Peel" candy. Please enjoy the whole bag as creatively as possible. Take a picture of different ways you can "wear" your "Pull 'n Peel" and send me a picture. The person who sends me the most creative "Pull 'n Peel" photo wins $5. Contest is only valid if at least three of you participate. Good luck, my favorite little people. I love you loads, tons, gobs, bushels, bags, and barrels.

Well, the photos I received from those ten-, seven-, six- and three-year-old children were absolutely hilarious. Best of all, I bet they raised their creativity quotients up a notch or two. Today, why don't you think of something that will stretch your child's sense of creativity?

Lord, thank you for little children who are truly creative. Help me to keep them that way ... and also, Lord, help me to be more like them.

I tell you as seriously as I know how that anyone who refuses to come to God as a little child will never be allowed into his Kingdom.　　　MARK 10:15

MAY 13

Did your ex-spouse remarry? Many times it's difficult to deal with the new stepmother or stepfather in your children's lives.

I have a stepmother. And instead of treating her like an outsider in my dad's home, my brother, sister, and I decided early on to accept and cherish her.

Over the years, Bev has totally changed our dad's life. Instead of feeling sad, lonely, and out-of-sorts like he was after Mother died, he is now vibrant, happy, and always on the go. Bev is a gem whose optimistic personality adds sparkle to Dad's life. Together, they travel the country by car or plane, more often than not, visiting *his* friends and relatives. She smiles and loves every minute of their life together.

I know it's not quite the same when your ex-spouse remarries, but I think stepmothers and stepfathers have generally been given a bum rap. Because stepparents are an important part of your child's life, and because letting go of any pent-up emotions toward the new spouse does you a world of good, treat that person with respect and kindness.

Let's pretend this is "Step-parent Day." If your children have a stepparent, encourage them to express appreciation and love. A homemade greeting card or a phone call just to say "hi" might be a good way to start.

Lord, help me to be a loving, considerate stepchild and/or to teach my children to be the same. Bless all the stepparents in the world who are trying to be good role models to our children.

May my spoken words and unspoken thoughts be pleasing even to you, O Lord my Rock and my Redeemer.   PSALMS 19:14

MAY 14

A high school cook won a million dollars in the Illinois state lottery a number of years ago. When I interviewed her for a local radio station, I was surprised that she had no intention of quitting her job. In fact, she continued on as a hard-working, hot-water-up-to-her-elbows, ever-smiling cook until she reached retirement age.

How would it change my life if I won a million dollars? Would I become a different person? Would I try harder to make even *more* money, or would I count my blessings?

Taking a good look at my life, I see that I am already wealthy in the things that really count. I have four happy, healthy children; loving relatives; devoted friends and neighbors; an active, concerned church; a comfortable home; and an interesting career. When I long for a newer, more comfortable car, a better wardrobe, or more luxurious vacations, I try to count my blessings instead.

What things in *your* life make you feel like a millionaire? Why not make a list of them and tape it over the kitchen sink? When you're having one of those "feel sorry for myself" days, it will remind you that being thankful for the things that really matter is a lot easier and more pleasant than being wistful.

Lord, you have blessed us with so many good things. On those days when my children or I start to dwell on what we don't have, help us to concentrate instead on the many blessings that we do have.

It is easier for a camel to pass through the eye of a needle, than for a rich man to enter the kingdom of God.   MARK 10:25

MAY 15

Once, when talking to my airline pilot friends, Dave and Lyle, I asked how pilots remain calm during disasters. They smiled and said, "The five step plan."

Lyle continued, "The same 'Five Steps to Problem Solving' the military uses: One … retain control; Two … define the problem; Three … review your objectives; Four … develop and evaluate the alternatives; Five … decide on a course of action."

"In other words," Dave added, "when you have an emergency, the most important thing is to not to get distracted and forget to fly the plane. Then you list the symptoms and get to the *root* of the problem. After reviewing your ultimate goal, you work out possible solutions. Finally, you decide on a course of action, which is usually to try one possible solution after another until the problem is solved."

I've concluded that the "Five Steps to Problem Solving" is the most logical way to solve problems with children as well. Think of any problem a child might have: a report card loaded with Ds and Fs; being disrespectful to a teacher or parent; drinking; cheating on a test at school; feeling unloved.

If you sit down with that child and write down the symptoms, possible causes, possible solutions, alternatives, and then decide on a course of action, you'll not only solve the problem, but you'll give your child an invaluable lesson in problem-solving that will last a lifetime.

Lord, when my life feels like it's in a tailspin and I'm about to crash, keep me calm, then help me find logical solutions to my problems.

When the queen of Sheba heard how wonderfully the Lord had blessed Solomon with wisdom, she decided to test him with some hard questions.

1 KINGS 10:1

MAY 16

When my four children were all still living at home, I seemed to worry about everything: my job, health, the bills, getting the children through college.

One day I interviewed Tom Trebelhorn, the manager of the Milwaukee Brewers baseball team, for a magazine article I was writing.

I talked to Treb about the Brewers amazing 1987 season when they fell from an incredible, history-making 13-0 season starter, right into a 12-game losing streak.

How did Treb keep going after such a downslide? He said with determination, "I live by 'The Ten-Day Plan.' If there's any way a problem will change or go away in ten days, I don't waste precious time even thinking about it, let alone worrying about it. Every spring I get hay fever so bad I could scratch my eyes out. But it never lasts more than ten days, so I refuse to worry about it. Truth is, if we have faith in the talent God has given us, practically everything is either solved or at least gets better within ten days, including the Brewers' win-loss record."

I decided to stop worrying about all the things that plague me as a single parent. Instead I concentrated on getting by for ten days at a time. Before I knew it, three years had passed, I'd had two raises at work, paid off my house, and had three kids in college ... and as far as I can recall, nothing happened during that time that ten days didn't cure.

Lord, give me a big dose of faith and trust. Instead of worrying, help me to keep plugging along, one day (or ten) at a time, with the talent and determination you've given me.

Commit everything you do to the Lord. Trust him to help you do it and he will   PSALMS 37:5

MAY 17

One day when I was still writing commercials for a radio station I found a note on my desk from one of the radio sales people. It said, "Pat, you are a gem and a treasure! Thank you for the super job you did for me on those two commercials last week!"

That note filled me up like a balloon and put a smile on my face that lasted all day. I pinned the note to my bulletin board, where it was a constant reminder that my efforts were appreciated. It made such an impression on me that I decided to give it a try myself.

To my daughter's piano teacher: "Sister Mary Ellen, you're doing such a great job with Jeanne. She doesn't even mind practicing anymore!"

To the paperboy: "Joe, thanks for bringing the newspaper right up to our door every day. You're such a fine, conscientious newsboy that someday you could be the editor!"

To my daughter: "Julia, thank you for taking such good care of your little brother after school. He loves spending time with you. Someday you will be a wonderful mother."

Little notes only take two or three minutes to write, but they're worth a fortune.

Give it a try. Today, write a couple short thank-you notes. You might be surprised what happens.

Lord, keep me mindful of all the nice things that are done for me and for my children. Nudge me to say "thank you" on paper.

And now God can always point to us as examples of how very, very rich his kindness is, as shown in all he has done for us through Jesus Christ.   EPHESIANS 2:7

MAY 18

I'd been feeling like an overloaded circuit about ready to blow. Single-parenting four children and working three part-time jobs left me absolutely no time for myself.

One busy spring day I looked out the window at our barn-sized willow tree and suddenly found myself inviting my youngest, six-year-old Andrew, to have lunch with me under the tree. We spread a blanket, ate, read stories, and tree gazed. It was wonderful.

After that I decided to make a conscious effort to slow down and smell the daisies at every opportunity. The next day, I pointed out a squirrel's nest full of babies to all the kids and we all enjoyed watching the little squirrels scamper about.

The following day while running errands with a car full of kids, I happened to see a family of woodchucks popping their heads up and down in a cabbage field. I stopped the car so we could watch their antics. That little reprieve from our rush-rush routine brought out all sorts of comments, questions, and later an encyclopedia session.

The kids learned about woodchucks, but I learned how important it is to take time from our busy days to enjoy the little things in life. Taking those breaks had somehow eased the stress and worry in my life.

Today, why don't you take one of the littlest bits of your life and just plain enjoy it? You might find that those big problems you thought you had aren't so big after all.

Open my eyes, Lord, to the little things around me that can calm me down.

And if God cares so wonderfully for flowers that are here today and gone tomorrow, won't he more surely care for you?   MATTHEW 6:30

MAY 19

When Jeanne, my oldest daughter, said she wanted to spend the summer studying art in Europe, my faith in the impossible did not stretch far enough to comprehend such an adventure. I suggested something more appropriate for her that summer—like a job at a fast-food restaurant.

Jeanne's faith, however, was a different matter. She even had the audacity to send off her application *without* the $35 application fee. I pointed out that the Open Door program probably wouldn't even look at it, much less consider it. Jeanne reminded me gently, "Mother, I'll never know if I can go if I don't try."

After many phone calls from the program director in New York, Jeanne received a scholarship and a large government grant. On a bright day in July, she left for Cologne, West Germany, to study art and architecture for six wonderful weeks.

Is there something you think is impossible in your life? A promotion at work? An exciting vacation with your children to a distant place? A long weekend by yourself in a cabin on a lake somewhere? Well, gather up your faith and *believe* that you can do it. Then make a plan. Write a letter or do the first thing that needs to be done to make your goal achievable. Do one thing toward your goal every day. Plug ahead like that little engine that said, "I think I can, I think I can."

Lord, when I'm tempted to say "I can't" give me generous doses of "I can do anything" faith, and a truckload of determination. Then watch me soar! Also, Lord, help me pass on my newfound "anything is possible" faith to my children.

"If you had faith even as small as a tiny mustard seed you could say to this mountain, Move! and it would go far away. Nothing would be impossible."
MATTHEW 17:20

MAY 20

Do you ever feel that life is dumping more on you than you can possibly handle alone? That feeling reminds me of the time, shortly after my friends, Bob and Betsy, were married, that Bob ordered twelve yards of dirt for his garden, not knowing how much dirt that really was. (He really only needed four yards of the stuff.)

A few days later a huge dump truck pulled up in their driveway. The driver hollered, "Where do you want it?" Bob pointed to the driveway. "You can put mine here. Where's the rest of that load going?"

As the man raised the back end and the dirt started sliding onto the driveway he grinned. "It's all yours. All twelve yards."

Bob could have fussed and fumed and made himself and everybody around him miserable. But instead, he and Betsy had a good laugh. Then he did four things to solve the problem:

First, Bob suggested that Betsy use some of the dirt to expand and enhance her flower gardens.

Second, Bob decided to double the size of his vegetable garden and share his bountiful harvest.

Third, Bob's brother happened to be visiting that week and moving, shovel by shovel, the "larger than life" load of dirt gave the two brothers something vigorous to do together.

Fourth, Bob offered free dirt to anyone up and down the street. In so doing, he got acquainted with much of the neighborhood.

Lord, when life dumps more dirt than I can handle, help me to find creative ways to make mudpies out of mud. Help me to be an optimist and put one foot in front of the other and just get the job done.

Hear me, Lord; oh, have pity and help me.

PSALMS 30:10

MAY 21

I'll never forget the first dance I ever attended ... at the end of my eighth grade year. I preened, primped, and pampered until I felt like Cinderella going to the ball. The billowing yards of net petticoat underneath my black and pink poodle skirt were starched to stand-out perfection.

As soon as the music started, Randolph, the grade-school fat person, came galumphing across the room to make me his conquest. He plopped his massive self down next to me and did his best to begin a conversation. I was mortified! There I was longing for Prince Charming and instead ending up with Randolph the Round. Figuring the rest room was my only haven, I stood up and lurched toward the door marked Girls.

Unbeknownst to me, Randolph had been sitting on a couple yards of my net petticoat. As I tried to make my getaway, I felt the swoosh of netting and saw to my horror the elastic waist and all twenty yards of the billowing petticoat dangling around my ankles. Blood rushed to my face and my heart beat so loud I was sure the band would stop playing.

Randolph just sat there with a silly powdered-sugar grin on his face. I tugged on the yards of netting until I was able to rip the petticoat away from his mighty thighs ... and then spent the rest of the evening huddled in the bathroom.

Of course Randolph grew up to be a handsome, successful businessman with a wife and a couple of kids. And I eventually grew up to be more accepting of all people. Now when I see someone that at first doesn't appeal to me, I take a closer look and try to start a conversation. More often than not, we're soon chatting like old friends.

Lord, help me keep an open mind and to remember that the way a person looks has nothing to do with what's in his or her heart.

Men judge by outward appearance, but I look at a man's thoughts and intentions.   1 SAMUEL 16:7

MAY 22

Even though I've lived in numerous places in four states, I have always lived within a mile of a body of water. In Illinois I grew up near the Rock River. When I was a kid my dad built an airboat that was the most fun anyone could have on the water. We skimmed across the mighty Rock, speared fish, water-skied, and in the winter sledded behind that airboat on the frozen river.

In Colorado and Missouri I lived within walking distance of creeks and park lagoons. There's just something cathartic about the water and I took refuge near its edge during the unhappy days of my first marriage.

I've lived in Wisconsin since 1980, just a mile or so from Lake Michigan, one of the mightiest of the Great Lakes. I treasure its sandy beach during the hot summer days. In the winter crashing waves demonstrate the lake's mighty power. No matter what the season, the water itself brings peace to my soul.

Over the years, I've always been amazed that no matter where I go, there's always a body of water somewhere in the vicinity. Isn't it wonderful that God provides us with everything we need everywhere we go, including the most basic need of all ... water?

Today, on National Maritime Day, talk to your children about the marvelous gift of water that we enjoy. Perhaps you could take a picnic to the nearest body of water. Take along a notebook so you can write about your feelings as you sit propped against a tree watching the gentle flow of the water before you.

God, thank you for your creations, especially water. Thank you especially for the beauty of the water near my home, and for the peace it gives.

Again, he turns deserts into fertile, watered valleys.
PSALMS 107:35

MAY 23

A number of years ago, a deadly tornado ripped through a tiny town in Wisconsin, killing nine people and destroying nearly everything in the little village.

A newspaper columnist visited the town to write about the devastation. At the local Catholic church he discovered one of the few things remaining was part of page 168 in a hymnal. On that page was a song, "O Come and Mourn With Me Awhile."

I often wondered if that small piece of paper was God's gentle, loving touch, reminding the people there that the time for mourning was with them and that it was all right to lose themselves in grief and sorrow … momentarily. That word "awhile" implies that it's OK to mourn, but not forever. It was as if God were saying, "Cry awhile, then get on with the business of starting again and rebuilding your lives."

Don't you think that also holds true in our lives as single parents? Yes, we've experienced the loss of a spouse, unhappiness, grief, denial, anger, depression … all the things a tragedy brings. But don't you think it's time to get on with the business of living, loving, and laughing again? Yes, yes, it is. It's time.

Lord, when I see someone caught in the web of grief, help me to bring your light into his or her life. And on those days when I still feel great sadness about my own marriage, please let me know that the time for mourning is over. The time for rebuilding is now.

But O my soul, don't be discouraged. Don't be upset. Expect God to act! For I know that I shall again have plenty of reason to praise him for all that he will do. He is my help! He is my God!   PSALMS 42:11

MAY 24

Today I give you a dozen dynamite directives written through the eyes of a child. They were found in the counseling department of a high school in New York.

MEMO TO: Parents
FROM: Your Child

1. Don't spoil me. I know quite well that I ought not to have all I ask for. I'm only testing you.
2. Don't be afraid to be firm with me. I prefer it. It makes me feel secure.
3. Don't let me form bad habits. I have to rely on you to detect them in the early stages.
4. Don't make me feel smaller than I am. It only makes me behave stupidly "big."
5. Don't correct me in front of people if you can help it. I'll take much more notice if you talk quietly with me in private.
6. Don't protect me from consequences. I need to learn the painful way sometimes.
7. Don't be too upset when I say "I hate you." Sometimes it isn't you I hate, but your power to thwart me.
8. Don't take too much notice of my small ailments. Sometimes they get me the attention I need.
9. Don't nag. If you do, I shall have to protect myself by appearing deaf.
10. Don't be inconsistent. That completely confuses me and makes me lose faith in you. When you say "no," mean "no."
11. Don't forget that I cannot thrive without lots of love and understanding.
12. Please keep yourself fit and healthy. I need you.

Lord, as I celebrate my parenthood, help me to be worthy of the job and to see the kind of parent I need to be through the eyes of my children.

Honor your father and mother, that you may have a long, good life in the land the Lord your God will give you.   EXODUS 20:12

Is there something you've always wanted to accomplish? Afraid time is passing you by?

I didn't know what I wanted to be when I grew up until I was thirty-five years old. After I wrote my first full-length article, "I'm going to be a writer," I told my family. "I mean it. I'm going to write every day, send manuscripts to editors, and I'm going to get published!"

The children nodded. "Sure, Mom. What time is dinner?"

They looked upon the hours I spent in my writing room as something akin to the hobbies friends' mothers did in their spare time. I never quite convinced them that writing can be time-consuming and often exasperating *work!*

A few months and hundreds of rejection letters later, I sold my first short article, and then another, and another. Finally, my family started referring to me as "Mom, the writer."

I still get rejection letters from editors, but because I refused to give up on this all-consuming passion, I finally earned the title *writer.* I also learned that no matter what we want to do with our lives, if we work hard enough, we can accomplish *anything*—no matter how old we are when we start.

Lord, thank you for showing me that determination, persistence, hard work, the ability to face rejection and start over again, and a strong belief in the talents you've given me are the main ingredients for success and happiness.

And let us not get tired of doing what is right, for after a while we will reap a harvest of blessing if we don't get discouraged and give up.   GALATIANS 6:9

Do you ever feel that you just don't have enough time to accomplish all that you want to? Wish you could learn to play a musical instrument, another language, the art of cake decorating, painting, carpentry, or ballroom dancing?

I used to say, "I'd do it, but I just don't have enough time," a lot. Then a dear family friend, Leo Walter, who was in his eighties at the time, heard me make that excuse. Leo looked at me, smiled, and pulled a tiny piece of worn paper out of his wallet.

"Pat," he said softly. "This is my favorite poem. I'll read it to you. Listen carefully. I don't know who the author is, but I'm sure it's been around as long as I have."

Only One Minute

I have only just a minute.
There's only 60 seconds in it.
I didn't seek it.
I didn't choose it.
Forced upon me, I must use it.
Just a tiny little minute
But eternity is in it.

The more I thought about Leo's little poem, the more I became aware of how much time I wasted. I decided to try to find eternity in a few of those wasted "tiny little minutes." I gathered them all up and before I knew it, I'd written my first book.

Aren't there a few little minutes in your day that you could put to better use?

Lord, help me not to waste time. Give me the grace and strength to use every tiny little minute to your glory.

Don't act thoughtlessly, but try to find out and do whatever the Lord wants you to.　　EPHESIANS 5:17

MAY 27

A few years ago, the developers of a large downtown mall-office-hotel complex held a contest. They were looking for an ordinary person to be the model for the life-size bronze statue to be placed in front of the new complex.

Four hundred and twenty applicants entered the contest by finishing the sentence, "I picture myself as a work of art because." The winner was a thirty-five-year-old woman named Julie. Julie's smile was as wide as her face, and her pixie haircut showed off her big sparkling eyes. She was a homemaker, mother of six … and a cancer survivor.

Julie wrote, "I picture myself as a work of art because the diagnosis was cancer on May 22, 1983. Here I still am alive and well, who'd have thought it could be? Seems that I'm the survivor type. That's why the statue should be me."

When she found out she had cancer, Julie's whole attitude about life changed considerably. While she underwent a year of radiation treatments and chemotherapy, people she didn't even know came to cut her lawn. Others brought meals over for her family. Friends and neighbors stood by her the entire year. Julie not only learned to rely on the help of people she'd never met, she also survived the radiation and chemo, truly earning the title, "survivor."

Lord, I know we can't all be immortalized in bronze, so help me become immortalized in the minds and hearts of others by the kind of life I lead. Help me, Lord, to help someone every day of my life.

And if the Spirit of God, who raised up Jesus from the dead, lives in you, he will make your dying bodies live again after you die, by means of this same Holy Spirit living within you.   ROMANS 8:11

MAY 28

I grew up in the fifties and sixties, the era of those aproned TV mothers from *The Donna Reed Show, Leave It to Beaver, Ozzie and Harriet*, and *Father Knows Best*. My mother, who could out-polish and out-shine June Cleaver any day of the week, tried her best to convince me that life for a woman centered around the three most basic human needs: cooking, laundry, and housework.

Around age twelve, I decided I'd have a career instead. When I became a mother, I tried to teach my children four things that really make a home sizzle: learning, loyalty, laughter, and love.

Learning. Get as much education as you can possibly afford to accomplish what you want to do in life. Prepare yourself to use the talents God gave you.

Loyalty. Be honest with and devoted to your family, friends, employers, neighbors, and to God. Loyalty raises you above the ordinary and breeds character and strength.

Laughter. Being able to laugh at yourself and see the humor in life will not only help prevent stress, it will keep you optimistic.

Love. The most necessary ingredient for success in life is certainly love. We must love ourselves, (after all, God doesn't make junk), and we must love our families and neighbors whole-heartedly, even the guy next door who drives us crazy. We must love enough to *want* to cook, launder, and clean for each other.

Lord, thank you for giving me more options in my life than my mother had. And thanks for all the machines that make the cooking, cleaning, and laundry care so much easier.

Stay away from any Christian who spends his days in laziness and does not follow the ideal of hard work we set up for you.   2 THESSALONIANS 3:6

MAY 29

My first husband's grandmother, Agnes Daubs, lived in a tiny town in southern Illinois. An active, independent woman, Agnes lived alone for over thirty years after her husband died. One of the most amazing things about Agnes was her garden. Even when she was in her eighties, Agnes planted, tended, and harvested that garden by herself.

Whenever Agnes' family visited, she produced meals fit for royalty, thanks to that garden. Real food. Tomatoes, lettuce, peppers, carrots, and onions, that she'd slice, toss, dice, boil, and cream into colorful, nutritious delights.

I don't have a garden or the desire to spend hours in the kitchen. Cooking, for me, is sometimes running hot water over a frozen bag of pasta salad. True, I have more time to spend with my children ... but on the other hand, didn't Agnes' family crowd into her kitchen "to help"?

And yes, I have more time to exercise ... but didn't all that plowing, planting, and weeding provide Agnes with plenty of exercise?

Sure, I have more time to be creative ... but what's more creative than taking a fresh ear of corn and turning out a melt-in-your mouth, fresh-from-the-oven corn pudding?

This year, Lord, I'm going to ask my son to help me with a little garden. It may just be a couple of tomato plants and a row of peppers, but it's a start. Thank you for the many blessings you give us when we use your good earth for its intended purpose.

And the Lord will bless Israel again, and make her deserts blossom; her barren wilderness will become as beautiful as the Garden of Eden. Joy and gladness will be found there, thanksgiving and lovely songs.

ISAIAH 51:3

MAY 30

Today is Memorial Day, the day we honor our loved ones who have died. It's also known as "Decoration Day," a day for decorating graves with flowers.

One day when I was doing dishes with my stepmother I looked out the kitchen windows and noticed that someone had put flowers on my mother's grave, which is right across the street from my dad's house.

Bev smiled. "Geraniums. Aren't they pretty? My sister and I put geraniums on the graves every Memorial Day and red ruscus and evergreens every Christmas. My first husband, Web, is buried in that cemetery, you know. And my sister's husband, and our mother, and of course, your mother."

Bev continued, "I wish I'd known your mother better, Pat. I met her a few times and she seemed like such a nice person."

I asked Bev to tell me about her first husband and she shared some of her happiest memories.

Bev and I sat in the kitchen for an hour, sharing memories of two special people in our lives. That bouquet on my mother's grave had given Bev and me a chance to grow closer to each other by sharing warm memories of two people we each loved very much ... people whose bodies were laid to rest across the street, but whose souls were celebrating eternal life in a distant place.

Today, Lord, I'm going to visit a cemetery with my children and teach them by my example how to honor and remember those who have died. Thank you for your promise of eternal life.

For God loved the world so much that he gave his only son so that anyone who believes in him shall not perish but have eternal life.   JOHN 3:16

MAY 31

When my ex-husband died in October, 1989, our nine-year-old son, Andrew, was devastated. Though Andrew and I attended the wake and funeral, we weren't able to go to the burial, held at Harold's boyhood hometown in southern Illinois, seven hours away.

All year, Andrew talked about wanting to see his father's grave. Finally, in August of 1990, we made the trip. The little cemetery was out in the country on a hilltop, surrounded on all four sides by cornfields. The smell of wild clover, the sound of birds singing as they flew among the enormous oak trees, and the warm summer breeze filled our senses. When we found Harold's grave marker, Andrew and I stood there, arms around each other, while Andrew talked aloud to his dad. Then Andrew and I recalled many special memories we had of his father.

Then I asked my young son to sit quietly with me under a shady tree and concentrate on locking that peaceful scene into his memory.

Once again, on that day I learned why people visit graves. It's a powerful way to remember the deceased. It opens up a flood of warm memories ... and some theraputic tears as well. Walking through a quiet cemetery filled with flowers and trees is the perfect setting for talking about what happens to our bodies when we die and for sharing with our children that powerful message of Christ's resurrection.

Lord, bless all who have gone before us to join you in Heaven. During this Memorial Day week, help me share the anticipation and promise of life eternal with my children.

O death, where then your victory?

1 CORINTHIANS 15:55

A Prayer for June

At last, Lord,
The laid-back days of summer,
Walks to take, vacations to plan,
Garage sales to visit, parades to watch,
Gardens to water, lemonade to sip,
Picnics to prepare, lakes to swim.

Yes, Lord, at last it's summer,
Keep these joys of summer filling
My head and my heart.
Push the heat, the mayhem,
The noisiness of the children,
The backdoor slamming, the flies,
The humidity and the mosquitoes
Out of my mind.

You suffered silently the thorns
In your crown, Lord.
Help me do the same with summer.
Help me to stop complaining
And to bask instead,
In the caressing warmth and sunshine
Of June.

JUNE 1

The first Sunday in June is Family Day. Sometimes I think we single parents forget that we are the head of a real honest-to-goodness working family. We often need to work harder to build a strong family, but we can have one. Some people assume that when two people have separated or divorced, or one parent dies, that it's end of a "family." Nonsense! This week do four things to help make your family strong.

Write love letters to your children. Place them on their pillows to read just before they go to sleep. Remind all of them how happy you are to have them as part of your family.

Ask your parents for some family heirlooms or mementos to pass down to your children. The items can be as small as a war medal from Grandpa or a teacup from Great-aunt Rose. Ask the oldest people in your family to talk about their ancestors and to share their stories with your children.

Make a family tree. Draw in branches and leaves and explain to your children how and where they fit in. Ask your children's other parent or grandparents to do the same for that side of their family.

Create a family code of honor. Write it on a beautiful sheet of paper, frame it, and hang it in a prominent place. Make it personal. An example: "In the Lorenz family we will respect and defend each other. We will phone each other if we're going to be late. We will help each other. We will tell the truth about each other, even if the truth is painful. Most of all we will love each other no matter what."

Heavenly Father, be with us every day as we work to make our family strong. Never let us forget that you are the head of our household.

He is a father to the fatherless; he gives justice to the widows, for he is holy. He gives families to the lonely.

PSALMS 68:5-6

JUNE 2

The world is full of temptations to be dishonest ... going thirty-five in a 25-mph zone ... bringing a few of the office supplies home for personal use.

When I was seven years old, my dad promised to take me for my first boat ride on the last day of a weekend camping trip. The anticipation was more than I could stand, and I woke Dad at 6:30 A.M. We watched the sun rise over the glassy Minnesota lake, then headed for the boat office to rent one of the rowboats lined up on the shore.

The sign on the office door said, "Open 11:00 A.M." My heart sank to my shoes.

I looked up through tear-clouded eyes in time to see my father pulling a dollar bill out of his wallet. Then he was writing a note. "7:00 A.M. One dollar for a one-hour boat ride. Hope this is enough." He signed his name and address then slipped the note and the dollar under the window.

It would have been easy for anyone to "borrow" one of the unchained boats that day. There wasn't a soul around for miles. But for over forty years that dollar bill and Dad's note is more vivid in my memory than the boat ride itself. That day I discovered that my father was, indeed, one of the good guys. Dad taught me that honesty means being honest *all the time*, not just when someone else is watching.

Heavenly Father, never let me be led into temptation to be dishonest. Help me to teach my children honesty by teaching them to do as I say and as I do.

But the good soil represents honest, good-hearted people. They listen to God's words and cling to them and steadily spread them to others who also soon believe.   LUKE 8:15

JUNE 3

When John, one of my little neighbor friends, was eight years old he discovered that the screen on his bedroom window could be taken off easily from inside his room. Craving the open spaces and freedom that a screenless window provides, John decided to hide the screen temporarily in the field next to his house.

One night, John's dad finished up his two-mile jog by cutting through that same field. When Bob came upon the window screen he picked it up and thought, *I might need some extra screening material someday,* so he pulled the screen out of the aluminum frame and then ripped the frame into eight strips for his aluminum scrap pile.

Well, you can imagine the scene that night when Bob discovered the missing screen in his son's room not long after he returned home with the pile of scrap aluminum. At first, Bob's voice shot into ballistic levels, but his incredible sense of humor caught him in the nick of time, and he spent the next three days laughing aloud every time he pictured himself ripping up John's good bedroom screen.

Aren't there times when you've felt like yelling at your child in anger or frustration? We've all done it at one time or another. Today and every day let's make a special effort to treat our children with dignity, love and, most importantly, with a sense of humor.

Lord, no matter what my children do, let me love and cherish them above all. Give me patience and most of all, Lord, help me to keep my sense of humor intact and to use it often.

There is a right time for everything:… a time to cry; a time to laugh;… a time to hug;… a time for loving ….
ECCLESIASTES 3:1, 4, 5, 8

JUNE 4

The summer of '88 in Milwaukee was the hottest on record. It was dry, too. The month of June brought in only 0.7 of an inch of rain. Naturally, a month before that drought began, I spent my entire savings on sod.

My backyard had been a homeowner's nightmare. The abandoned garden had weeds the size of Frisbees; the two-foot drop-off from the patio to the trees was an eroded mess of mud and rocks; the old sandbox pit was a dirt-and-sand pit three times its original size.

The first of June, when the landscapers placed the thick, green sod on the yard, it looked like a golf course. I had visions of *House and Garden* coming to take pictures. They said to water it every day for a week if it didn't rain. It didn't, so I did. When I had to leave town my neighbors brought over their hoses and sprinklers ... three fountains spewed fresh water on my new grass. By mid-June they'd given up on their own dry, brown and parched yards. But they made sure the sprinklers continued day and night in mine. That sod was going to grow roots or else!

By the end of Milwaukee's "hottest summer ever" my yard was still like a giant emerald dropped on the desert. All summer I was reminded that God often doesn't "send down the showers and make the green grass grow" as we'd like. But he certainly gives us the means to find other solutions to our problems.

Lord, remind me that the seeds of your goodness are planted in the hearts of my neighbors. Help me think of something special to do for them today.

He covers the heavens with clouds, sends down the showers and makes the green grass grow in mountain pastures.   PSALMS 147:8

JUNE 5

We've all served on committees at one time or another. I was on one at church once that really irritated me. Most of the time only half the members showed up. Those who did come never seemed to be prepared. Too much time was spent criticizing people, ideas, or programs. I was ready to drop out.

Then a "garden planting schedule" appeared in our church newsletter. After I read it I decided to get down to business and maintain a more prepared, positive attitude at all my meetings. It even helped in family meetings.

If you belong to any organization, perhaps you can use this to help strengthen the group.

Garden Planting Schedule

First, plant four rows of *peas*: *P*resence, *P*romptness, *P*reparation, and *P*erseverance.

Next, plant four rows of *lettuce*: *Let us* obey rules and regulations; *let us* be true to our obligations; *let us* be faithful to duty; *let us* be loyal and unselfish.

Then, plant three rows of *squash*: *Squash* gossip, *squash* indifference, *squash* criticism.

Finally, plant four rows of *turnips*: *Turn up* for meetings; *turn up* with a smile; *turn up* with new ideas; *turn up* with a determination to do the job.

Lord, help me to be a ready, willing, and able committee person. Help me to "harvest the crop" of success with appreciation for your being the head gardener.

And the Lord will guide you continually, and satisfy you with all good things, and keep you healthy too; and you will be like a well-watered garden, like an ever-flowing spring.   ISAIAH 58:11

JUNE 6

It was one of those weeks when Murphy's Law prevailed in my household. The TV and stereo both broke within two days of each other. Before I could take them in to the repair shop, my computer stopped computing. The next day the garage door broke ... with my car stuck inside.

The following day a friend at the radio station where I worked dropped a piece of paper on my desk. It said:

God is like Ford ... He has a better idea.
God is like Coke ... He's the real thing.
God is like Pan Am ... He makes the going great.
God is like Alka-Seltzer ... try Him, you'll like Him.
God is like Bayer ... He takes the pain away.
God is like Tide ... He gets the stains others leave behind.
God is like Hallmark Cards ... He cares enough to send
    the very best!
God is like Frosted Flakes ... He's grrrrrreat!

My friend's list changed my thinking and lifted my spirits. Soon I decided I could be a little more like Timex—I could take a lickin' and keep on tickin'.

Lord, when things go wrong and stress piles up, help me to remember that you love me, no matter what!

"Then who in the world can be saved?" they asked. Jesus looked at them intently and said, "Humanly speaking, no one. But with God, everything is possible." MATTHEW 19:25-26

JUNE 7

I bought a used computer for Andrew the summer before he started high school. Before long, that machine was a source of contention between us.

"Two hours a day on the computer is enough," I told him. He would have been happier with twelve.

When I reminded Andrew that there was too much life outside the front door to spend the summer cooped up in the computer room, he thought for a minute and asked, "Mom, what did you do for fun in the summertime when you were a kid?"

I told him about the airboat my dad built and how we skimmed the backwaters of the Rock River in northern Illinois looking for carp. Another summer I'd organized a whole neighborhood full of kids and we'd put on a circus in our backyard and given the money to charity.

I remembered how my folks had worked to help us create outdoor family fun. That week I started planning special things for Andrew and me to do that summer. We designed and created a new flower bed. One weekend we drove to Chicago to see the sights and eat Chicago-style hot dogs. We drove to a nearby college town to explore the campus.

It takes time, effort, and organizational skills to plan family events. But the memories you give your children will last a lifetime.

Lord, help me find ways to get my children away from the TV, computer, and video games and to create their own real-life action. And thank you for such a wonderfully incredible world in which to do it.

Teach a child to choose the right path, and when he is older he will remain upon it.   PROVERBS 22:6

JUNE 8

How many times have I been upset because no one in the family emptied the dishwasher, or picked up newspapers scattered all over the living room, or folded the laundry piled high on my bed?

Perhaps you've heard the old saw "Whose Job Is It?"

This is the story about four people named everybody, somebody, anybody, and nobody. There was an important job to be done so everybody was sure somebody would do it. Anybody could have done it, but nobody did it. Somebody got angry about that because it was everybody's job. Everybody thought anybody could do it, but nobody realized that everybody wouldn't do it. It ended up that everybody blamed somebody when nobody did what anybody could have done.

Perhaps you need to call a family meeting. Explain to the children that it doesn't matter who the job belongs to ... what matters is that the job gets done and that each member of the family pitches in. When we parents see a child doing a job that was not assigned, an immediate reward is certainly in order, say, an extra special bear hug.

Today, let's all find one task that's really not our job, and do it anyway with a smile and without expecting any gratitude. And tomorrow, let's find another chore that needs to be done ... and do it. If it gets to be a habit, just imagine what we can accomplish in a year's time!

Lord, today I'm going to take your command to love your neighbor and stop fussing about whose job it is and just do it myself with a smile ... and I won't ask anything in return.

Everyone's work will be put through the fire so that all can see whether or not it keeps its value, and what was really accomplished.   1 CORINTHIANS 3:13

JUNE 9

Seven years after she graduated from high school, my oldest daughter, Jeanne, graduated from college. She had spent a year in Yugoslavia as a foreign exchange student, then attended a junior college, and finally received a bachelor of arts degree in fine art from the California College of Arts and Crafts in Oakland.

During those years, Julia and Michael also started college. For four years all three were in college at the same time. I was so busy working, filling out financial aid forms, and encouraging them through a maze of grants, scholarships, loans, work-study programs, and part-time jobs that I barely had time to breathe. But in the spring of '94, when Jeanne graduated, she gave me a beautiful card with this message:

Dear Mom,
    Today on my graduation from college I want to thank you. From the first days we spent together you've been nurturing me. You read to me, gave me piano lessons, encouraged me to draw. You taught me how to follow my dreams, to turn them to reality. Without you this education would never have been possible. So today as I graduate, know that I love you and am grateful for what you have given me.

Jeanne

Jeanne's words meant more to me than anything I've received before or since. My daughter's simple acknowledgment turned all those struggles into joy.

Today, why don't you write a note to someone who has supported you during the hard times?

Lord, thank you for getting me through the tough college years with my children. Help me to continue to share with them how important they are in your world.

Go ahead and prepare for the conflict, but victory comes from God.　　　　　PROVERBS 21:31

JUNE 10

A "keeper" is something worth holding on to. We know how it works in the fishing world. "Hey, son, that fish you just caught is most definitely a keeper. It's almost a foot long!"

Seems like most folks have "keepers" in their lives. My friend Alice told me about her husband's "keeper," a 1970 Oldsmobile that's as big as a barn. "He takes good care of it and even though it costs a lot for insurance and oil, I know he could be spending a lot more on other hobbies. Besides, that old car gives him so much joy."

My "keeper" is the big old blue bicycle I received from my folks on my seventh birthday, over forty years ago. It was a used bike, already five years old, purchased by my dad for a song and then lovingly fixed up. The fat balloon tires cushioned my way over many country gravel roads. I was forty-six when I received my first brand-new bike, but I still can't get rid of "Old Blue." So there she hangs over the car in the garage, a monument to my childhood, teenage, and young-married days.

If you're like me, sometimes you feel like tearing out your hair when you go into your childrens' rooms and see all the junk they've collected. "Clean up! Get organized! Get rid of this stuff! Throw it out! Give it away!" we holler. But quite often, buried in the mess, is a "keeper." We need to respect it and our children for wanting to cherish it.

Lord, when I nag at my children to get rid of their "junk" remind me that I may be speaking about a precious "keeper." Thank you for giving us tangible objects where we can store our happiest memories.

Wherever your treasure is, there your heart and thoughts will also be.　　　　　LUKE 12:34

JUNE 11

Whenever I see notices of high-school reunions I think back to my own high school experience and remember the teachers who made an indelible mark on my life.

Freshman algebra would have been a dark curse if it hadn't been for Sister Leorita. She was able to take my unmathematical, right-brained mind and help me grasp algebra and its systematical approach to life.

Sister Clarice, my Latin teacher, was relentless. If we couldn't answer her questions, she'd launch into a fifteen-minute tirade. "Latin is the most important course you'll ever take," she'd exclaim. "It'll help you understand the English language for the rest of your life!" I laughed at her words, but Sister was right. Many times since, those two years of Latin helped me figure out the meaning of English words.

English class was taught by Sister Mary Rhodes who demanded massive amounts of reading, ten-page term papers, daily sentence diagramming, and daily essays. At the time I felt tortured, yet no college-level English class taught me so much.

I spent lots of time complaining about algebraic equations, Latin, and English class. But each time I've attended one of my reunions, I appreciate more and more what gifts those teachers gave me.

Lord, now that my own children are sometimes terrorized by the learning process, help me to reassure them that someday they'll appreciate their hard work and the tremendous effort their teachers put into it. Encourage me to send a kind note to their teachers every now and then.

Therefore the desire of wisdom brings one to the everlasting kingdom.   WISDOM 6:21

JUNE 12

Are you a collector of sayings, like me? I snip them out of magazines, newsletters, and church bulletins and keep them in a folder. Sometimes I memorize them so I can pass them on to my children. Once in a while I'll tape them to the front of the envelope of a letter I'm sending to the older children, hoping that all the mailmen from here to there will enjoy the pearls of wisdom as well.

Here are a few examples of my favorites:

- We don't laugh because we feel good. We feel good because we laugh.

- No matter how long you nurse a grudge, it won't get better.

- If you must speak ill of another, do not speak it; write it in the sand near the water's edge.

- Age is a matter of mind; if you don't mind, it doesn't matter.

- In life, the destination will take care of itself if the journey is done well.

Over the years I've learned that other people's wisdom helps me, as a single parent, to make a point without belaboring the issue. When Andrew missed getting his swim-team letter by three points his sophomore year I posted this one on his mirror, "Success is not permanent ... and neither is failure."

Lord, thank you for the wise words of others, words that often help me do a better job of parenting.

Write this down, for what I tell you is trustworthy and true.   REVELATION 21:5

JUNE 13

Right after fifteen-year-old Andrew talked me into practically shaving his head at the beginning of the summer, he talked two of his friends into doing the same thing. Safety in numbers, I presumed. "Please, Mom, Brian and Paul really want you to cut their hair like mine. School's out. It'll be cool!"

I looked at the boys, each sporting sun-streaked, four-inch-long haircuts.

"It's OK, Mrs. L. Shave it off!"

I insisted they call their parents for permission and then for the next hour, I ran my hands and my electric clippers over each head until just an eighth-inch of fuzz remained. During each haircut I got to know my son's friends much better. I became very well acquainted with Paul's two stubborn cowlicks, and I nicked Brian's ear, then heard about his plans for the future and about his family. His gentleness and quiet sense of humor impressed me.

That night after the boys left, Andrew asked, "Mom, do you like my friends?"

I suddenly realized I'd never told my son what I thought about any of his friends. I sat down with Andrew and went down the list, pointing out what I thought were the nicest qualities of each. Bert's friendliness, Tracy's bubbling personality, Paul's thoughtfulness....

"Andrew, your friends are great. They're exactly the kind I would choose for myself if I were your age."

Throughout the school year, Andrew's friends filled our home with their infectious laughter, constant chatter, and empty stomachs, and by its end, they had become my friends, too.

Lord, help me to be a friend to my children's friends and to welcome them into my home and heart.

A true friend is always loyal, and a brother is born to help in time of need.   PROVERBS 17:17

It's difficult for me to pray for people I don't know. Blanket prayers, I call them. Praying for the sick, the lonely, the poor, the depressed is a noble gesture but I've always wondered, *Who are these people, anyway?*

Then I heard about a young woman who'd been frozen solid. If she lived, the doctors were sure her legs would have to be amputated. When a prayer chain was put into motion and thousands of people started praying for her, she survived without any ill effects whatsoever. Those who were praying knew her name, the circumstances of the emergency, and were kept up-to-date on her condition.

Later I wrote a "how-to" article on starting a church prayer chain. When it was published, my own "blanket prayers" disappeared.

Linda called from southern Wisconsin, torn apart because her husband had walked out on her and the children for no apparent reason, after twenty-three years of marriage.

Ann, a seventy-three-year-old widow from Illinois, wrote begging for prayers that she might sell her house so she could move back to her hometown and start a new life with old friends.

May, from Florida, had had a stroke and was having trouble breathing and walking.

Suddenly, praying became more relevant. When I prayed for Linda, Ann, or May I was able to pray specifically for their needs … bullet prayers directed at their problems.

Lord, let me be aware of the specific needs of others, and to pray for them with all my heart. Help me teach my children to do the same.

Always keep on praying.   1 THESSALONIANS 5:17

JUNE 15

This week as we celebrate Father's Day, I'll be honoring the man who is, in my opinion, the best father in the world … my dad. Most of the happy memories of my childhood center around my dad. He spent hours with me every day because his job as a rural mail carrier ended around 2:00 P.M.; Dad and I went sledding and skating in the winter, and swimming and boating in the summer. We read comics, built kites, planted gardens, mowed grass, and talked about everything under the sun.

When I was in high school Dad never complained about working two jobs so I could go to college. He taught me about honesty, loyalty, hard work, friendship, faith in God, and how to have fun, and instilled in me a sense of adventure and love of travel. I believe that my relationship with my father is the most fundamental reason why I am a happy, well-adjusted person.

Chances are, if you're reading this book, you are either (1) a single mother who may or may not get along with your children's father; (2) a single father who may or may not be a good father to your children; or (3) my dad. If you belong to group one, please encourage your ex-husband to spend time with your children by showing appreciation when he does. If you belong to group two, please put your children first in your life. They'll be grown before you know it, and they need you desperately now. If you're group three, I'd just like to say, "Dad, thank you for being the wind beneath my wings. I love you."

Heavenly Father, you loved your Son more than anyone ever loved a child. Teach us to be like you in the way we love and parent our children.

We are children of the same father, Abraham, all created by the same God. And yet we are faithless to each other, violating the covenant of our fathers!

MALACHI 2:10

JUNE 16

I'll never forget a conversation I had with my then thirteen-year-old daughter, Julia, while I was still married to Harold. I'd asked Julia to vacuum the family room. When she turned the vacuum cleaner off, she said, "You know, Mom, Dad sure makes a mess around his chair. His mess is completely different from anybody else's in this family.

"It starts with his Carmel Nip wrappers on the floor. Then the Big Red chewing gum wrappers. You'd never know there was a wastebasket right next to his chair.

"Then come the popcorn kernels. I love that sound when they all go click-click-clicking up the vacuum cleaner. I bet Daddy eats a gallon of popcorn every night!

"Of course we can't forget Dad's toothpicks. I found three or four broken ones beside his chair. I guess anybody who eats as much popcorn as he does needs lots of toothpicks."

Julia continued her tirade. "Then, Mom, you should see all the pencils around that chair! Must be from all those lists Dad makes. I found pencils under his chair, in the chair, under the cushion, and on the table next to his chair. I put them all in the pencil holder on the end table. Sure hope he notices.

"You know what, Mom? It's nice to have the family room clean again, especially around Daddy's chair. But if you ask me, I like it better when he's home messing it all up again!"

Lord, when I grumble about my messy house, remind me that the clutter is created by busy, active, hungry, hurried, or exhausted people. Help me not to get so uptight and to concentrate, instead, on having pleasant, loving conversations with my children. Bless our home with its lived-in look.

She watches carefully all that goes on throughout her household, and is never lazy.   PROVERBS 31:27

JUNE 17

When Michael was a high school sophomore he changed from an interesting, talkative, fun-to-be-around kid, to an often sullen, withdrawn, and uncooperative one. Some weeks, no matter how hard I tried, he'd just grunt (was that a yes or a no?) then walk away.

One day during this trying time, I read Andrew the story about the Trojan horse from Greek mythology. The Greeks fooled the Trojans by building a massive wooden horse and filling it with armed soldiers. The Trojans, who thought they'd won the battle against the Greeks, had fallen asleep after too much celebrating. During the night the armed soldiers came out of their wooden horse and captured the city.

As I read the story I wondered, *Couldn't I recapture Michael's heart by putting on my own "wooden horse"?* I put on the armor of patience and waited until he felt like talking to me. I donned a breastplate of caring, making sure I said at least one complimentary thing to him every day. I wore a helmet of determination by refusing to give up on him no matter how argumentative he became.

Within a few months, Michael's contagious smile returned and he started talking in paragraphs again. I had won the battle with God's armor.

Lord, during trying times when my loved ones seem foreign to me, restore our relationship with the armor of your goodness.

So use every piece of God's armor to resist the enemy whenever he attacks, and when it is all over, you will still be standing up.   EPHESIANS 6:13

JUNE 18

Slippery When Wet, Winding Road, and *Yield to Pedestrians* tell us to proceed with caution. Tornado warnings give us time to prepare for bad weather. Tiredness, irritability, and pain can also be warning signs, telling us to change the pace of our lives.

Once a single-parent friend told me about her hectic life. Her full-time job, the social activities her career demanded, the responsibility of caring for three children, and her involvement in church and professional groups spread her time so thin that she had nothing left for herself. Her health suffered. Tiredness, depression, lingering guilt, anxiety, and constant self-criticism became a way of life. Finally, she realized she was on overload.

The woman took a week's vacation. One day while she and her children were at a nearby beach, she made a list of all the things she *wanted* to do in her life, not the ones she felt she *had* to do. She discovered that spending more time with her children was very important to her. She also liked her job even though it didn't leave much time for cleaning the house, cooking, and doing laundry.

Rather than cutting back on her career, she gave up the job of superwoman and hired a woman to clean the house twice a month, budgeted money so she and the children could eat out twice a week, and set up a chart that divided kitchen responsibilities among her teenage children.

My friend found time every week to smell the flowers and bask in the knowledge that she didn't have to be or do everything.

Lord, help me to stop being superwoman and to take time to smell your flowers and enjoy your world with my children.

Oh, for wings like a dove, to fly away and rest!

PSALMS 55:6

JUNE 19

Do you ever get tired of nagging your children to do their chores? I think we parents spend far too much time nagging. Many parents don't know how to avoid the "nagging" part of the operation.

An easy solution is the "when/then" method. Nagging, yelling, arguing, and bitter feelings can be avoided if you simply say, "When the trash is out, then you may use your computer." Or, "When your homework is finished, then you may phone your friends." Or, "When the kitchen is clean, then you may go to the mall." Or try a general choice, "When your chores are all finished, then you may choose whatever you want to do for the rest of the day." You get the idea. Good discipline is really just putting the ball in your children's hands. Let them decide when they want to get the chore done. If being with their friends, watching TV, or any other child-determined necessity of life is part of the deal, they'll usually get the job done in a reasonable time so they can enjoy the fruits of their labor.

Giving our children chores gives them a sense of family cooperation, responsibility, and self-esteem. Don't forget to say, "Thanks for helping me clean the garage. You're a good worker. Let's go for ice cream!"

Lord, it's hard being the custodial parent who must insist that my children do their chores. Give me the courage to be firm, but loving, with them and to let them know exactly what I expect so that I won't be tempted to nag. Remind me to praise my children for a job well done.

Praise God forever! How he must rejoice in all his work!　　　　　　　　　　　　　　PSALMS 104:31

JUNE 20

I was exhausted from eight hours of writing radio commercials and rushing home to take Jeanne to piano lessons. I had to fix supper for the family, eat, and get ready for a meeting. So there I was frying hamburgers, barking orders to the children to set the table, wash hands, and hurry up because I had to leave soon.

In the midst of all that I told the kids that I'd received a long-overdue raise at work. I expected accolades or at least a "way to go, Mom!" Instead they started bombarding me with requests of things they wanted to use the extra money for.

"Tell it to the property-tax man," I barked. "The whole raise is going to help pay the house taxes."

I started getting depressed and wondered why so many of our evenings ended up like that.

That night I paged through my Bible and came across Psalm 62:5, "I stand silently before the Lord, waiting for him to rescue me. For salvation comes from him alone." I read that verse again and again and then realized, when it finally sank in, that whenever I felt unappreciated by the whole world, God, in all his infinite love was still there for me, cheering me on, blessing every minute of my days.

Lord, help me to slow down. Teach me to share my feelings with my children. Give me the courage and energy to have a family meeting tonight, Lord, so that we can all air our gripes and start liking each other again. Most of all, Lord, thank you for being there for me and for holding me in such high regard.

But I stand silently before the Lord, waiting for him to rescue me. For salvation comes from him alone.

PSALMS 62:5

JUNE 21

The foam-stuffed cushions on the pine furniture in our family room were in embarrassing condition. I wanted ready-made replacements, but couldn't find the correct size anywhere. A friend suggested Mrs. Pascolini. "She's hard to understand ... came over from Italy a dozen years ago. But you'll like the work she does."

When she arrived with her enormous material sample books, her expressive eyes and constant arm motions helped solve any problems of communication. I chose a pattern while she measured the furniture.

A few weeks later she asked me to come to her house to inspect the material. During that visit she poured me a generous glass of grape juice, dribbling from the grape press that had come with her family from Italy.

A few days later Mrs. Pascolini came to my house to remake the bottoms of the furniture. "Can't put new cushions on broken wires. I make new foundation." With that she hammered in new wood supports, wove yards of heavy rubber stripping, and upholstered each chair bottom with extra cushion material.

When she delivered the finished cushions and tucked them into the pine furniture, I could feel her sense of pride when she stepped back and said, "You like, no?"

Indeed I did. The workmanship was exquisite. The radiance that beamed from my new friend's face when she saw her completed project showed me that she *knew* she'd done her best, as well.

Lord, thank you for the talents you've given each of us. Give me the energy to develop mine to the fullest, to your glory.

Work hard so God can say to you, "Well done." Be a good workman, one who does not need to be ashamed when God examines your work.
2 TIMOTHY 2:15

JUNE 22

Do you ever wonder what kind of a job you're doing as a parent? Do you spend enough time with your children? Do you discipline them fairly? Are you demonstrative enough with your love? Do you help develop their natural talents?

Goodness knows, parenting is the most difficult, most awesome job in the world.

Today I want you to read something written by Abraham Lincoln. Try to remember it when you're tired of being a parent or when your children are giving you fits, and you wish you could just turn the responsibility over to someone else.

A child is a person who is going to carry on what you have started. They are going to sit where you are sitting, and when you are gone, they will attend to those things which you think are important. You may adopt all the policies you please; but how they are carried out depends on them. They will assume control of your cities, states, and nations. They are going to move in and take over your churches, schools, universities, and corporations. All your books are going to be judged, praised, or condemned by them. The fate of humanity is in their hands.

Lord, it's an awesome job, this parenting thing. Give me the grace, goodness, and determination I need to do the best possible job, no matter how tired or frustrated I get. It's up to you and me, Lord. Be with me every step of the way.

For he gave his laws to Israel, and commanded our fathers to teach them to their children, so that they in turn could teach their children too. Thus his laws pass down from generation to generation.

PSALMS 78:5-6

JUNE 23

I have a friend who writes beautifully. She has boxes and boxes of stories, poems, and journals tucked away in a closet. "Why don't you send those things out to editors and get them published?" I asked her.

"Oh, I don't write for anybody but me," she said. "Besides, I'm not sure my writing is good enough to be published."

"Then why write it in the first place?" I asked.

Her response reminded me of a poster I'd seen: a giant, fluffy, dandelion seed ball glistened in the sunlight next to a dried-out, withering daisy. The caption read, "We are either in the process of being born or in the process of dying."

The continual process of being born includes developing the talents God has given us, and sharing them with others. Dying begins when we bury our talents and turn selfishly inward.

Do you know someone who plays the piano but for years hasn't touched a key? Or an artist who hasn't painted a picture since art class?

It's simply the natural order of things that writers write to be read, that singers sing to be heard, and that artists paint to have their paintings seen by others. Since each of us is a unique expression of God, shouldn't we share our talents with others?

Lord, help me overcome any fear I have that keeps me from expressing the talents you've given me. Help me teach my children to share their talents as well, so that we can all stay in the process of being born, rather than in the process of dying.

For the man who uses well what he is given shall be given more, and he shall have abundance. But from the man who is unfaithful, even what little responsibility he has shall be taken from him.

MATTHEW 25:29

JUNE 24

Have you ever run across another single parent who is so sad, depressed, stressed, and beaten down by life that a black cloud seems to hang over her head? She's often tired, irritable, crabby with family members, neighbors, and co-workers. She seems to have a chip on her shoulder. Her problem is negative thinking.

When it comes right down to it, human beings can have only two kinds of thoughts. We can think negative thoughts and wallow in self-pity, guilt, self-criticism, and inferiority. Or we can think positive thoughts and celebrate and bask in our goodness and in the joyous aspects of everything around us. I choose the latter.

If we want to become positive people, we must learn to forgive others just as Jesus forgives us. That means forgiving everybody who ever did anything to us that made us unhappy, including our parents and perhaps that ex-spouse who still gives us a lot of grief. Then we must forgive ourselves for every dumb, unkind, or foolish thing we've ever done. Most important, if we've hurt another person, we need to apologize.

After we've cleaned all the cobwebs out of our lives, we need to live kindly, positively, joyously. We need to think of ourselves as being good, worthy of love and free to enjoy all the joy and wonderment that's out there for the taking.

Lord, thank you for life and for the exquisite beauty and goodness around me. Help me to be a positive person and to give my children the gift of a positive self-image.

And their prayer, if offered in faith, will heal him, for the Lord will make him well; and if his sickness was caused by some sin, the Lord will forgive him.

JAMES 5:15

JUNE 25

Today is the anniversary of Custer's Last Stand. In 1874, General George Armstrong Custer was placed in command of an expedition to the Black Hills, a sacred portion of the Sioux Indian reservation. When gold was discovered there, the Sioux Indians refused to sell or lease their land to the miners who converged on their territory. So the United States government ordered the Sioux to abandon the land. They refused, and General Custer's troops were sent to force their retreat.

On the Little Bighorn River, on June 25, 1876, Custer and his men rode right into an ambush led by chiefs Sitting Bull and Crazy Horse. All of Custer's men (over 250) were killed in the last major Indian victory in North America.

Today, an enormous granite sculpture of Chief Crazy Horse is being created in the Black Hills, a fitting tribute to all Indians who were pushed out of their homelands by white settlers. Korczak Ziolkowski (1908-1982), the sculptor who began the dream of creating the monument, wrote, "To you I give this granite epic for your descendants to always know—'my lands are where my dead lie buried.'"

How painful it must have been for the Indians to be pushed out of the land they loved. So many times single parents feel the same anguish as they're booted out of their homes because of a separation, death, or divorce. If you had to leave, may God give you strength and courage to make a new home for yourself and your children. If you were able to stay in your home, perhaps today you could try to make life a little happier or nicer for the parent who had to move.

Lord, thank you for my home, no matter where it is. Help me to make it a happy place for my children.

You will live in joy and peace. The mountains and hills, the trees of the field—all the world around you—will rejoice.   ISAIAH 55:12

JUNE 26

"Hi, how are you?"

"Fine, thanks. How are you?"

"Fine."

How many times have we had that conversation? *Do* we always feel "fine"? Are we sure the person we ask is truly "fine," as they say? Or do we say "fine" though we feel lousy, lonely, depressed, disillusioned, or even fabulously wonderful?

As single parents we generally don't have the luxury of living with another adult who can read our moods, hear our sneezes, feel our fevered brow, or sense our needs. So when another adult asks how we are, wouldn't it make more sense to "open up" to another human being who's as tall as we are and has been around the block a few times?

Let's practice. You're in the grocery store, and you bump into your best friend's spouse.

"Hi, Joe, how are you?" you say.

"Fine, how are you?" he says.

"Well, I'm glad you asked. Not so good. My mother's been sick. And my clothes dryer won't work."

"Sorry to hear about your mother. I'll tell Jane to give you a call. What's wrong with the dryer? Did you check the fuse box? Maybe the belt broke. I'll stop over and look at it."

Believe me, it works. Next time a friend asks how you are, tell him honestly. And if you're having a great day say, "Thanks for asking! I'm feeling fabulous."

Lord, help me communicate honestly when people ask how I'm doing. Thank you for friends who care.

These teachers will tell lies with straight faces and do it so often that their consciences won't even bother them.   1 TIMOTHY 4:2

JUNE 27

In 1991, from June until December, I lost forty pounds, mainly because I fast-walked, roller-skated, or rode my bicycle at least four to five times a week. But that winter, I let my exercise program slip. Over the next couple of years I gained back those pounds. Every time I looked at my exercise bike I shuddered and walked right past it.

In January of 1996, I heard that it takes three weeks to make a habit. So I decided to get back on that exercise bike at least three times a week for three weeks to see if I could, indeed, get back into the exercise habit. Sure enough, by the end of the third week I didn't even have to drag myself downstairs to that bike. It became automatic. Get up. Get Andrew off to school. Fix a cup of tea. Then downstairs to watch the news on TV while I rode six or eight miles on the stationary bike. It was a routine I looked forward to.

I not only started losing weight, I gained lots more energy and confidence in myself. As soon as the warmer weather hit I simply took my act on the road ... fast-walking in the beautiful outdoors. I still love and cherish my solitary morning walks.

Is there a habit you'd like to acquire? Drinking more water, perhaps? Or reducing fat and sugar from your diet? Finding more time for daily exercise? Phoning a lonely friend or relative once a week? Well, just *do it* for three weeks and form a lifelong habit.

Lord, in addition to building my body into a "home of the Holy Spirit," help me create spiritual habits as well, such as morning and evening prayer and being a more frequent volunteer at church.

Haven't you yet learned that your body is the home of the Holy Spirit God gave you, and that he lives within you?   1 CORINTHIANS 6:19

JUNE 28

Do you ever lose your patience with old people?

Married or single, at some time we all have to help with the elderly. And they can be exasperating. My great-aunt Peggy, born in 1900, lives in a nursing home and is nearly blind, hard of hearing, very frail, and as cantankerous as they come.

One time my dad and his sister, Helen, went shopping to buy Great-aunt Peggy a new bathrobe. Because Peggy is extremely picky about everything, they asked her exactly what she wanted. They found the perfect one and then had to pay lots more than they expected for it. When they gave it to her, she said it was fine.

A few weeks later, Dad asked, "How's that new bathrobe working out?"

"It's too long and the sleeves get in my way," she groused.

Dad opened her closet door and saw that Peggy had cut a foot off the bottom of the robe and cut the sleeves up to the elbows. She'd completely cut off the beautiful, lace-trimmed collar.

Dad was furious. "Where are your scissors! I'm taking them home! You have no business cutting up your clothes!" He collected the scissors and stomped out the door.

The next time he visited he was amazed to see Peggy wearing the ratty-looking bathrobe. But it wasn't so ratty looking. One of the aides on Peggy's floor had taken the robe home, evened up Peggy's cutting job and then stitched new hems on the bottom, sleeves and collar. Great-aunt Peggy was enjoying her new robe with style and gusto.

Dad's gotten lots of mileage out of that story, and by now he thinks it's pretty funny. Our oldsters may be crotchety and hard to please, but getting old is not easy. The aches and pains alone would make anyone hard to get along with. And when the only thing different in your life is a new-fangled bathrobe, who wouldn't want to customize it?

Lord, give me patience and caring when I'm needed to help with people whose lives are not as exciting or busy as mine.

And now, in my old age, don't set me aside. Don't forsake me now when my strength is failing. PSALMS 71:9

JUNE 29

The first thing one sees when entering my home is the white dry-erase board just inside the front door, forever filled with messages, reminders, and schedules. Granted, it's not the most attractive thing I could have on that wall, but after more than a decade of single-parenting I don't know how I could survive without it. If I didn't write notes to myself every day, I'm sure I would have made a mess of things.

When my four children were all still in school I remember the dry-erase board being filled with times for pick-up and delivery for basketball, band practice, music and swim lessons, and religious-education classes. Or the board contained notes to the children arriving home on the school bus, letting them know where I was and when I'd be back. Sometimes I'd write "congratulations" notes. Most of the time one side of the board was reserved for the kids' chore list. Phone messages were left on the dry-erase board. Lists of things I had to do on the weekend were written on the board.

Today, why not take stock of how your family really communicates with each other? Perhaps you need to purchase a blackboard, note center, or dry-erase board and place it in a strategic location in your home so each of you can communicate better on a daily basis.

Lord, let me teach my children that open communication is vital to a family. And let my directives to them also include "I love you!" "Way to go!" and, "Thanks for your help!" messages.

Say only what is good and helpful to those you are talking to, and what will give them a blessing.
EPHESIANS 4:29

JUNE 30

During his sermon one Sunday, our pastor talked about Jesus "robed in majesty and strength" (Psalm 93:1). I looked down at my own clothing and smiled. Here I was, wearing a skirt that had belonged to my mother five years earlier. The sweater vest had also been hers, and even though it was a little frayed, I wore it more often than some of the more stylish, newer things in my wardrobe.

The silver bracelet on my wrist had been a gift from my dad to my mother before they were married. My watch had been on my mother's wrist. And the scarf around my neck had belonged to my grandmother.

I was a walking sentimentalist. Why did I cling to the clothing and accessories of my departed loved ones? Did I feel closer to them with their "things" next to me? I think so.

In a way, Mother's clothing, her jewelry, and Grandma's scarf were my pieces of armor, giving me comfort and a sense of protection. I liked wearing their things and being constantly reminded of the goodness of these loving souls.

If you have cherished items that once belonged to another family member, get them out and share them with your children. Treasure them. Use them. Wear them. Let them help you become whole again.

Lord, as we use and enjoy the clothing, accessories, and treasured knickknacks left by our loved ones, let these items be a reminder for us to take on the good qualities of the people who once owned them. Let their "things" be our armor against evil, our protection against temptation, and a joyful reminder that someday we'll rejoin our loved ones in paradise.

Jehovah himself is caring for you!... He keeps his eye upon you as you come and go, and always guards you.
PSALMS 121:5,8

A Prayer for July

℃

O Lord, thank you for my country,
For America.
For this Fourth of July.
Thank you for freedom
To believe in my God, without fear.
Thank you for a country that accepts
Every race, every nationality.
Thank you for confidence
That our leaders will keep us strong.

Yes, Lord,
As I raise the stars and stripes
On the pole near the front door,
Keep me proud of my country.
Help me to be a good citizen,
An informed voter,
And to help change those things
That need to be changed
Help me to teach my children
About patriotism.

Yes, Lord, thank you
For my America
And for the beauty of this land
And the potential of our people.

JULY 1

The Monday before my son Michael's wedding, the white dry-erase board in my front hall listed seventeen preparations I needed to make for the rehearsal dinner at my house the following Friday and for the sixteen houseguests who would begin to arrive in three days.

I shuddered and asked God to send me a guardian angel. That morning, Wally and Shirley Winston pulled up in their RV.

Shirley immediately saw the list on the board. "Well, let's get to work," she said.

Wally gathered up brooms, the hose, and fifteen-year-old Andrew and headed for the backyard patio to get it ready for the rehearsal dinner.

Shirley and I headed for the grocery store. Then we started cooking. She thought up fabulous entertaining and food ideas and organized everything while I was at the wedding rehearsal. She and Wally even cleaned up after the dinner party.

The whole wedding week was a great success, but I could never have pulled it off alone. Through Shirley, Wally, and my reminder board, God showed me that guardian angels don't always have wings.

These days when I'm feeling stressed and overworked, I simply make another list on the reminder board so Andrew or any guardian angel who sees it can feel good about offering to help.

Lord, give me courage to admit that I can't do it all alone. Help me swallow my pride and allow others to help me when I'm feeling stressed.

He calms the storm and stills the waves. What a blessing is that stillness, as he brings them safely into harbor!   PSALMS 107:29-30

JULY 2

My grandmother, Emma Schwamberger Kobbeman (1890-1970), watched our country change from horse-and-buggy to men-on-the-moon. When I was a child, Grandma Kobbeman presided over our annual family reunion at Sinissippi Park in Sterling, Illinois, every summer ... surrounded by her five children, their spouses, and her twenty-four grandchildren.

One year, when Grandma was well into her seventies, she decided to ride her grandson's motorized go-cart. We held our breath when she squeezed into the seat, pressed the accelerator to the floor with her heavy brown oxfords, and threw that little engine into world-cup competition.

Grandma flew across the track and onto the baseball field, barely missing the popcorn stand. As she headed for a row of poplars at the edge of the Rock River she suddenly released her foot from the accelerator and came to an abrupt halt at the edge of the water.

Once I asked Grandma, "Why aren't you afraid to try new things?"

She just smiled and said, "Faith in the Lord is all you need, honey."

I'll always be grateful for Grandma's example. Since her death in 1970, I've soared down a steep water slide with my children, taken a helicopter ride, and guided a two-person ocean kayak. A hot air balloon ride and parasailing are on my "to do" list of adventures.

Isn't there something you've always wanted to try but were afraid? Do what Grandma did. Depend on your faith in the Lord and then plop down on that go-cart!

Lord, let me give my children a sense of adventure by being a bold example for them.

Yes, be bold and strong! Banish fear and doubt! For remember, the Lord your God is with you wherever you go.

JOSHUA 1:9

JULY 3

I collect antique hat pins, unusual napkin rings, and beach glass. *Beach glass?*

Yes ... right off the shores of Lake Michigan, close to my home. I've gone collecting by myself, but mostly with the children or a visiting friend. At the shoreline I immediately start walking with my head down. "What are you looking for?" one friend asked.

"Beach glass. Little bits of glass, probably from old bottles, that's been worn down smooth as a pebble by the waves—I sort them by colors and keep them in tall glass jars at home in a window."

"Oh, here's one," she exclaimed.

"Nope, it's too sharp. Still needs a few years of waves lapping across it to smooth it out."

"Reminds me of my rough edges when I shout at the children," she says.

"Or me when too many repair bills turn me into a raving maniac," I say.

"Or when I'm cranky at work for no particular reason. Guess we all need to smooth out our rough spots. Think I'll take this rough piece of beach glass home with me as a reminder."

Today, Lord, I'm going to put a rough stone in my pocket to remind me to be a little kinder, softer, gentler ... as I deal with others. Each time I touch it, Lord, remind me to smooth out my rough edges.

Then he picked up five smooth stones from a stream and put them in his shepherd's bag and, armed only with his shepherd's staff and sling, started across to Goliath.   1 SAMUEL 17:40

JULY 4

My aunt, Mary Kobbeman, is one of my most amazing single-parent role models. A farm accident killed Uncle Harry in 1958, when their eleven children ranged from six months to nineteen years. Aunt Mary kept the farm and went back to college to get her teaching degree. Then she taught fourth grade and raised those children by herself in that big white farmhouse, while her older sons kept the farm going.

Our family lived in town, about five miles from Aunt Mary's, but my dad and I often went out there so he could help the older boys with a farm project every now and then. I loved playing in the creek along the farmhouse, in the haymow, or in the barn. Of course, riding Queenie—the fattest, most gentle horse in the world—was the most fun of all.

Not long ago, I spent the Fourth of July on the farm with Aunt Mary and my cousins, who are now in their forties and fifties. We ate a huge meal, then gathered outside for a rousing baseball game. We chose teams, made jokes, then hooted and hollered our way through nine innings as the hot July breeze caressed the knee-high corn in the fields around the farm.

After cold drinks, ice cream and watermelon, we watched the fireworks show that some of my cousins put on for all of us.

It was the most perfect Fourth of July ever because I got to spend it on the farm with Aunt Mary, my most amazing role model. As I drove home that night, I realized I'd just experienced what America is all about ... the freedom and independence that a strong family creates.

Lord, thank you for a free country where all people, even widows with eleven children, have the chance to grow and succeed and maintain their dignity.

Dear brothers, we are not slave children, obligated to the Jewish laws, but children of the free woman, acceptable to God because of our faith.

GALATIANS 4:31

JULY 5

It was one of those summers when the houseguests came in overlapping waves. First Lynn Archer, an actress friend from New York, arrived for a weekend. The morning after she left, my sister-in-law Linda and her five-year-old arrived for three days. Then my sixteen-month-old granddaughter, Hailey, began her first four-day visit without her parents. Two days before Hailey left, Rusty, one of the pilots using my home as his Milwaukee-area "crash pad," flew his wife Heather and eight-week-old daughter Anna in from Kansas City to stay at my house while they looked for a home in Milwaukee. During that time, my daughter Julia came to get Hailey, and she stayed for two days. Before Heather and Anna left, my sister Catherine, husband Bill, and their two children arrived for three days.

As I was tossing another load of sheets and towels into the washer and trying desperately to pick up the clutter, Heather put it all into perspective, "Pat, you have made my coming to Milwaukee the nicest experience. You've been given this big home so you can fill it with people. You're certainly being obedient to his command in Hebrews 13:2 to be kind to strangers."

When I read about "entertaining angels without realizing it" I understood how blessed I was. I'd been given laughter, interesting conversations, and the fun of visiting antique shops and local restaurants with the various "angels" in my home.

These days I look forward to as many "angels" as I can pack in. Nobody seems to mind if peanut butter and jelly or frozen pizzas are on the menu. What's important is that my guests feel welcome.

Today, Lord, make me thankful for all those who fill my life and my home ... and for the joy they bring to these walls.

Don't forget to be kind to strangers, for some who have done this have entertained angels without realizing it! HEBREWS 13:2

JULY 6

When a couple separates or divorces, there's always a period where feelings, emotions, and even physical endurance seem to be ripped to shreds. Time heals these hurts, but our financial life often takes longer to heal. After all, when you take one household income and suddenly have two rents or house payments, and two sets of utility and repair bills ... it can be a financial problem of monumental proportions. Suddenly, money worries invade our every waking moment.

We scrimp, budget, whine, cry, and despair. We wonder if we'll ever be able to buy luxuries again. We may get jealous if others are doing well financially while we're struggling from paycheck to paycheck.

But we humans only need three things in order to be happy: something to do, someone to love, and something to hope for.

By those three standards I was a rich woman. I certainly had plenty to do, raising my children, working, and running the household. I also had four someones to love ... my children. Something to hope for? I wanted to write and sell a book more than anything in the world. I dreamed about it and worked on it, and finally, after ten years of being a single parent, I did it. I'm also "hoping" to meet someone special one of these days ... a man with whom I can enjoy the rest of my life.

Lord, give me the grace to stop worrying about money and to concentrate on something to do, someone to love, and something to hope for. Thanks for making me a happy person, Lord.

The man who knows right from wrong and has good judgment and common sense is happier than the man who is immensely rich!   PROVERBS 3:13

JULY 7

I remember saying good-bye to a co-worker who was leaving to take a job in another city. Knowing that I would probably never see him again all I could think to say was "Jim, have a good life."

Over the years I've had many such "for a time" friendships. Thousands of people have moved in and out of my life.

I wonder how many of them even remember me. Did I make an indelible mark on their minds? I hope so. Some have certainly made a mark on mine.

In Colorado in the late sixties, I met Paula at my first job. Though she was my mother's age, Paula accepted me as a friend on equal terms. I appreciated her gentle way of giving sound advice on the ways of the world.

In the early seventies when I moved to Missouri, I met Louise in the church nursery. Within a few months we were soul mates. Her infectious laugh and generous spirit eased me through many of the rough days when my marriage started falling apart.

In the late seventies after I moved to Illinois, Sister Giuseppa welcomed my children into her kindergarten class with the widest arms and biggest heart of any teacher I'd ever known. I was a divorced mother of three young children, and busy Sister Giuseppa found time to stop by my home to share more of her special brand of love with my children.

I'll probably never see these people again, but they remain locked in my memory because of their special gift for selfless giving.

Lord, help me to be the kind of person who doesn't fade from the memory of others. Help me give unconditional love to everyone who passes through my life.

There are "friends" who pretend to be friends, but there is a friend who sticks closer than a brother.
PROVERBS 18:24

JULY 8

My whole life was one big "hurry." I hurried to take the children to games and music lessons and my teenagers to the orthodontist, then shopping so I could hurry home to fix supper. Every minute of every day was programmed. My head and back ached, my whole body felt tense, yet I still hurried to work, hurried home, raced to the grocery store, threw another load of clothes into the washer, ran to my night class, and flopped into bed at night, too exhausted to even think.

One day I spotted a two-person, white rope hammock in a catalog and ordered it on impulse. When it arrived, Michael and I drilled holes in two backyard trees and mounted the screws and hooks that would support this new lap of luxury. We rewarded our efforts with an inaugural rest and chatted about other projects we might tackle together. He talked about school and the excitement of the home run he'd made the day before.

Andrew came bounding out of the house for his first "ride" in the hammock. Michael gave up his spot and Andrew climbed aboard. The two of us stared at the leaves above us. "Mommy, look! There's a squirrel," Andrew giggled. We watched the brown fur streak from limb to limb. I closed my eyes as a breeze rocked me toward slumber. Andrew's little body hardly moved from the curves of my own as we snuggled in the hammock.

An hour later, I realized that I was, for the first time all summer, totally, completely relaxed. The hammock was also the perfect place to talk to the children one-on-one, to open up our hearts, and to grow closer as we really listened to each other. Somehow our lives haven't been quite the same ever since the hammock became part of our family.

Lord, let me rest and bask in the beauty of your world, so I can emerge refreshed and ready to be a better single parent.

Stop awhile and rest here in the shade of this tree.

GENESIS 18:4

JULY 9

After our long, cold winters, summertime in Wisconsin is welcomed like a long-lost friend. Fresh breezes from Lake Michigan temper the sunny eighty-degree days. One glorious July day I sat on my deck, just soaking in the sounds of summer.

First I heard the roar of a jumbo jet that had just taken off from Milwaukee's airport.

Then the melodic bluejays, twittering finches, cawing crows, all scarfing up vittles from my bird feeders.

Next I heard the man down the hill making sad, guttural, unintelligible sounds caused by the debilitating stroke he'd suffered the year before.

Finally, the magnificent electronic carillon of the church down the block. Twice a day, four or five music pieces carry with the wind across the fields and roads. It lifts my spirits.

As I listened carefully to those four sounds, it seemed that the voice of God was giving me some powerful advice:

Stop complaining about the airplanes overhead. Airplane noises don't upset you when you're a passenger in one. Be patient now and let these passengers enjoy their travel.

My birds are chirping happily because you feed them. Don't neglect them in the winter.

The man down the hill needs your patience and your help. A kind word to his wife and an offer to mow their yard would be a good idea.

You've never met the pastor and his wife at the church with the magnificent bells. It's time you introduced yourself.

Lord, open my ears to really hear the sounds of your world, to listen for your voice and to act on your goodness.

Blessed are those who hear the joyful blast of the trumpet, for they shall walk in the light of your presence.

PSALMS 89:15

JULY 10

Ominous black clouds rolled in over Milwaukee's famous annual Summerfest ... a ten-day music, food, and entertainment extravaganza on the Lake Michigan shore. The wind howled, tornado warnings came over the loudspeaker, and the rain poured down in wild sheets. At one end of the grounds, five or six hundred people crowded elbow-to-elbow under a permanent shelter near a stage.

Suddenly a young man with a guitar jumped up on a picnic table at the front of the shelter. As the rest of us shivered he played songs from the fifties, sixties, and seventies. Within minutes we were all smiling, clapping, and singing our favorite old standards with gusto. An hour later we'd ridden out the storm amidst gales of music and laughter.

It happens in church, too. Just when I'm feeling overwhelmed by the week's chores, my numerous part-time jobs, and the children's constant needs, I raise my voice in song in the Lord's house and invariably my worries weaken and blow away. Somehow singing the praises of the Creator helps me to calm down and fill up the never-ending well of strength every parent needs.

I'm not sure what it is about singing, but it sure works. Give it a try this Sunday. Sing out loud and clear, and just watch those black clouds roll away!

Heavenly Father, when I'm down and out, help me to shout out your praises in song.

But as for me, I will sing each morning about your power and mercy. For you have been my high tower of refuge, a place of safety in the day of my distress.

PSALMS 59:16

JULY 11

Did you know there are 150 babies born every minute? On July 11, 1987, eight-pound Matej Gaspar, born in Zagreb, Yugoslavia, was proclaimed by the United Nations Fund for Population Activities as the five-billionth inhabitant of the earth. But by the year 2000 the world population will reach 6.2 billion. What will happen to all these babies?

Barely measuring three inches wide across her back, my granddaughter, Hannah, was born a month prematurely. Her skinny little legs and arms were as big around as my fingers. A full head of inch-long red hair stood straight up all over her baseball-size head.

Hannah was fortunate to have been born in America. Two nurses in the neonatal intensive-care unit cared for her full-time, each on a twelve-hour shift. Wires attached to Hannah's chest recorded every heartbeat, every breath. For a few days she was fed with a tube directly into her stomach.

As I watched the care Hannah was given, I thought about the other 149 babies born in the same minute as Hannah. How many would die because of squalid living conditions or of starvation before their second birthday? How many would grow up uneducated, forced to beg in the streets for a living?

Today talk to your children about the expanding world population. Consider taking them to a hospital nursery to see how well newborns are cared for in this country. Talk about ways we can help the others, in countries far away.

Heavenly Father, help my children and me find ways to make life easier for babies who won't stand a chance unless we do something.

Children are a gift from God; they are his reward.
PSALMS 127:3

JULY 12

A few years ago, I attended a celebration of the 125th anniversary of the Milwaukee archdiocesean newspaper, *The Catholic Herald.* Feeling somewhat cocky because I was one of the paper's regular columnists, I introduced myself to a number of guests. Then, nibbling on a piece of cheesecake, I studied the mementos and photos chronicling the newspaper's history. A tall, good-looking gentleman on my left was also looking at the display. Thinking perhaps he was on the paper's staff, I asked, "So what do you do here?" He smiled and said with a twinkle, "I empty the wastebaskets."

When he turned to face me, I noticed his Roman collar.

Just then an acquaintance on my right said, "Your Excellency, I'd like you to meet Patricia Lorenz. Pat, this is Bishop Sklba."

The color drained from my face, then immediately a whole new blood supply rushed upward. "Oh, Your Excellency, I'm, I'm...."

Bishop Sklba interrupted with a hearty laugh as he put his arm around me. "Pat, it's my pleasure to meet *you.* And you know what? I really *do* empty the wastebaskets!"

As the Bishop moved on to meet other people, I was moved by his humility, his humanness, and his sense of humor.

I learned a good lesson that day. I learned not to take myself or my position so seriously. Bishop Sklba taught me that a sense of humor and the ability to laugh at oneself is the mark of a truly great person.

Today, Lord, help me put others at ease by being humble and humorous.

The more lowly your service to others, the greater you are. To be the greatest, be a servant.
MATTHEW 23:11-12

Years ago, a police chief in a neighboring community let me observe an undercover drug operation. I interviewed the team, went on patrol for three nights, and even got to go on the early-morning drug raid.

What impressed me most was the frustration each police officer experienced during those days. The chief had been ordered to end the successful undercover operation after only three months because of the city's financial difficulties. But the undercover officers hadn't even made a dent in the drug dealing, because they hadn't had enough time to round up the big dealers who were bringing drugs into the city. The officer in charge of the unit knew that most of those arrested would be set free on bond, and their cases would be plea bargained to lesser charges.

Fortunately, a local radio and TV station picked up on the police department's efforts and aired public service announcements congratulating the men. People all over town started complimenting them on their fine work. Flowers arrived at the police station. A story appeared in a local paper.

All it took to erase many of the officers' frustrations was a little recognition.

You know people who are feeling particularly frustrated. Today reach out and remind them of their strengths and all the good things they do.

Lord, today let me reach out to another single parent and acknowledge what a great job he or she is doing.

Dear brothers, warn those who are lazy; comfort those who are frightened; take tender care of those who are weak; and be patient with everyone.

1 THESSALONIANS 5:14

JULY 14

When Michael and his bride, Amy, returned from their honeymoon, they stayed at my house before moving across state to the town where they both had secured jobs.

One night, Amy, who'd been giving Michael haircuts all through college, said, "Don't you need a haircut, honey?"

Michael said, "Good idea. I'll call the barber for an appointment."

Trying to be a frugal wife, Amy said, "Michael, that's ten dollars! I'll cut it."

We all went out on the patio. Amy started clipping; Michael started grumbling. I was watching.

Michael began. "Put the other attachment on the clippers. You're going to make it too short."

"No, I'm not. This is the attachment I always use."

"No, it isn't. You're not going to get it right."

"You wouldn't talk to the barber like that. Why can't you be nice and just tell me how you want it?" Amy pleaded.

"I'd be happy to tell the barber what I want, but you won't let me go."

At first I wanted to side with Michael. *Maybe he should have gone to the barber. She's obviously not cutting it the way he likes.* Then I was on Amy's side. *She's doing a great job. Why can't he just appreciate her efforts?* I changed the subject to break the tension and before long, all three of us were chatting like old friends.

Before supper that night, Michael scooped his wife into his arms, apologized profusely and told her it was one of the best haircuts he'd ever had. He promised never to complain again when she got out the clippers.

Lord, when my children want to bicker with me or with each other, help me to use words that heal instead of adding fuel to the fire.

Help me, Lord, to keep my mouth shut and my lips sealed.

PSALMS 141:3

JULY 15

One of the most difficult things I had to put up with was the "Disneyland Dad" syndrome. Many divorced couples know how it works. If Mom gets custody of the kids, Dad gets them on weekends. (Or vice versa.) When one parent gets to do the majority of the disciplining, weekdays often become a stressful, hurry up, do this, don't forget that, stop fighting with your brother, rules are rules kind of life. But on weekends ... the other parent takes the kids to the movies, to the park, to ride bikes, and shopping.

My ex-husband took my young son to the museum to see the new mummy display, to the performing arts center to see *The Nutcracker,* and yes, even to Disneyland. He got to have all the fun with his child and none of the craziness.

Naturally, at times I was resentful that I couldn't *afford* to take my child to the symphony or the circus. But then I read that once A.J. Foyt won the Indianapolis 500 by a mere five seconds ... pretty amazing when you consider the race lasted over three and a half hours.

Endurance and determination could mean the difference between success and failure. If I simply kept on being the best parent I could be weekday after weekday, giving my son the daily stability he needed in his life, perhaps in the end he would view my efforts as valiant and successful as his "Disneyland Dad's."

And you know what? He did.

Lord, give me the courage to be strong and determined as I parent my children and not to buy their love with gifts and adventures. Help me to give them loving stability instead.

As Christ's soldier do not let yourself become tied up in worldly affairs, for then you cannot satisfy the one who has enlisted you in his army.   2 TIMOTHY 2:4

JULY 16

July 16, the anniversary of the world's first atomic bomb explosion, unleashed a power everyone has a reason to fear.

But do we also have a time bomb ticking inside our bodies? Once I was in a fast-food restaurant with my friend Sharon. I'd just complained about all the high-school kids around us who were smoking on their lunch hour when Sharon ran into Mr. Schmidt, who had just celebrated his eighty-fourth birthday. He started talking about Germany and Russia during World War II.

Mr. Schmidt looked around the restaurant. "Look at these kids smoking. I remember my uncle telling me about a prisoner of war camp in Russia. As a German soldier he wasn't treated too well by the Russians. Every day they gave the prisoners a little water, a piece of bread, and tobacco. Some prisoners were so hooked on cigarettes that they traded some of their bread for my uncle's tobacco. My uncle never smoked. Well, they all died of starvation, except my uncle. Can you believe all they had was a little bread—and they gave it up for more tobacco?"

I looked at the teenagers puffing away. "Yes, Mr. Schmidt, I can believe it. Things aren't much different today, are they?"

Lord, you've given us life and a beautiful world. Why are so many of us bent on self-destruction? Help me teach my children to respect and protect their world and their bodies.

Wisdom is better than weapons of war, but one rotten apple can spoil a barrelful. ECCLESIASTES 9:18

Many single parents have difficulty finding the time to fix proper meals. Because nutritious meals and snacks always seem to take more planning and time than we can spare, we often end up in the drive-through lane of the nearest fast-food restaurant. Fast food generally contains alarming amounts of fat, which can be disastrous to your family's good health.

Still not convinced? Here's a list of all the premature aging symptoms caused by the gradual accumulation of cholesterol deposits in your blood vessels: graying and thinning of the hair; wrinkled skin; loss of hearing; poor eyesight; dry, less pliable skin; arthritis; decrease in muscle tone; decline in breathing capacity; slow metabolism; decline in kidney function; less resilient cartilage; age spots; decline in sexuality; increased blood pressure; hardened arteries; heart disease, stroke, and senility risks.

Today, make a list of good-for-you foods, let the children help you shop, and start slicing and dicing. Tonight could be "huge garden salad" night. Add whole-grain bread, a protein food, skim milk for the beverage, and fresh fruit for dessert. You're on your way to a whole new healthy family!

Heavenly Father, today and every day let me use your bounty of fresh fruits, vegetables, and grains to feed my children. Keep us healthy, Lord.

And look! I have given you the seed-bearing plants throughout the earth, and all the fruit trees for your food.   GENESIS 1:29

JULY 18

In 1995 I received a letter from the medical director of a Texas health center, asking me, "What is the key to contentment, fulfillment, or happiness in life?" He was preparing a book that would contain the answers to that question from "leaders and personalities all across our nation."

Well, I knew I wasn't a leader, so feeling rather perky that he'd proclaimed me, a mom from Oak Creek, Wisconsin, a "personality" I set out to answer the doctor's great question.

First, I pontificated about how one of the main purposes of education should be to help us discover the unique talent God has given each of us. I continued, "Next, we need to find a career that utilizes our particular talent. When we work at something we're naturally good at ... contentment, fulfillment, and happiness automatically follow. For me, chocolate chip cookies and naps work well also."

I'm not sure I captured exactly what the good doctor had in mind, but the more I thought about it, the more I decided my last sentence was the most important.

Lots of other "little" things make me happy: the giant willow tree outside my office window. A good steaming cup of Irish Breakfast tea. My son Andrew's big hug every morning as he leaves for school. All these "little" things and hundreds like them make me happy, contented and fulfilled.

Lord, help me start each day by thinking about all the wonderful "little" blessings you've provided that make me happy.

But as for me, my contentment is not in wealth but in seeing you and knowing all is well between us.

PSALMS 17:15

JULY 19

When Andrew was in junior high school he had to read twenty statements and check whether or not he believed each statement would happen in his lifetime.

Some things Andrew did not think would happen were: "Church attendance will increase and more people will believe in religion. Starvation in the world will be eliminated. Pollution on the planet Earth will be completely eliminated."

Some of the things he thought *would* happen in his lifetime are, "Students will take all courses through home TV sets or computers. All nations will agree to destroy all nuclear weapons. Women and men will be treated as equals in all matters. Life will be discovered in outer space."

It's hard to imagine what life will be like for our children when they're our age. Look at how drastically the computer revolution has changed our lives.

We need to give our children vision and the education necessary to make their dreams come true. We also need to keep up with technology ourselves. That's why, after using the same dinosaur computer for fourteen years, I decided to join the twenty-first century and buy a new one. If I didn't, how can I expect my children to believe that one is never too old to learn?

Lord, give me the courage and mental prowess necessary to learn all about my new computer. Help my children and me to be enthusiastic about learning new things now and for the rest of our lives.

Wear my yoke—for it fits perfectly—and let me teach you; for I am gentle and humble, and you shall find rest for your souls; for I give you only light burdens.
MATTHEW 11:29-30

JULY 20

One day my pastor, Father Ron, visited a store that sold beautiful life-size brass and bronze original art statues purchased from museums all over the world. As Father Ron turned the corner at the end of an aisle he saw the angel. Four feet tall, cast bronze, with a six-foot wing span and the most beautiful face Father had ever seen. He gasped when he turned over the price tag, $7,000.

Just then a tall, striking gentleman of Middle Eastern descent walked up. "The angel, she is beautiful, yes?"

"The most beautiful I've ever seen," Father. Ron said wistfully. "We want to build a memorial," Father began, "but we don't have that much money...."

The man persisted. "What is it you need the angel for?"

"My parish. I'm the pastor of St. Mary's Catholic Church in South Milwaukee. We want to build a memorial/hospitality room in the back of church, a place where we can remember deceased members of our parish. I've been hoping to find an angel to preside over this place of prayer."

"I see," said the tall, serious man, whose name was Ali, as he pulled a calculator out of his pocket. He punched numbers on his calculator, then cleared the total and started over. Father thought, *Even if he gives us a discount of 20, 30, or even 50 percent, we still can't afford this angel.*

Ali held the calculator in front of Father's eyes. "How does this look? I will deliver the angel to your church for you personally," he said.

"Sixteen hundred dollars? But why ... ?" Father stammered.

"I would rather see this angel in a house of prayer than in someone's home. All I ask is that on the day you put this angel in your church you ask your people to pray for Ali."

Lord, bless Ali and all the others like him who are your messengers of love.

Yes, bless the Lord, you armies of his angels who serve him constantly.　　PSALMS 103:21

JULY 21

When she was eighty-six years old, my Aunt Helen sent me this anonymous prayer that a friend had sent her.

Lord, you know that I'm growing older. Keep me from becoming talkative and possessed with the idea that I must express myself on every subject. Release me from the craving to straighten out everyone's affairs. Keep my mind free from the recital of endless details. Give me wings to get to the point. Seal my lips when I am inclined to tell all my aches and pains and when my love to speak of them increases with the years. Teach me the glorious lesson that occasionally I may be wrong. Make me thoughtful but not nosy. Helpful but not bossy. Help me to be silent when listening to others even through it does seem a pity not to use all my vast store of wisdom and experience. But Thou knowest, Lord, that I want a few friends at the end.

I've decided that this is a great prayer for single parents as well as for older people. Try it. Just change the first line to read, "Lord, you know that I'm a single parent."

Lord, help me to make my prayers more personal, to acknowledge my faults and to work on changing them.

Listen to me! You can pray for anything and if you believe, you have it; it's yours! But when you are praying, first forgive anyone you are holding a grudge against, so that your Father in heaven will forgive you your sins too.   MARK 11:24-25

JULY 22

Do you ever get bogged down by all the clutter in your house? Are you still collecting it and adding to the "stuff" in your home … or have you tired of "things" and wish you'd never bought and saved it all in the first place?

For me, the collecting bug, the nesting instinct, the decorating mania … whatever you want to call it, ended around age forty-five when I discovered that I had too many "things" and not enough space. I started giving away my less-than-perfect furniture to my college-age children. When they got married or moved into their own places, I gave them some of my antique dishes, decorative serving pieces, and family heirlooms. I had annual rummage sales after cleaning out closets and storage spaces. Everything that didn't sell I gave away. Once I gave away 133 books and eight sweaters. Another time at a luncheon I passed around two dozen pairs of earrings that I wanted to get rid of. That year I also vowed not to buy any more clothes for myself for three years just so I could wear out the things I already had.

I still have lots more "stuff" than I need to survive. But now, instead of collecting more, I spend more time playing outdoors and enjoying God's world with the people I love.

Lord, help me to stop buying and start sharing instead. Give me the wisdom to spend my life enjoying your wonderful world instead of looking for more "stuff."

I'll tear down my barns and build bigger ones! Then I'll have room enough.… But God said to him, "Fool! Tonight you die. Then who will get it all?" Yes, every man is a fool who gets rich on earth but not in heaven.
LUKE 12:18, 20, 21

JULY 23

When my four children were all still living at home I was the sole caretaker of their transportation problems because the father of the three oldest ones lived six hours away and the father of the youngest died when Andrew was nine years old. As the sole parent I spent hours in the car, grumbling all the way to soccer practice, Little League games, music lessons, and trips to visit their friends, who all seemed to live four or five miles from our house. I started to feel as if that car was my second home.

I stopped grumbling after my friend, Wade, told me about the time he drove his teenage son, Trevor, home from a friend's house. Trevor started telling his dad all about the party he and the friend had attended the night before. Wade knew they'd be home long before the story ended, so he purposely made a wrong turn and kept driving on and on, listening intently to Trevor's animated story. Wade didn't often have a chance to talk with his son one-on-one, and he simply didn't want the trip to end before Trevor was finished telling the story.

Are you a happy chauffeur? If you are, you've probably already figured out that the time you spend in the car together may be the only chance you have all day to talk one-on-one with your teen. Each of you is a captive audience, so to speak. What a blessing.

Heavenly Father, thank you for all the times I get to be in the car with my child. Help us use that time productively.

Listen to my counsel—oh, don't refuse it—and be wise. Happy is the man who is so anxious to be with me that he watches for me daily at my gates, or waits for me outside my home! PROVERBS 8:33-34

JULY 24

In his book *Living Faith,* Jimmy Carter tells of the arguments he and his wife Rosalynn used to have. Because they were very headstrong, sometimes their stony silence would last for days after a particularly bitter argument. Jimmy tried to find a way to end their arguments in a more timely fashion. One night, Jimmy, who is quite a carpenter and loves to work with wood, carved the following words on a thin sheet of walnut the size of a checkbook ...

> EACH EVENING, FOREVER, THIS IS GOOD
> FOR AN APOLOGY—OR FORGIVENESS—
> AS YOU DESIRE. JIMMY

Jimmy presented the little wooden check to his wife, thus allowing her to decide each time they had an argument if Jimmy would be the one to apologize, or if he should forgive her indiscretion.

When tensions rise between you and your children, wouldn't it be nice to let each child fix the problem before bedtime by asking for forgiveness for their own bad behavior ... or by asking for an apology from you? You certainly don't have to carve the check out of wood. Draw, paint, color, or computerize the sign on paper and laminate it with clear adhesive-backed paper. Make one for every member of the family. And tonight, before you go to bed, if you've had unkind words with one of your children today, get ready to forgive or apologize ... and then dream sweet dreams because all will be right in your world.

Lord, give us the wisdom to forgive those who trespass against us ... and the courage to apologize when we are the culprits.

Rebuke your brother if he sins, and forgive him if he is sorry. Even if he wrongs you seven times a day and each time turns again and asks forgiveness, forgive him.   LUKE 17:3-4

JULY 25

If you live in the northern part of the United States, as I do, July, August, and September are harvest months. No longer do we have to rely on Texas, Florida, and California to provide us with fresh fruits and vegetables. At last, we can enjoy fresh, healthful, home-grown eating.

I heard once that half our grocery money should be spent in the produce department. Next time you and your kids are wandering up and down the aisles, why don't you wow 'em with these seven fruit and vegetable facts?

(1) A red bell pepper has twice as much vitamin C as an orange. (2) A small sweet potato has twice the recommended daily allowance of vitamin A ... and only 140 calories. (3) A large baked potato has twice as much potassium as a medium banana. (4) If you drink tea (regular or decaf, hot or iced) with food it can cut your iron absorption by 85 percent. (5) A whole orange has a third more nutrients than orange juice. (6) The more colorful a vegetable is, the more vitamin A it has. Look for bright orange carrots, bright green broccoli, dark romaine or escarole (instead of pale iceberg lettuce). (7) Lima beans have seven times more fiber than green beans.

Lord, thank you for the fresh produce that's so abundant this month and for the rest of the summer. Thank you for the earth, wind, rain, and sun that grow the crops you've provided for us. Help me to teach my children about good nutrition by feeding them with your bounty.

The eyes of all mankind look up to you for help; you give them their food as they need it. You constantly satisfy the hunger and thirst of every living thing.

PSALMS 145:15-16

JULY 26

"Mom, you're supposed to do *Hawaii Five-O* when you turn fifty. It's a tradition. I'll pay your airfare," my oldest daughter, Jeanne, gushed.

So we went, Jeanne and her boyfriend Canyon, both twenty-six, my youngest son Andrew, fifteen, and me, on a dream vacation to Hawaii for fifteen glorious days. On the morning of day twelve we rented ocean kayaks, the only way to get to the most spectacular snorkeling spot on the Big Island. We kayaked a half mile across the bay and spent the day underwater smiling at a gazillion technicolor fish.

Around 4:00 P.M. we climbed into our kayaks for the return trip, the only living souls in that part of the Pacific Ocean. Exhausted, we lollygagged across the calm, crystal-clear water.

Suddenly huge fish were popping out of the water just ahead of us. Fish? They were dolphins! Dozens of them … perhaps a hundred. We paddled like crazy to get closer, then sat silently when we reached the spot where they were playing.

I looked at Jeanne and Canyon. They were speechless. As we sat motionless in that great ocean, the dolphins jumped out of the water, did spins in the air, and dove back in headfirst. They seemed as happy to see us as we were to see them and for thirty minutes or so we four were spellbound. I felt as if I'd been transported to another world, something akin to heaven.

Finally Canyon whispered, "This is unbelievable. It's definitely a 'God moment.'"

I nodded as six sleek dolphins, perfectly synchronized, glided within feet of the kayak Andrew and I were in, wiggled their fins almost in a wave, then headed out to sea.

Lord, thank you for the "God moments" here on earth that are a preview of what eternity with you in heaven is all about.

O Lord our God, the majesty and glory of your name
fills all the earth and overflows the heavens.

PSALMS 8:1

JULY 27

It had been one of those weeks that single parents experience more often than we like to admit. Nothing was going right. Not only had it rained every day, there was simply too much to do and not enough time to do it. The older children snapped at me, I snapped at them.

At church our pastor challenged, "Each time someone hurts you, snubs you, is unkind to you, or puts you down, give that person a sincere compliment that same day."

Give that person a compliment! I thought. *Impossible!*

By midweek life was so grumpy I decided to give it a try.

I left Michael a note, "Thanks for making your bed. Your room looks great!"

The next time Andrew threw a temper tantrum I scooped him off the floor, told him I loved him, and read him a story.

When the girls complained about chores, I changed the subject. "You girls sure are good baby-sitters. Two people have told me this week how good you are with their children."

It worked! Michael gave me a spontaneous hug on his way out the door to play baseball. Julia offered to watch Andrew so I could go grocery shopping. Andrew asked me if he could help set the table for supper. And Jeanne invited me to a summer-school musical production with her.

Lord, when I'm hurt by those around me, help me to fight fire with water and to find creative ways to show my love.

How wonderful it is to be able to say the right thing at the right time!   PROVERBS 15:23

JULY 28

Let me tell you about two friends of mine whom I met in San Francisco. I met Bill Lombardo on the Bay Area Rapid Transit train. He's in his early fifties, a percussionist, married twenty-seven years, and has two children. He used to play in his uncle Guy Lombardo's band, then started his own fifteen-piece orchestra. Bill was in my state of Wisconsin only once that he can remember, years ago when he spent the night with a friend in the tiny town of Cuba City.

When Bill told me that, I couldn't believe it. You see, that very day, my son Michael, also a percussionist, was moving to Cuba City to take over the high school band director's job. Bill and I had a lot to talk about.

My other friend is Vivian Su, born in Canada and of Chinese descent. She's sixty-seven years old but looks and acts fifty, because she fast-walks a mile and a half around the lake in Oakland every morning. She's been a homemaker all her life, and her two sons still live at home because they like her cooking. Vivian and her husband have visited China twice, climbing the Great Wall both times. We met in the bargain basement of a department store the same week I met Bill.

What's so unusual about Bill and Vivian? Well, I only knew them for twenty minutes each. We just started talking, and before I knew it, I felt as if we were old friends.

I'll tell you one thing ... I remember those twenty-minute conversations in greater detail than I remember Golden Gate Park or Chinatown.

Lord, wherever I may be, open my eyes, ears, and heart to the people you have put in my path.

When she speaks, her words are wise, and kindness is the rule for everything she says.   PROVERBS 31:26

JULY 29

It's a fact that we single parents need each other. Check out the singles group in your community or church. Find some other single parents who live near you and ask if they'd be interested in a sort of job-share program. You could offer to help her with extra carpooling. Watch his children once a week in the evening so he can volunteer at church, go to the library, or go shopping by himself without worrying about the children. He, in turn, could do the same for you.

Invite a single-parent neighbor for dinner some Saturday evening when her children are visiting their dad.

Single parents should get in the habit of visiting each other, especially in the evenings. It may just meet that need for adult conversation after the children are in bed. Pick up the phone and chat with a single parent who may be feeling particularly lonely at night.

Offer to trade mending or cooking skills in exchange for snowblowing your driveway or helping with your household repairs. Oh, and don't forget to compliment your single-parent friends on what a great job they're doing as parents. We all desperately need positive reinforcement.

Lord, there are so many single parents like me. Keep me aware of ways I can help other families like mine to feel whole, strong, intact, and appreciated.

When I come, although I can't do much to help your faith, for it is strong already, I want to be able to do something about your joy: I want to make you happy, not sad. 2 CORINTHIANS 3:24

JULY 30

"Hey kids, turn off that TV! It's been on too long!"

"Mom, there's nothing to do!"

"There's plenty to do!"

"Like what?"

"OK, take your pick. We're going to get in the car and do one of the following: visit a pet store and just *look* at the animals; visit a police or fire station; visit someone in a nursing home; go to the library; visit a farm; go to an art gallery; watch construction workers build a building; or drive to another town and just explore."

"Mom!"

"Wait, there's more. You can each take a friend along and on the way home we'll stop for ice cream."

"Cool. Who decides where we go?"

"We're going to write each possibility on a little piece of paper and draw from a jar."

Creating a special summertime memory for your children is simple. It's just a matter of getting out there and doing something different. Rainy day? No problem. Here's a list of inside activities: make candles, explore the attic, make popcorn balls, plant a small indoor herb garden, build a huge Tinkertoy tower, learn how to build a birdhouse, make a kite, have a checkers tournament, or have a water balloon fight outdoors in the rain.

Lord, thank you for your bounty of things to do with my children this summer. Give us the energy to be active all summer long.

I have learned how to get along happily whether I have much or little.　　　PHILIPPIANS 4:11

A few years ago someone faxed me a list of "100 things we didn't have 25 years ago." Some were things we certainly could have done without like crack cocaine, AIDS, Legionnaires' disease, and direct-mail advertising.

But I can't imagine *not* having home computers, answering and fax machines, VCRs, no-smoking sections, Post-it Notes, rollerblades, microwave ovens, fat-free foods, pocket calculators, and bread machines.

How many single parents whine and complain if we can't have the latest electronic invention? Worse, how many of us work extra hours so we *can* buy our children all the latest gadgets? Perhaps we feel guilty because we think we've messed up their lives by making them live in a single-parent family.

All I can say is *nonsense!* Don't fall into the "things mean love" trap. Time with your child means love. Period.

When I look at the "things we didn't have 25 years ago" I have to laugh, because I *still* don't own a CD player, a car with air bags, a video camera, on-line computer service, a mini-van, a cellular phone, or designer jeans. I feel rich, though, because I have time to spend with my children, time to take a hike after supper, watch my son add a few boards to his tree house, and give him a driving lesson. Time is the most valuable asset we have. The latest "things" aren't important at all.

Tonight, why don't you turn off the VCR and shut off the computer and lob a few balls to your child in the backyard?

Lord, keep my priorities strong. Help me make the time I spend with my children the most important and most "time consuming" thing in my life.

And so since everything around us is going to melt away, what holy, godly lives we should be living!
2 PETER 3:11

A Prayer for August

Dear God, it's so hot today!
Pavement scorches my bare feet.
My body drips with perspiration.
Sometimes it's easy
To long for the cool
Kite-flying breezes
Of last spring.
Or the crisp-cold
Snow-crunch days
Of last winter.

Father, teach me to love
Each season *while I'm in it.*
Help me not to be
Forever wishing
For the last season
Or dreaming of the next.
Help me to be patient
With the children
During these scorching days.
And Lord, help me to bask
In the warmth of your love
365 days a year
No matter what the weather!

AUGUST 1

What is the one thing we all have that when we give it away it makes us happy, and when we get it back (which we almost *always* do), it makes us even more happy? Ask your children that question and see if they know the answer. Be sure you have a big *smile* on your face when you ask the question. Maybe if you hold a banana in front of your mouth in the upward *smile* position they'll get it.

When I take my daily morning walk, I smile and offer others a hearty "Good morning!" and without fail, I get a smile and a greeting in return.

When I'm in the car and someone cuts me off or commits some other irritating driving sin, instead of growling, frowning, and offering an unsavory piece of my mind, I smile a real, genuine smile. Then I say a quick prayer. Something like, "Lord, help that driver to be a little more careful so he or she won't be a danger behind the wheel."

The first week in August is National Smile Week. Try one on for size. Take your children along next time you run errands and make it a game. Count how many people you can get to smile at you. If nothing else you'll teach your children what a positive attitude is all about. Together create a little smile magic and make the world just a bit nicer.

Lord, thank you for such a simple way to change an attitude, lighten a load, lift a heart, or touch the lonely.

How we laughed and sang for joy. And the other nations said, "What amazing things the Lord has done for them."　　　　　PSALMS 126:2

AUGUST 2

We single parents often have to rely on "quality" time with our children rather than "quantity" time. That's because most of us work to make ends meet. Time alone with the children is at a premium, especially if visitation with the other parent enters into the picture.

Why not make August the month you organize at least one "quality time" activity a day. Start an ongoing jigsaw puzzle. Take turns reading a book out loud, one chapter a day. Or make up your own family game. Here's one to get you started. Write down the following fifteen things: *Ohio furnace, steam furnace, tater patch, black hollow, rock hollow, deep cut, front end drive, chenoweth fork, serpent mound, union hill, sunfish creek, gingersnap, crabtree hollow, hackleshin, plum run.*

Ask the children, "What do these fifteen things have in common?" Let each child have five guesses. Write down all their answers. What are they? Brand names of old-fashioned toys? Indian burial grounds? Great names for dogs?

Lots of laughs and mental exhaustion later, tell them the answer: they're all names of roads near the Ohio/West Virginia border. If you have an Ohio or West Virginia road map you might even look for the roads.

Lord, I know it doesn't take much to create "quality" time with my children. Just help me to do it, every day. Help me, as parent, grow the fabric that weaves us together as a family.

You must think constantly about these commandments I am giving you today. You must teach them to your children and talk about them when you are at home or out for a walk; at bedtime and the first thing in the morning.   DEUTERONOMY 6:6-7

AUGUST 3

Dating for single parents can be the pits. But the possibility of meeting someone nice to enjoy the social side of life is just too tempting. But dating when you're thirty, forty, or fifty is often crazy and uncomfortable. Most of the time we don't even know what the rules are anymore.

For over a dozen years, I've found the personal ads in the local newspaper to be a fun way to meet interesting people. After years of having lots of "first" dates through the personals I met Jim, a bank executive with whom I seemed to have a lot in common.

After two long dates and umpteen hours on the phone I learned that he was looking for someone to start a full-blown intimate relationship with, now, right now. "I'm so lonely," he said. Amazingly Jim and his second wife had only been separated for three months, and their divorce wasn't final. So I wrote him a letter pointing out that I thought he had his priorities out of order and gave him suggestions on putting his life in order, working through the grief, and *then* finding intimacy and happiness through a lifelong marital commitment.

Jim never responded to my letter. Maybe he didn't follow my advice. But after putting my feelings in writing, I knew *my* intimacy and happiness lay in my relationship with God, and for the time being I could be happy with that.

Lord, let me be careful out there. Remind me that total commitment is the only sure way to guarantee true happiness when it comes to love.

I say it again, that if your aim is to enjoy the evil pleasure of the unsaved world, you cannot also be a friend of God. JAMES 4:4

AUGUST 4

After writing over 40,000 radio commercials, it became more and more difficult to keep from repeating myself. One day I was writing ads for two different bottled water companies. Although they sounded suspiciously alike, I turned them in.

At bedtime, ten-year-old Andrew and I rattled off the Lord's Prayer, paying little attention to the words. It reminded me of those bottled water commercials. Would anyone hear the sponsors' messages?

The next day I creatively rewrote the commercials so listeners could really hear them.

Andrew and I also became creative about bedtime prayers. Sometimes we'd read a psalm and talk about how we could practice its message.

One night we read Psalm 27:14, concentrating on the lines "Don't be impatient. Wait for the Lord." Andrew, who had been talking for days about his lost Cleveland Indians baseball cap, asked God to help him find it. I knew Andrew had listened to the psalm because he stopped talking about the cap. A few days later, he told me, "Look, I was patient and I waited ... and found my cap."

Our Father, who art in heaven, help us find ways to get closer to you each day. Help me to talk to you as my friend.

Don't recite the same prayer over and over as the heathen do, who think prayers are answered only by repeating them again and again.   MATTHEW 6:7

AUGUST 5

Ten years ago when I was up to my eyeballs in single parenting, I read a column by a woman who said that a single parent is a prisoner locked into a life of sacrifice and guilt. I agreed that most of us do sacrifice a life of our own. Because so often we must leave our children with day-care workers or baby-sitters, we wouldn't dare think of going out at night. So we sacrifice. Then we feel sorry for ourselves and we get irritable with the children. So we feel guilty.

But I began to notice the same two qualities in two-parent families. I remembered when I was married and leaving my preschooler with a baby-sitter while I worked. I didn't feel I could go out at night then either. And I certainly got just as irritable when I had a husband at my side. When you're raising kids, sacrifice and guilt just come with the territory. They aren't just single-parent things.

Children are our greatest joy as well as our greatest challenge. Raising them is the most thought-provoking, mind-boggling, stress-causing adventure of our lives. And whether we're doing it alone or with a spouse, it's also the most joyous.

Lord, thank you for my children. Never let me lose sight of the fact that they are my greatest treasures.

Any of you who welcomes a little child like this because you are mine, is welcoming me and caring for me.   MATTHEW 18:5

AUGUST 6

I've always liked rocks. Granite, sandstone, limestone, quartz, shale, mica, pumice, slate, geodes ... I like them all, especially if they're colorful and have great texture.

Ten feet from our front door is a large, odd-shaped rock garden. The rocks are all shapes, sizes, and colors. When my children were young, every time we visited Lake Michigan we collected rocks that had washed up onto the beach. The county work crews spent hours with huge machines getting rid of those rocks, so I figured we'd help out by taking some of them home for our rock garden. I kept six or seven gallon-size buckets in the trunk of the car for rock gathering.

I'd say to the children, "I'll take you to the beach today if you each promise to fill two buckets with rocks and deliver them to the car." They'd moan and groan but after they tested the icy cold waters and built huge sand castles, they'd start their rock safari, oohing and aahing over each beauty they collected. After a few years we had enough rocks for rock gardens in both the front yard and backyard.

It's been years since we gathered those rocks and lugged them home, and they are still beautiful, but even more so are the memories of the summers when my children and I collected them.

What can you and your children build or gather or collect today that will provide warm memories for years to come?

Lord, building a family takes work. Help me to know that, rock by rock, brick by brick, each day is a gift, a new chance to build memories for my children.

All who listen to my instructions and follow them are wise, like a man who builds his house on solid rock.
MATTHEW 7:24

AUGUST 7

My daughter Jeanne had procrastinated until she had only two days to get ready to spend a year in Yugoslavia as a foreign exchange student. Then the day before she was to leave, came the call from the program director in New York.

"Where's Jeanne? She wasn't on the plane this morning."

"She's coming tomorrow, Mr. Lurie, August eighth."

"No! She was supposed to be here this morning! She's already missed half the orientation!"

I had booked that morning's flight months earlier but had mistakenly put it on the wrong date on the calendar.

The next two hours were a whirl, with me blubbering to the airline about the horrible mistake I'd made, them telling me to bring Jeanne to the airport *right away* to fly standby. I then had to drive home from work and FIND Jeanne (who was out cavorting with her friends), watch as she packed everything she would need for the next year in twenty minutes, and blubber some more as I apologized for my horrendous mistake. Jeanne, bless her, just hugged me and said, "It's OK, Mom. Maybe it's better this way." We then dashed to the airport in a frenzied rush, and I was just explaining our situation for the fourth time that day to the airline officials when I realized that we'd left her airline tickets on the counter at home … So we dashed back home, and returned to the airport just in time for me to watch my beautiful first-born child walk down the corridor to board the plane.

By the next day the panic of those few hours turned into a hilarious Three-Stooges-movie memory that none of us will ever forget. Next time something goes awry, take a deep breath, say a few prayers, and know that God truly does send angels down to shield us.

Lord, if I have a disaster today, get me through it with a chuckle instead of a curse.

He will shield you with his wings! They will shelter you. His faithful promises are your armor.

PSALMS 91:4

AUGUST 8

When Terry Meeuwsen was a small girl she wanted to be a famous star and sing her way around the world. At nineteen her professional singing career began, and two years with the New Christy Minstrels brought international travel and seven recordings.

As Terry jetted from country to country, rubbing elbows with big stars, she discovered that those famous people were often confused, depressed, or downright angry about their lives.

She said, "My own career started to feel like a vacuum. I wondered, *Is this all there is?* Then something happened that spiraled me into the worst depression of all. In Hawaii, while waiting to leave for a singing tour of Japan, I was sexually molested. Suddenly I realized that nothing, absolutely *nothing* belongs to me. Anyone bigger or stronger can take away everything I have.

"Not long after that, after singing at a Bible college, a coed started talking to me about Jesus. She made me realize that I'd pushed the Lord out of my life to make room for my career. Then she gave me a pamphlet to read that said 'God is the God of a second chance.' I wondered, *Can I commit myself to the Lord and make Him number one? Can I forgive my attacker and gain a second chance at life with Jesus at the helm?*

"I decided to give it a try. Before long, I began to feel really good about myself because I was feeling so good about the Lord. I was singing for His glory and not mine."

Even the song Terry sang at the 1973 Miss America pageant, "He Touched Me," was about the Lord. And for the first time in the history of the pageant the audience gave a standing ovation. Terry won the pageant and continues to share the goodness of the Lord on TV and in many singing and speaking engagements.

Lord, help me not to give up no matter how many bad things happen in my life. Help me to remember that You will always give me a second chance ... and a third ... and a fourth ... and....

When I pray, you answer me, and encourage me by giving me the strength I need.   PSALM 138:3

AUGUST 9

One day when I was recuperating from a bad summer cold I flipped on daytime TV and watched the talk shows for a few hours. I watched children on one show spewing venomous words on the side of the racist KKK. In another, out-of-control teens who "slept around," did drugs, and physically abused their siblings and parents were trying to explain why.

What happened to the days when workers worked, God's laws were cherished and obeyed, marriages endured, neighbors helped one another, and children were taught to respect their parents and themselves?

As single parents, we want those values in our children's lives. Though we may do a good job of parenting, doing it alone is not the ideal way to do the job. Everyone has a mother and a father. God intended for both to raise their children. That's why we must make a special effort to teach that model to our kids. How can we do it? By staying friends with many married couples and inviting them to our homes often so our children can see them relating to each other and to their children. Our children desperately need to see how a two-parent family works and plays together.

If our parents or our ex-spouse's parents are alive and still together, we should include them in as many of our family activities as possible. We may be doing this parent thing solo, but we still owe it to our children to show them how the ideal situation works.

Heavenly Father, bless and protect the marriages of all the couples we know who are still together. Let them be an inspiration to my children and to me.

Honor your marriage and its vows, and be pure ...
HEBREWS 13:4

AUGUST 10

I was driving my beautiful eighteen-year-old niece, Kirstie, and my fourteen-year-old son, Andrew, home after visiting my brother and his family in Louisville for a week. Near Chicago, I had to change highways, but unfortunately, got off the interstate at the wrong exit. I ended up on a deserted, dead-end dirt and gravel road. As I got off, I noticed a car following me down the deserted road. Quickly I made a U-turn just as the other car sped up and pulled along side me. Five or six loud, jeering men who didn't speak much English started to get out of their car.

Terrified, I locked my car door and gunned the engine, spewing dust and rocks behind me. I raced back toward the interstate, praying like gangbusters, drenched in fear. Five minutes later the right exit appeared and we headed home, out of danger.

For the next hour I said prayers of thanksgiving and took lots of deep breaths. I started thinking about fear and how powerful it is. I recalled stories my dad tells about his experiences as a World War II fighter pilot in the South Pacific.

"Weren't you scared?" I'd ask. He'd say he just remembers flying one mile after another, getting closer and closer to his destination, trying not to think about what *could* happen, knowing that God was his copilot.

Whether we're facing an enemy in war, an ambush on a deserted dirt road, or struggling to make it through to the next paycheck ... if we just have faith that God is there, guiding us mile after mile, we'll make it to safety.

Lord, help my faith to grow so that I can reach out to you and find comfort, no matter how dangerous the waters are.

Peter went over the side of the boat and walked on the water toward Jesus. But when he looked around at the high waves, he was terrified and began to sink. "Save me, Lord!" he shouted. Instantly Jesus reached out his hand and rescued him. "O man of little faith," Jesus said. "Why did you doubt me?"

MATTHEW 14:29-31

AUGUST 11

This quote by Paul Dudley White is taped to the inside of my front door: "A vigorous walk will do more good for an unhappy but otherwise healthy adult than all the medicine and psychology in the world." Exercise is a *must* for single parents.

So what's your excuse for not exercising? In a recent survey, other Americans gave these:

1. They don't have the time.

2. They don't have the willpower.

3. They don't feel like it.

4. A medical reason keeps them from exercising.

5. They don't have enough energy.

But before you tape your favorite excuse to your front door, here are seven reasons most people *do* exercise regularly.

1. It makes them feel better physically and mentally.

2. It relaxes them.

3. They sleep better.

4. It improves their concentration, self-image, and their ability to cope with pressure and stress.

5. It makes them more productive.

6. It makes them more creative.

7. It gives them more energy.

Which list do you want? Next time you're feeling "down and out," give a little shout and lace up those walking shoes. I'm here to tell you, it *works!*

Lord, take away my laziness and help me create a new habit that includes daily exercise. Thank you for the great outdoors that I can enjoy every time I take a walk.

Spend your time and energy in the exercise of keeping spiritually fit.   1 TIMOTHY 4:7

We all have friends or acquaintances who forever gripe about their childhood. Their parents didn't show them enough love. Or they were abused as children. Or their family or religion made them feel guilty. Always critical of themselves and others, they worry, fret, and slowly turn their children into little versions of themselves.

If you tend to be a negative person, maybe you experienced destructive criticism as a child or were the spouse of an abusive adult. Stop using anyone else as an excuse for your own behavior.

Brian Tracy's tape, "Accepting Responsibility and Taking Charge," from his excellent *The Psychology of Achievement* series, relates four things we must do to erase a negative self-image. "First," he said, "we have to forgive our parents for everything they ever did that caused us any unhappiness. Second, we have to forgive everybody else—every single person who has ever hurt us in any way. Third, we have to forgive ourselves for every wicked, senseless, foolish, brainless, cruel, ridiculous thing we have ever done. Finally, if we feel we have done or said anything to anyone else that causes us to feel uneasy inside, we have to go to him and apologize."

Today, I give you Brian Tracy's wisdom and ask that you act on these steps.

Lord, let me forgive and forget and to take responsibility for my own happiness. In the meantime, help me to pass generous doses of self-esteem onto my children.

Stop being mean, bad-tempered and angry. Quarreling, harsh words, and dislike of others should have no place in your lives. Instead, be kind to each other, tender-hearted, forgiving one another, just as God has forgiven you because you belong to Christ.

EPHESIANS 4:31

AUGUST 13

Did you ever play the "what if" game? Write down these four questions:

1. What if I had three wishes that could all come true? What would they be?

2. What if I could choose to have a great talent? What would it be and how would I use it?

3. What if I won a million dollars. What would I do with it?

4. What if I only had six months to live. How would I spend my time?

Our answers to these questions can show us what our personal goals are.

God gives us a great start on achieving goals by giving each of us certain talents or abilities. To find out what our talents are, we simply need to look at what we enjoy doing in life, things we're good at or that set us apart from others, and the skills that seem to come easy to us. Education helps us discover our talents. But it's up to us to make the most of them.

Why don't you play the "what if" game with your children today? Uncover some talents God has hidden in your lives!

Lord, help me to be the person you envisioned when you created me. Help me to set my sights on noble goals and give me the grace and stamina to fulfill them. Help me teach my children to do the same.

So I run straight to the goal with purpose in every step. I fight to win. I'm not just shadow-boxing or playing around.   1 CORINTHIANS 9:26

AUGUST 14

Not another dental appointment! I'd already been to the dental clinic four times that week. On Monday, Jeanne had her monthly checkup on her braces in the orthodontist section. Tuesday, the three younger children had been to the dentist for cleaning, X-rays, and checkups. I waited for two hours in the waiting room. Wednesday, I took Jeanne back for her checkup in the adult section. Thursday, Julia had to get her new retainer checked. Then I noticed Jeanne had to go back *again* the following week to get her retainers after two and a half years of braces. I was starting to hate the dental clinic.

That afternoon I spotted a middle-aged woman in the clinic with a large fabric bag at her side. First she pulled out a notebook and made a list of some sort. She was engrossed in her project and seemed delighted when she finished the job and tucked the notebook into the bag. Next, she pulled out a granola bar and munched away, enjoying her mid-afternoon snack. Finally, she pulled out a skein of colorful yarn and began work on a knitted baby blanket. Forty-five minutes later, when her teenager appeared from the orthodontist's office she was all smiles and ready to go.

I am the master of my days, hours, and minutes, and I can choose to spend them wisely or can fuss and fume over time wasted. It's up to me. By the way, I now have my own fabric bag full of goodies and projects, including stationery for letter writing.

Lord, help me to stop complaining about the times I have to wait. Help me use my time wisely by planning ahead.

That is why I wait expectantly, trusting God to help, for he has promised.   PSALMS 130:5

AUGUST 15

Winners and losers … it's all a matter of attitude. I found the following list of differences between winners and losers in a newsletter. The author is unknown. You might want to copy it and make bookmarks for your children. Clear contact paper works great for a project like this.

A loser always has an excuse.
A winner always has a plan.

A loser says, "That's not my job."
A winner says, "Let me help you."

A loser says, "It may be possible, but it's too difficult."
A winner says, "It may be difficult, but it is possible."

A loser is always part of the problem.
A winner is always part of the answer.

Next time your children squabble about whose turn it is to do the dishes … remind them that a winner says "Let me help you." If your child complains because he just doesn't know how to get started on the science project, remind him that a winner says, "It may be difficult, but it is possible." When your daughter rolls her eyes and growls when you remind her of the family meeting that afternoon, remind her that a winner is always part of the answer and that you're all going to work together to find the answers to some family problems.

Lord, help me to be a winner and let my positive attitude rub off onto my children.

But with God, everything is possible.   MATTHEW 19:26

AUGUST 16

Sometimes we get so wrapped up in our own worries that we think we're the only ones with problems. But our kids have problems as well. I'll never forget the summer of '89 when Andrew was nine and had so many worries that I bought him a set of eight tiny, inch-tall Guatemalan "worry dolls" at the state fair. The directions said to place a doll under your pillow for each worry you had and that they would worry for you. That night Andrew put all eight under his pillow.

"Mom, here are my worries," he said very seriously.

On lined paper he'd scrawled: (1) Dad has leukemia, had surgery. (His dad died two months later.) (2) I have chicken pox. My cousins might get it. (3) Don't want Mom to get sick. (I assured him that one doesn't get chicken pox twice.) (4) Climbing tree ruined. (His older brother trimmed the tree, not knowing he removed Andrew's best climbing branch.) (5) Jeanne's in California. (He missed his oldest sister, who'd been gone for over a year.) (6) Julia's leaving for college. (In two weeks Julia, who spent lots of time with Andrew, would be three hours away.) (7) Michael joined the army. (Andrew's older brother, a high-school senior who'd joined the National Guard band, would be gone one weekend a month and would leave for basic training the following summer.) (8) Fight with Dad about the curly perm. (Andrew's Dad had gotten a curly permanent earlier that summer and now wanted Andrew to get one as well.)

As we placed all eight worry dolls under his pillow, Andrew talked about each concern. I listened and assured him that the worry dolls would do the worrying, but that Jesus would hold Andrew in his care.

Lord, don't ever let me think that I'm the only one in this family with problems. Let me listen to and comfort my children and to teach them to share their problems and to come to you with everything that's in their hearts.

Commit everything you do to the Lord. Trust him to help you do it and he will.　　　PSALMS 37:5

AUGUST 17

Are you and your children creative? Of course you are! Everyone is. It's all there, inside us, like a great glob of unformed clay, just ready to be stimulated and ignited. Wish you could design a really neat single parents' newsletter? In the midst of a big project at work and it all just seems so hum-drum? Children dreading going back to school and you need something to pump them up? Wish you could make every holiday all year long something special instead of celebrating everything the same old tired way you've always done? Then it's time for you to learn how to tap your creative well.

Motivational speaker and seminar leader Brian Tracy says there are three passive techniques for stimulating creativity:

Solitude. Sit quietly in silence for 30 to 60 minutes with no interruptions, no reading, no coffee, music, or eating. Keep your mind blank, and before long creative solutions to your problems will appear.

Deep relaxation. Count down from 50 to 1 then meditate for 10-20 minutes. Ideas will come.

Surround yourself with nature. Listen to tapes of water, birds, wind, or the seashore. Go for a walk in a quiet park or visit a body of water. Hike in the woods. Relax in nature and often creative solutions will come for your most serious problems.

Learning how to clear the mind of all peripheral clutter is a must if we're going to allow new, highly creative thoughts into our subconscious. Today, take your children into nature and tell them you're all just going to sit quietly for thirty minutes. You may be surprised what comes of it!

Lord, teach me to practice the art of doing absolutely nothing so I can discover creative ideas that you have placed in my heart.

I thought about the wrong direction in which I was headed, and turned around and came running back to you. PSALMS 119:59-60

AUGUST 18

In the movie *Amadeus,* Emperor Joseph II criticizes one of Mozart's compositions for having "too many notes." History has shown that none of Mozart's compositions contained too many notes. In fact, they were brilliant masterpieces!

Sometimes I think we single parents have "too many notes" in our lives. Too many commitments, too many meetings, too many shopping trips and social events.

"Too many notes" cause a cacophony in our lives that leaves us crabby, stressed, and out of sorts. Since this is "back to school" season let's set aside some time with our children to set up a calendar of activities. Let's talk to them about which after-school activities they'll participate in. Don't let them spread themselves too thin. After all, kids need time to be kids ... to read comics, jump rope, blow bubbles, stare into space, and "hang out" with their friends.

We parents also need time where nothing is programmed or expected of us. Instead of signing up for that three-nights-a-week business class, perhaps you should plan to fix three great meals a week and dine in style with your children, with a promise to help with homework after everyone helps with the dishes.

Keep it simple. When the children are grown, you'll have time to take that class, join that club, or volunteer at church. If there are "too many notes" being played in your family, turn down the volume, simplify, relax, and enjoy each other.

Lord, this school season, help me be a good parent by eliminating the stress in my life.

Be beautiful inside, in your hearts, with the lasting charm of a gentle and quiet spirit which is so precious to God.   1 PETER 3:4

AUGUST 19

Today, August 19, is the birthday of America's first pilot, Orville Wright ... and National Aviation Day.

Flying and pilots have been a big part of my life. My dad was a P-39 fighter pilot in the South Pacific during World War II. Uncle Jim, a major general in the air force, commanded a number of air force bases and was the chief of staff of the Strategic Air Command. Uncle Ralph, also a World War II pilot, retired as a colonel in the air force. Uncle Francis flew "the hump" over the Himalayas. My brother Joe is a captain for UPS and flies all over the world.

In high school I took flying lessons from my dad, although I never soloed. Today seven airline pilots use my home as their Milwaukee area "crash pad." Flying is my favorite mode of transportation; it is in my blood.

But the thing that instilled this love of air travel in me was my first time in a small, single-engine plane with my father at the helm. As I looked down at the Illinois corn, wheat, and soybean fields, they were suddenly transformed into a patchwork quilt, handcrafted by God himself. I saw the whole world from the viewpoint of heaven.

Today, call a local airport and ask what they charge for a ride in a small plane. Put it in your budget. Giving our children the gift of seeing the world from God's viewpoint is something *all* parents should do.

Lord, your world is so beautiful when seen from the sky. Help me to treasure and protect it when I'm back on earth.

I am creating new heavens and a new earth—so wonderful that no one will even think about the old ones anymore.   ISAIAH 65:17

AUGUST 20

When I was little I wondered how they fit all those people and records inside the family radio. Around first grade someone told me about radio stations and said that the people who worked there sent their voices and the music through the air on sound waves right into our kitchen radio. I couldn't figure out how the sound waves worked. I still can't.

In high school I wondered how disc jockeys had enough hands to play records, answer phone calls, play commercials, whip up sound effects and talk to people. After college I worked for a radio station and learned all about the electronic wizardry that made the announcer's job easier.

These days, every business has blossomed into the age of computer prowess. The postal service can sort thousands of letters a minute. The phone company service rep can have your complete phone history in front of her by the time you finish giving her your phone number. Complete inventories can be taken in minutes. Child support records can be accessed in seconds.

However, no matter how important computers become, none of it would happen without the human element. Somewhere a radio announcer pushes buttons and talks into the microphone. That someone has a family, friends, pays income tax, maybe child support, and wishes the weekend would last longer. He's the heart behind the machinery.

Lord, keep reminding me that even though our high-tech computerization makes life incredibly easier, the human element will always be there with a warm hand and a kind heart to help me over the rough spots.

And the one sitting on the throne said, "See, I am making all things new!"　　REVELATION 21:5

AUGUST 21

Today, August 2lst, is the anniversary of the founding of the American Bar Association in 1878. I chuckle when I think about the relationship between single parents and attorneys. Happily married couples rarely need an attorney, unless for a business matter or to draw up a will. But we single parents, whether we're widows, widowers, legally separated, or divorced, are on close terms with members of the bar association.

When my husband and I divorced in 1975, my attorney made it possible for my three preschoolers and me to move out of state that very day. Two years later, when my ex-husband stopped making payments on our home and then abandoned it, my attorney arranged for the sale of my ex's half of the house on the courthouse steps. Nobody showed up to buy half a house, so my attorney bought it in my name for a dollar. While I scraped up money for back payments, my attorney took over the care of my house because I lived out of state. He paid all the bills, hired a real estate company to sell it, then sent me a check for $14,000, enough for the down payment on my house in Wisconsin.

Often, lawyers are the brunt of jokes, the bane of many going through a divorce, and come off as being greedy.

But if you're lucky enough to have an attorney like mine, instead of the stereotyped version, pick up the phone and let him or her know you appreciate what's been done for you and your family.

God, sometimes I feel like it's me against the world. But then I remember all those people you've put in my corner to help me achieve justice. Thank you for their wisdom, Lord.

One of them, a lawyer, spoke up: "Sir, which is the most important command in the laws of Moses?" Jesus replied, "Love the Lord your God with all your heart, soul, and mind."   MATTHEW 22:36-37

AUGUST 22

Dr. Norman Vincent Peale's wife, Ruth, wrote about the stories Dr. Peale made up for his three children. Their favorite was about Larry, Harry, Parry, and the magic airplane they could carry in their pockets, take out, blow up, and sail into the clouds. Dr. Peale added to the story every night at dinner, much to the delight of the children.

Once two of my children and I went on a trip with my brother, sister-in-law, and two of their children. In my brother's comfortable van, we laughed and lounged our way through Kentucky, Tennessee, and Alabama until we reached the shores of the Gulf of Mexico, where we frolicked for a week. Along the way we made up a silly song, each of us coming up with different lines, giggling all the while. Before long, we had three or four verses, including: "My name is Doc-tor Funk. I've got a dead body in my trunk. My girl's name is Ed-na Fay. She likes to drink bug spray. Oh ya." Pretty dumb, I admit, but our song is a golden thread in the fabric of the relationship of the seven of us who took that trip.

Tonight ask one child to give you a funny name of a person or a character. Ask another to give you a place where that character can have an adventure. Then, just start telling a story. Continue the story every night at dinner. It's a wonderful way to cement your family together.

Heavenly Father, fill my children and me with heaping globs of creativity so we can laugh and learn and love together in a way that will be unique and precious to our family.

Sing a new song to the Lord telling about his mighty deeds! PSALMS 98:1

AUGUST 23

In 1976, as a divorcée with three young children, I had an income of less than $7,000 a year. One Saturday the four of us piled into our little, red, ten-year-old Volkswagen bug and set out to do the weekly errands.

First stop was the drive-in window at the bank. I made out a withdrawal slip for $80 to pay the bills and to buy groceries for the coming week.

When I counted the money I found $90 in my hands. A simple mistake on the teller's part, yet before I could stop myself I started thinking about how that extra $10 could buy more fruits and vegetables or an extra-nice cut of meat and maybe even the makings for oatmeal cookies. But as quickly as those thoughts came to mind, another thought slammed into my head. *Here is the first opportunity you've ever had to teach your children about honesty from a real-life situation.*

I showed my four-, five-, and seven-year-old children the withdrawal slip and explained how I had asked for $80 to be taken out of the account. The receipt showed that $80 *was* taken out. I counted out loud the nine $10 bills and said, "See, the lady gave me one too many. We have an extra $10 bill. What should we do with it?"

"Give it back to her!" they shouted in unison.

When I told the teller about the mistake I was rejoicing not only for my own good feeling of doing the right thing, but even more so because my children had already learned the lesson of honesty.

When we left the bank we finished our errands, bought the groceries, and went home and made oatmeal cookies anyway.

Thanks, Lord, for providing those "teaching by example" opportunities so I can show my children all that is right and good in the world.

God is more pleased when we are just and fair than when we give him gifts.　　　　PROVERBS 21:3

AUGUST 24

Having a bad day? Just so you don't lapse into the "feeling sorry for myself" routine, I'm going to tell you about the most amazing single parent I ever met.

In 1989, Jan Turner, a single mother of two handsome adopted sons, busy full-time music teacher at a grade school, and the music director at her church, had a life that was full beyond measure. Then Jan contracted pneumococcal pneumonia, a swift and deadly bacterial infection. Two weeks later both arms and both legs had to be amputated—arms at mid-forearm, legs at mid-shin.

It took months of rehabilitation, determination, prayer and just plain guts, but Jan learned to live joyously with four prosthetics. Today she walks, works, drives a car, flips pancakes, plays ball with her boys, and takes them and their five dogs hunting and camping. Jan also went back to college, got a degree in communications, and now works for a radio station. She's also since been ordained the children's pastor at Triumphant Life Church in Wilmar, Minnesota.

Jan's strength came from her deep faith in God. She believes that God only gives good gifts and even her misfortune has been turned into goodness by the fact that she is able to share her faith-filled story to inspire and uplift many others.

Lord, when things don't go my way, give me courage to know that you never send more than I can handle. Help me handle it with dignity and determination.

Don't copy the behavior and customs of this world, but be a new and different person with a fresh newness in all you do and think. Then you will learn from your own experience how his ways will really satisfy you.   ROMANS 12:2

School is starting and we'll all be changing our routines somewhat. Ah-ha, the perfect time to start a new exercise habit!

I get up at 6:15 A.M. each school day and jump into my casual clothes and walking shoes. Then I fix Andrew's breakfast and my tea. As soon as he's out the door at 7:05, I take off fast-walking. Usually I'm wearing a radio headset. Sometimes, I leave the radio at home and meditate, plan my day, mentally outline an article that I'm going to write, or just commune with nature. It's a great way to start the morning.

Half an hour later, I'm back at the house to shower, eat breakfast and head for my office. That's *my* back-to-school exercise routine.

Now let me tell you about Anne Clark's exercise habit. She's competed in more than 500 running races worldwide and is the proud owner of more than 30 age-related running records. Amazingly, Anne didn't start running until she was 69 years old, and in 1996, at age 87, she was still running races. Anne says running has cured her age-related aches and pains. To look at her sleek physique and rosy complexion, you'd think she was in her early sixties.

Anne Clark reminds me that God meant for our bodies to remain young and healthy well into old age. But we have to do our part. It's never too late to begin a fitness habit. Let's start today ... for the rest of our lives.

Lord, help me to cherish the body you gave me by keeping it active. Don't let me be a slacker. Keep me walking, running, skating, swimming, whatever ... all year long.

I will give you back your health again and heal your wounds.   JEREMIAH 30:17

AUGUST 26

We've all heard the stories of broken marriages. One man I heard of pays so much support to his ex-wife that he's practically living in poverty. As a condition for accepting the large monthly spouse-support payment, the court ordered her to return to college. Three years later she still hasn't started school and refuses to support herself.

It reminds me of something Plato once said. "Good people do not need laws to tell them to act responsibly, while bad people will find a way around law."

We humans probably do not need the thousands of laws that are set before us. Good people will automatically live lives as fair, just, honorable, honest citizens. Those who are not so good will lie, cheat, steal, abuse, and demand that the rest of us support them. They'll inevitably find ways around the law.

We single parents must make sure our children grow up to be among the "good" people, by making sure we are "good" people, doing the right thing. Ask yourself these questions: Am I paying or receiving a *fair* amount of ex-spouse and child support? Am I treating my ex with respect and dignity? Am I being the absolute best parent I can? Or am I wasting time arguing about money and putting my ex down?

Lord, I want to be one of the "good" guys. Help me to treat my children and my ex with dignity and respect.

Because of this light within you, you should do only what is good and right and true.   EPHESIANS 5:9

Do you have a favorite tree? When I was a kid, mine was a huge, many-limbed maple down the road at the McKee's house. One or more of the ten McKee kids and I would climb high into that tree and survey the estate below ... which, in reality, was nothing more than their small two-story green house, a white frame garage, and a gravel driveway. But from up in the tree it seemed palatial.

When I was a newly single parent, my favorite tree was one my children and I adopted at a park five miles from our home. We'd go there often because this tree had about eight trunks that wove in and out and around each other, some almost parallel to and just a few feet above ground. The children and I could easily find a comfortable spot in that tree or climb willy-nilly throughout its branches.

These days my favorite tree is also my least favorite tree. It's a gigantic willow right outside my office window at home. Big, old willow trees like this one are messy. A pain in the neck. If the wind blows up even a little cough, the next morning we find a gazillion sticks and branches all over the yard. Picking up all those sticks before we mow is a pain.

On the other hand, that old willow is a keeper. When Michael was ten, he designed and built a crude fort in its branches. When Andrew was fifteen, one of our pilot houseguests helped him design and build a fancy wooden floor between the three giant sections of the tree, complete with supports and a side rail. Andrew and his friends "hung out" on the tree floor every now and then, but these days, I mostly just look at the birds and squirrels playing in the tree from the luxury of my hammock below as I enjoy the willow's enormous shady cover. Actually, it's a pretty good old tree.

Lord, thank you for all the favorite trees of my life. Help me to pass on to my children a love of nature that includes claiming "favorites" from among your creations.

They shall thrive like watered grass, like willows on a river bank.   ISAIAH 44:4

AUGUST 28

Researchers say that the average American now has five hours of leisure time a day. I can already hear you busy single parents laughing over that one.

Think what our lives would be like without computers, fax machines, and microwaves. With these we can accomplish tasks in nanoseconds, things that used to take hours. But single parents are still left with much less than five hours of leisure time a day.

That means we just have to eliminate some other elements in our lives that take up time. Your mother expects to have you over for dinner every Wednesday and for you to invite her over for dinner every Sunday. If that tight schedule causes you stress perhaps you need to adjust the meal thing to once a week, taking turns every other week, and suggesting that you and your mom just take a leisurely walk together on Sundays. Don't be afraid to break tradition and eliminate some of those occasions you *thought* were obligations.

Learn to *relax!* Take a walk by yourself. Read a novel, not another self-help book, but a real make-believe novel. Lather on sunscreen and flop into a lawn chair for an hour. You don't have to accomplish *anything* during your leisure time. You just have to relax.

Settle me down, Lord, and make me take time every day to do absolutely nothing. Teach me the art of relaxation.

He lets me rest in the meadow grass and leads me beside the quiet streams. He restores my failing health.   PSALMS 23:2-3

AUGUST 29

After fourteen years on an old archaic computer, I bought a new one with all the bells and whistles one could imagine. I was astounded at what it could do! Whole days simply disappeared into a maze of new learning and excitement. I'd look up and Andrew would be home from school already. Two hours later I'd dash upstairs to throw supper together before he had to leave for band practice. Then I'd spend the entire evening attached to my new best friend, Mr. State-of-the-Art Computer. By midnight my eyes burned, my neck ached, but I didn't care.

As I was contemplating becoming a new Internet user, my friend, Jean, loaned me a book called *Silicon Snake Oil*, by Clifford Stoll. Page after page Clifford jolted me back to reality.

He warned, "A computer network is, indeed, a community. But what an impoverished community!... What's missing from this ersatz neighborhood? A feeling of permanence and belonging, a sense of location, a warmth from the local history. Gone is the very essence of a neighborhood: friendly relations and a sense of being in it together ... we chat without speaking, smile without grinning, and hug without touching."

After that, I turned my computer off when my work was completed. I fixed better meals, took longer walks, talked to my son more, hugged better, read more books, and enjoyed my friends. I did *not* take up surfing on the Internet as a replacement for real life.

Lord, as a single person, sometimes, in the late evenings, my computer does seem like my best friend. But don't let me become addicted to its intrigue. Let me live life ... the real thing, not just what's in cyberspace.

We have come to bring you the Good News that you are invited to turn from the worship of these foolish things and to pray instead to the living God who made heaven and earth and sea and everything in them.   ACTS 14;15

AUGUST 30

One hot day in August I took my youngest child to a day-care preschool for the first time. I was glad it would only be for two mornings a week. After all, he was only three.

Andrew's preschool was operated by a church, and I was glad for the Christian influence. As we walked in and out of the rooms I could feel Jesus' love for little children. But as we walked, Andrew's little hand tightened its clasp in mine. After all, he was only three.

In the large colorful playroom filled with happy three- and four-year-olds we met Miss Marie, who said the children would be making giant banana splits out of construction paper that day. I wondered if my son even knew what a banana split was. There were so many things he hadn't experienced. After all, he was only three.

It was time for me to leave. I bent down and gave Andrew a kiss. His eyes clouded with tears; a look of panic set in. But I knew I had to leave without making a fuss. As I walked up the stairs Miss Thelma scooped him into her strong, gentle arms and carried him to the section of the room where he could choose the race car of his dreams. After all, he was only three.

At work I sat down with a cup of tea and wondered if my son was really being cared for properly. Then I remembered a plaque I'd seen on the wall of the school ... a quote from 1 Thessalonians, "We were as gentle among you as a mother feeding and caring for her own children." And I knew that Miss Marie, Miss Thelma, and all the others would love and care for my child during those hours each week. After all, Andrew was almost four and ready to have some adventures of his own!

Lord, I know I can't teach my children everything they need to know in this world. Help me to let them go ... so they can grow under the wings of others. Protect them, Lord.

But we were as gentle among you as a mother feeding and caring for her own children. We loved you dearly, so dearly that we gave you not only God's message, but our own lives too. 1 THESSALONIANS 2:7-8

AUGUST 31

My friend Betty, another single parent, phoned at the end of a busy summer. We hadn't seen each other for a few months because I'd been out of town a lot and she worked full-time.

After we caught up with each other's lives I noticed a depressed twinge to her voice. Finally, she told me, "I've been alone in this house for six years now. It gets so lonely sometimes. Your house is different. You've always got people over there."

I wanted to shake her and shout, "That's why I'm not lonely! I make an effort to have people in my home!" But I just let Betty get all her misery out and told her she'd probably feel better when she started a different shift at her job.

Later, I wished I'd told her to take charge of her loneliness. A few years earlier I, too, had suffered bouts of severe loneliness. That's when I organized the Swill Gang, a group of interesting women who meet at my house once a month. (Swill stands for Southeastern Wisconsin Interesting Ladies League.) I also volunteered my family room as a meeting place for a church group. I started inviting friends and neighbors over for tea or lunch. Sometimes all they got was leftovers, but it didn't seem to matter, because the conversation was more important than the vittles.

I called Betty back and suggested she invite neighbors and friends to her home one evening a month and start her own little monthly get-together. She did, and her social life picked up considerably.

Today, Lord, remind me to be thankful for a world full of wonderfully interesting people and for the many ways I can make their acquaintance.

I am like a vulture in a far-off wilderness, or like an owl alone in the desert. I lie awake, lonely as a solitary sparrow on the roof.   PSALMS 102:6-7

Prayer for September

Heavenly Father, at last
I kissed the children good-bye
As they headed back to school.
The summer is over.
Finally, we have a routine again.

But why is it,
That I miss them?
When for weeks
I couldn't wait for September.
I miss the banging screen door,
The wet bathing suits,
Their friends, their music.

Father, help me
Ease their return
Back to the real world.
Help me to spread
Your love and mine
Around them like a shield.
During this school year
Help me to grow in your love
So that I can
Share that love
With my family.

SEPTEMBER 1

This week, as we take a break from work to celebrate "Labor Day" let's think about whether we're working too much or not enough and whether or not the hosts of heaven and earth will say that we're doing our job well.

I remember when my neighbor dropped her wee first grader off at my house every school morning at 6:40 A.M. to wait for his school bus. Next, she dropped her preschooler off at the baby-sitter's so she could drive twenty miles to her job and be there by 7:30 A.M. Her husband had a well-paying job from 8:00-5:00. Plus he worked a manual-labor job from 2:00 A.M. till 7:00 A.M.

Those people labored too hard ... and for what? Was there time for a long walk for this couple "just to talk" or for a leisurely bedtime story with the children? Hardly.

When I became a single parent I knew my most important job was raising four children, so I tightened my budget and continued to work part-time. I've never regretted it.

Today, take inventory of how hard you work and why. Perhaps a change in your work habits will make all the hosts of heaven and earth proclaim, "Here lives a great single parent who works, raises children, and still has time to enjoy life."

Father, help me not to labor so hard that I have no time to enjoy this wonderful world and the people I treasure most.

For God is not unfair. How can he forget your hard work for him, or forget the way you used to show your love for him—and still do—by helping his children?
HEBREWS 6:10

SEPTEMBER 2

I can close my eyes and still remember the *Good morning! Good-byes* during the 1985 school year. It was the first year of the separation that led to my divorce. That September the four children were in four different schools.

Jeanne attended the Milwaukee High School of the Arts and was picked up by her bus at 6:25 A.M. The aromas of the delicious breakfasts she fixed woke me up. I stood there foggy-eyed in my flannel pajamas as she stepped into the darkness.

Julia, a freshman at our suburban high school, was next. Her bus came at 7:00 A.M. For fifteen minutes before she left we talked about school and cheerleading practice. Julia kissed me good-bye, then bounced out the door … blond hair, braces, and pom-poms all shining.

Andrew, who was in kindergarten, was my first responsibility of the day. I fixed his breakfast and ate with him. Saying good-bye to Andrew was a routine that never varied. A kiss and a hug, then he was out the door. He insisted I watch him from the kitchen window until the bus actually came, then I had to tear over to the front door and wave vigorously and blow kisses as he scooted into his seat. He, of course, waved back.

I'd watch Michael, a thirteen-year-old eighth grader, cook, eat, and chatter about basketball, homework, and girls. At 8:00 A.M. he was out the door. Once in a while I got a peck on the cheek. "Bye, Mom, see you tonight."

Four unique routines. Four separate needs.

Today, think about your children's different needs. To accommodate them, do you need to revamp your morning routine?

Lord, thank you for giving me that hour-and-a-half each morning to be present for my children and to send them into the world each day with love.

Let me see your kindness to me in the morning, for I am trusting you. Show me where to walk, for my prayer is sincere. PSALMS 143:8

SEPTEMBER 3

I'll never forget my youngest child's first day of first grade. Andrew was excited about going to school for a whole day, but I had some misgivings. My work hours had increased at work to thirty or more a week, which meant I wouldn't be home when Andrew got off the school bus. His sister Jeanne, eleven years older than he, would be there to watch him. But I wanted to hear his excited chatter, look at his papers, and help him get started on his homework. I couldn't imagine not being there for him.

Well, when I finally did walk in the door around 5:00 P.M., Andrew burst into the kitchen, "Hi Mom! Jeanne made cookies for me and milk and she gave me a big hug when I got off the bus! I like coming home to Jeanne!"

Another time, I remember Julia asking if she could stay after school a couple of nights each week to work on her sewing project in home arts class in junior high. I eventually discovered that it was Julia's teacher, Mrs. Wise, that Julia really wanted to spend time with. Later, at a parent-teacher conference, I learned how much both my daughter and her teacher enjoyed each other's company.

I learned something valuable that year. It's this: WE CAN'T DO THIS JOB OF PARENTING ALONE. We actually need to encourage our children to seek out other adults to spend time with, and we need to let those other people know how much we appreciate the time and role modeling they give.

Tonight, Lord, remind me to phone at least one of my children's mentors and thank them for their help.

Whenever we can we should always be kind to everyone, and especially to our Christian brothers.
GALATIANS 6:10

SEPTEMBER 4

I didn't like Phillip, age thirteen, from the first day I saw him at the bus stop. He was rude and unkempt. He swore. He darted in and out of the street, daring drivers to sideswipe him, then he'd laugh uproariously.

One morning just after the bus had picked up my children, the doorbell rang. It was Phillip, out of breath. "Where's Julia and Michael? Did I miss the bus?"

I assured him he had and started to close the door. "Oh, no!" Phillip pleaded. "I can't wake up my dad. What'll I do?"

"What about your mother? Can't she take you?"

"My folks are divorced. Dad works nights, and he's asleep. He'll kill me if I get him up."

"All right, Phillip. I'll take you on my way to work," I grumbled, knowing the school was in the opposite direction of my job.

On the way, Phillip chattered nonstop. He even told me about the time he ate a hundred pills of his brother's prescription when he was three years old.

Could the accidental drug overdose have caused his behavior problems? After months of disliking him, I began to understand: He lived alone with one parent who worked nights and slept days. His brothers and sisters had grown and moved away. He was slow in school and unaccepted by his peers.

But here he was, open, friendly, and talking up a storm to a woman he must have known didn't like him very much.

When we arrived at school, Phillip jumped out of the car with a hearty "thanks!" flashed a big grin in my direction and ran up the steps two at a time.

Lord, help me not to be so critical of others. Let me walk in their shoes for a while so I can be a kinder, more giving person.

Don't criticize, and then you won't be criticized. For others will treat you as you treat them. MATTHEW 7:1-2

An old man's grandchildren *are* his crowning glory. But grandparents are also a treasure beyond measure for *youngsters*, especially for children who live in single-parent families.

When Jeanne was born she had five living grandmothers—two grandmothers and three great-grandmothers—all of whom adored her. But when Andrew was born eleven years later, none of his grandmothers was alive.

When my dad married Bev in 1982 she became an "instant" grandma. But they live in Illinois, and we're in Wisconsin, and we usually only see each other three or four times a year.

An older woman who lives in Wyoming phoned me to say she'd read some articles I'd written about single-parenting and wanted me to know that she had raised two boys and two girls alone.

Barbara and I talked for over an hour. After that, we corresponded. Once she sent me flowers when I was having a bad week. After she had eye surgery and was feeling depressed she spent a few weeks with us.

Andrew suddenly had another "grandma" who showered him with lots of hugs, devoted attention, and great stories. "Grandma" Barbara came back for another visit a year later, and in 1993, Andrew and I visited her in Cheyenne on our way to California. These days our letters and phone calls keep our warm friendship flowing across the miles.

It's not hard to find a grandma or grandpa. Dozens probably attend your church, live alone, and would love to be "grandma" or "grandpa" to your children.

Lord, help me to bring grandparents and children together, even if they're not related.

An old man's grandchildren are his crowning glory.
PROVERBS 17:6

For over a year, seven of my writer friends and I gathered on the first Thursday of the month for a "read and critique" session. When we met in September, after taking a break for the summer, they all brought me gifts ... because I was the hostess every month, they said.

Shirley brought a bag of her home-grown salad tomatoes. Nancy gave me an exquisite napkin ring she'd bought on vacation. Pearl, who was born in England and truly appreciates my passion for tea, brought three flavors of fresh loose tea: bing cherry, orange spice, and apricot. Marjorie brought a copy of a book she and Nancy wrote together. Sue, who has MS, appeared at my door without her cane! What a gift that was to see her walking—slow perhaps, but straight and tall. Sharon came with the news that she had just sold her children's book to a big New York publisher. We all cheered.

My writer friends are among my most treasured gifts (even when they don't bring presents) because they encourage, help, gently criticize, and prod me forward when I need a good push.

What's one of the most important things in your life? Music? Computers? Quilting? Preschoolers? Bible study? Why not get a few people with the same interest together at least once a month? Talk about your passion. Encourage each other's creativity. Exchange ideas. Then just watch how you grow!

Lord, bless my writer friends. Be with us and give us the grace to help each other become the best we can be.

To enjoy your work and to accept your lot in life, that is indeed a gift from God.　　ECCLESIASTES 5:19

SEPTEMBER 7

I could hardly believe it. All three of my older children were in college. In one day I'd driven over 400 miles to get two of them settled in two different University of Wisconsin campuses. On the way home that night I wondered how I'd fill up my time. Sadly, I wondered, *Will the big kids "need" me anymore? Are my "mothering" days for my three older children over?*

The next week I sent all three "college kids" a three-page "Welcome to College" letter. I sent airline tickets to Jeanne in California so she could fly home for three weeks at Christmas. I mailed Julie a box of snacks along with a check to cover the tuition increase she hadn't counted on. Then I got a pleading phone call from Michael asking me to send him a batch of my homemade granola for late-night snacks. I lit the oven and started mixing the ingredients.

Doing those things made me feel so "needed" that I sailed through that first year of "missing" them without a hitch. I discovered that if a relationship is going to be kept alive, it's up to me to keep it that way.

When was the last time you sent a surprise letter, a newspaper clipping, a family photo, or homemade cookies to an elderly parent, your child, or other relative who lives in another state? Send something today, and strengthen the tie that binds.

Heavenly Father, when I miss someone who is distant, let me keep the relationship strong. Today I will send something to someone far away.

They should be rich in good works and should give happily to those in need, always being ready to share with others whatever God has given them.
1 TIMOTHY 6:18

A friend left a message on my answering machine saying I could "return his call twenty-four, seven."

Twenty-four, seven? I didn't get it. Was it his strange way of saying "over and out" or "that's all folks"?

I felt pretty silly when I asked him and he said, "I meant that you could call me anytime, twenty-four hours a day, seven days a week, that's all!"

Since then I've often thought that "twenty-four, seven" is a terrific way to abbreviate the way we must love our children. We owe them unconditional love twenty-four hours a day, seven days a week.

But we busy parents sometimes forget three other ways to love children: physical contact, eye contact, and focused attention.

Physical contact means we give them lots of hugs, squeezes, and pats on the back. Physical contact is necessary for human survival. Between parents and children it's a direct self-esteem feeder tube.

Eye contact is vital because it tells our children that we're really listening. It shows that we're paying attention to them. Eye contact with a loving glance or a big smile attached says we find them absolutely charming and love the persons they are.

Focused attention is giving each of our children 100 percent of ourselves. It may not be for long, but it needs to be done every day with every child. Maybe it's sitting on the edge of their bed in the morning for three minutes just to chat. Or cuddling up together on the sofa to talk in the evening. Focused attention lets our children know they are appreciated and cherished as individuals.

Lord, help me to love my children all ways, always, twenty-four, seven!

You must love others as much as yourself. Mark 12:31

The big yellow school bus swallowed Andrew as I dashed for the front stoop to wave vigorously, blow him a kiss, then end the routine with more wild waving as the bus moved forward.

"Why do you do that silly waving routine every morning, Mom?" asked sixteen-year-old Julia.

"Every single day since Andrew started kindergarten two years ago he has left the house with the words, 'Wave to me when the bus comes ... and don't forget the kiss part.'"

"You didn't wave to *me* every day when I was in first grade," reminded fifteen-year-old Michael.

"That's because you had your two older sisters to get on the bus with. Andrew needs to know he's not alone when he leaves. One of these days he'll get on the bus and forget to even look for me. But for now, I *like* feeling needed."

You know what? After that conversation Julia started giving me a quick kiss on the cheek as she bounded out the door for the bus, and Michael made sure to holler, "Bye, Mom!" even if I was in the bathroom getting ready for work.

I like the "leaving routines" our family has every morning that tie us together with a string of love and caring. This week, why not form a new good-morning, good-bye routine with your children?

Lord, thank you for hands that can wave, arms that can hug, and lips that can kiss.

Then he took the children into his arms and placed his hands on their heads, and he blessed them.

MARK 10:16

In her book *No Greater Love,* Mother Teresa tells a story about a wealthy Hindu woman who asked how she could share in Mother Teresa's work. As the two women talked, Mother Teresa commented on the woman's beautiful sari. The woman confessed that she had a weakness for elegant saris, and often spent 800 rupees for them. Mother Teresa mentioned that her saris cost 8 rupees. Then Mother Teresa suggested that the next time the woman bought a sari, that she only spend 500 rupees on it and use the extra 300 rupees to buy saris for the poor. Mother Teresa said, "The good woman now wears 100-rupee saris.... She has confessed to me that this has changed her life. She now knows what it means to share. That woman assures me that she has received more than what she has given."

On Labor Day in September, 1995, I made a promise to myself that I would not buy any clothes for three years (with the exception of shoes and underwear). I work in my home office, and can wear bedroom slippers and jogging outfits to work every day if I want to. Why should I spend money on clothes I don't need? I knew the only way I'd get rid of the clothes I had was to actually wear them out. I figured three years would do it. Then I could get rid of it all and start over with a few basic outfits.

As I write this, I still have over a year to go on my promise. At first it was difficult. Every time I went into a store I'd naturally gravitate to the sale racks. Then I'd say to myself, *What am I doing here? I can't buy anything.*

At the end of one year, half of one closet full of clothes went to Goodwill and two huge boxes full were given to two friends who truly needed the clothes worse than I did. These days, like the Hindu woman, I have received much more than I have given.

Lord, thank you for showing me how having less really means having more ... more time, more money to spend on worthwhile projects and donations, and certainly a neater, more organized closet!

The armies of heaven, dressed in finest linen, white and clean, followed him on white horses.

REVELATION 19:14

SEPTEMBER 11

A few years ago, in Ann Landers' column, I read: "The Lord gave you two ends. One for sitting, and one for thinking. Your success depends on which you use. Heads, you win. Tails, you lose."

It struck a note because the previous year after I quit my job at the radio station I started spending too much time in front of the TV, especially during the daytime, mesmerized by all the talk shows.

When Andrew started high school, I decided to clean up my act. When he started a new schedule, I did too.

Andrew's bus picked him up at 7:10 A.M. I started getting up at 6:30, spending forty minutes with Andrew, then taking off on a 30-45 minute fast walk as soon as he left. By 8:00 A.M. I was back home, full of energy, and ready to use the "right" end—the thinking end—in my home office.

By October my morning routine had become a habit and that year I didn't even have to think twice about taking my morning walk … or getting to my office by 8:00 or 8:30 A.M.

If you're having a hard time getting started on a task, why don't you give a brisk morning walk a try? It's a surefire way to jump-start your day, give you extra energy, and keep the TV turned off. It's also a marvelous time to say your morning prayers.

Lord, bless this brisk walk and these feet of mine that keep me from sitting. Fill my head with lots of ideas later on when I get to my office. Heads I win, tails I lose.

Take a lesson from the ants, you lazy fellow. Learn from their ways and be wise! For though they have no king to make them work yet they labor hard all summer, gathering food for the winter.

PROVERBS 6:6-8

SEPTEMBER 12

We single parents who work full-time don't have time to volunteer at our children's schools. Or do we?

When Andrew was in preschool, he rode to school with his teacher every day because she lived in our subdivision. One day she told me she'd be out of town on Monday, and I'd have to drive Andrew myself. She also asked me to be a driver for the day's field trip to the local police station. I agreed, grudgingly, after I managed to get the morning off from work.

When we arrived at school Andrew grabbed my hand and proudly announced, "This is my *real* mom! She's going to be a driver for the field trip!"

Andrew, Chris, Justin, Davey, and Jack climbed into our car. Andrew made the introductions. "These are my friends," he sang.

At the police station, Andrew quickly laid claim to my free hand. Together we inspected the squad room, the incoming-calls station, the fingerprint device, the jail, the target practice room, and the breathalyzer machine. Then we met the police chief, who gave us all baseball cards.

"Aren't you glad you came, Mom?" Andrew asked, beaming.

I drove the troops back to school where I chatted with six or eight other mothers. When Andrew bounced out of the classroom and saw me standing there waiting, his smile spread clear across his face.

I learned never to get so bogged down with my work schedule that I lose track of all the important things that need to be done with my children, including being a volunteer.

Lord, thank you for a boss who encourages me to be a good parent, even when I'm supposed to be working. And thank you, especially, for those jolts of pure joy that radiate from my children when I am.

He is my strength, my shield from every danger. I trusted in him, and he helped me. PSALMS 28:7

When Andrew was sixteen he and twenty-six of his classmates went to Germany for two weeks with the high school German Club. I was one of the chaperones. Before we left, the German teacher gave each of us a list of the "Traveler's Ten Commandments." Here are a few examples:

- Thou shalt not expect to find things as thou hast them at home, for verily, thou hast left home in order to find things different.
- Thou shalt not take anything too seriously, for a carefree mind is essential for a carefree vacation.
- Thou shalt not let other tourists get upon thy nerves, for thou art paying out good money to enjoy thyself.
- Thou shalt not worry, for he that worrieth hath no pleasure—and few things are ever fatal.
- Thou shalt not judge the people of a country by the one person who has given thee trouble.
- Remember that thou art a guest in foreign lands—and he that treateth his host with respect shall be honored.

The Traveler's Ten Commandments apply to single parents as well. When we become "single again" and suddenly find ourselves in new waters, it can be discouraging. But if we just remember this advice from the Traveler's Commandments we should be OK: (1) Try not to expect things to be exactly the way they used to be. (2) Lighten up. (3) Don't let the turkeys get on your nerves. (4) Don't waste valuable time worrying about anything. (5) Don't waste time judging your ex. (6) If you're newly separated or divorced, you are a guest in a foreign land. Respect yourself enough to act in a dignified manner.

Lord, help me respect myself and others so much that I will always act with dignity, good judgment, and a well-tuned sense of humor.

By traveling together we will guard against any suspicion, for we are anxious that no one should find fault with the way we are handling this large gift.

2 CORINTHIANS 8:20

SEPTEMBER 14

While Jeanne was in Yugoslavia, I prepared for her college career at our hometown University of Wisconsin in Milwaukee. I brought in slides of her artwork; they offered her a scholarship. I filled out pages of forms; the government gave her a grant. I even arranged for free room and board in a home near campus, in exchange for minimal child care. A year that would have normally cost $8,000 was handed to Jeanne for the cost of her books.

Two weeks after the semester began, Jeanne moved to California. She phoned a few days later. "I couldn't say good-bye ,Mom, because I knew you wouldn't understand, but I need to be more independent. I really want to get into an art school out here. I'll find a job. Don't worry, Mom, I can do it. I love you."

I felt betrayed. I worried. I began to understand how Mary felt when Jesus ran away. Slowly, I began to see Jeanne learning and growing in California. Had I suffocated her with my control, disguised as "help"?

Jeanne finally graduated with honors from one of the finest art schools in the country. Two years later she was accepted to Yale for graduate school.

As I watched my daughter thrive so far from home, I learned that if we truly love those closest to us, we will set them free to allow them to be all that God has planned for them.

Today, Lord, help me release the people whose lives I may be controlling. Give me the courage to let them make their own decisions so they can grow and learn and become whole.

Three days later they finally discovered him. He was in the Temple, sitting among the teachers of Law, discussing deep questions with them and amazing everyone with his understanding and answers.

LUKE 2:46-47

SEPTEMBER 15

I love September because the fresh produce is delicious and plentiful. Many days I become a vegetarian.

I read a newspaper article about the quest for the perfect foods. *The Milwaukee Journal/Sentinel* tallied the top twelve most perfect foods—the "dynamite dozen" I like to call them. They are: whole-grain breads, skim milk, nuts, fish, beans, prunes, bananas, peppers, carrots, brown rice, tofu, and tomatoes.

When I see the kinds of foods many of the children of my friends eat I am astounded: french fries, hamburgers, soda, chips, pizza, candy. Nothing on the "twelve most perfect foods" list! These kids' diets center around fat and sugar instead of nutrients, minerals, vitamins, and protein. We are raising a generation of eating misfits. If that's not child abuse, what is?

Too many times I've seen families allow the children to choose the foods they want to eat from the time they're off the bottle. No wonder they choose the high-fat, high-sugar foods. They aren't given an opportunity to learn to like foods that are good for them.

Have you been slipping lately in the nutritious foods department? Then scoop up your children and take them to a large farmer's market. Choose some fruits and vegetables they've never even tasted. Make it an adventure! As a parent, please have the courage to say "no" to the junk food and incorporate the "dynamite dozen" into your family's regular eating habits.

Lord, thank you for your bounty. Help me to prepare good-for-you meals from your harvest and to say no to my children's demands for junk food.

And he said, "Let the earth burst forth with every sort of grass and seed-bearing plant, and fruit trees with seeds inside the fruit, so that these seeds will produce the kinds of plants and fruits they came from."

GENESIS 1:11-12

SEPTEMBER 16

My personal appearance had slipped since I stayed home and worked in my home office. Sweatsuits and slippers had replaced dresses, heels, and pantyhose. What little makeup I had went unused.

Just before my forty-ninth birthday, my sister Catherine arrived for a weekend. She plopped a gift bag filled with eight little presents on my lap. "Happy Birthday. Here's to a new you!" she said, her eyes twinkling.

I opened box after box. Lipstick, eyeliner, blush, eye shadow, little brushes to apply them all, and a case to keep them in. Before I could protest, she whisked me into the bathroom and applied touches of highlighter, shadow, and liner to my eyes. When Catherine finished my makeover I couldn't believe my eyes. Literally. They looked bigger, brighter. Nice. I liked it—the whole look.

"It takes a little time every morning, but if you do it every day it'll become a habit," she advised.

The next morning I peered at my reflection in the mirror. It occurred to me that even something as trivial as putting on makeup could be a time to talk with the Lord. I added a touch of eye shadow and prayed, "Lord, please let these eyes of mine see the needs of others and respond accordingly."

With the blush brush in hand I said, "Lord, my cheeks are pretty full. Help me to watch the fat grams today and exercise."

Finally, the lipstick. "Lord, help me to use my mouth and the words that come out of it to your glory. Help me to speak only with kindness."

My makeup routine is now a habit. So are my morning make-up prayers.

Thanks, Lord, for all the daily reminders to come to you in prayer. Thanks also, for a sister who wants me to be the best I can be!

Charm can be deceptive and beauty doesn't last, but a woman who fears and reverences God shall be greatly praised.   PROVERBS 31:30

My daughter Julia seemed to get herself into more trouble than the other three.

One day when I was cleaning out a dresser I was planning to give her, I came across a funny, old mug. It looked as if the potter had stepped on one side of it when the clay was still wet. Lopsided and wrinkled, it proclaimed on its front in shiny letters, "Nobody's Perfect." I knew instantly that mug had to find a home with Julia. When I sent it to her I tucked in this note:

Dearest Julia:

Over the past few years I've heard you put yourself down a number of times as the one kid of my four who screwed up more than the others. I just want you to remember, Julia, how strong you really are. Yes, you've made your share of mistakes along the way, but I want you to know that I am so proud of the way you continually pick yourself up and forge ahead with such gusto. I want you to remember, also, when you look at this mug that "Nobody's Perfect"—not me, not Jeanne, Michael, Amy [my daughter-in-law], or Andrew. None of us are perfect ... we're all just working hard, like you, to get there.

As you get settled into your new apartment and new job and new life, please look at this mug every day and know that you're now moving forward in your life ... getting a little more perfect every day. And that's what the rest of us are doing as well. I love you and am very proud of you.

Mom

Lord, help me to be a better person, a better parent, and a better friend every day. Help me to encourage others to forge ahead through the hard times.

> "All right, hurl the stones at her until she dies. But only he who never sinned may throw the first!"
> JOHN 8:7

For single parents who feel betrayed by a broken marriage or relationship, I share this story, told to me by professional story-teller Art Beaudry.

Native Americans have a long tradition whereby teenage boys or young men go into the woods on a vision quest. They fast and meditate about the meaning of life and their role on this great earth.

One young Indian boy had the same dream every night. It was about two dogs. One was a young, gentle dog. The other dog was mean. The evil dog would goad the good dog into a fight, night after night. Sometimes the friendly, good-natured dog would win. Other times the mean, evil, cruel dog would win.

When the young man returned to his people, he told a respected elder about his dream and asked, "Which dog will become victorious? What does this dream mean?"

The old man smiled and said, "Son, within you live the two dogs. You ask which dog will survive the final battle? That depends on which one you feed."

If we continue to concentrate on the unhappy aspects of life, then those bitter feelings will take over our lives. If we feed the good dog instead, we'll emerge winners ... people who are happy, positive, energetic, spiritually connected, and full of life and love.

Which dog are you going to feed?

Lord, give me the grace to concentrate on the good things in my life and to stop feeding into the bad with my thoughts, words, or deeds.

All these vile things come from within; they are what pollute you and make you unfit for God.   MARK 7:23

SEPTEMBER 19

Do your children ever lie to you? Though I tried to impress upon my children that if they lied to me it would be hard to trust them, they still told an occasional lie. At one time or another, most kids tell lies in order to save their skins. Over the years I learned that sometimes you have to do a little "creative sleuthing" to get to the truth, when more than one child is involved in the lie.

As assistant principal of a local high school, my ex-husband Harold held the "Golden Spyglass" award for his ability to ferret the truth out of unsuspecting teenagers. One day, four senior boys sauntered in around 11:00 A.M. "Mr. Lorenz, we had a flat tire and had trouble getting it changed," the boys chorused.

"OK, men, follow me," Harold replied. He placed each boy in a different room and told each one, "Son, I'm going to give you a little test. Simply write down on this piece of paper which tire was flat."

When Harold collected the four papers he learned that the "front right," "back left," and "back right" tires had all been flat. Each boy served time in detention without so much as a complaint.

Next time your children gang up on you, separate them and go room to room asking them individually for the real story. After being "caught" a few times, your kids might find that the truth has become a habit.

Lord, it's not easy to get to the bottom of things around here sometimes. Give me generous doses of patience, justice, and a huge sense of humor.

Stop lying to each other; tell the truth, for we are parts of each other and when we lie to each other we are hurting ourselves.   EPHESIANS 4:25

SEPTEMBER 20

When my co-worker Dan learned that his fourteen-year-old daughter had run away from home, he was frantic. One of Trina's friends called to say she'd heard that Trina was taking off for Florida or California. After calling the police, Dan called the bus and train stations for schedules. There was a bus leaving for Orlando at 11:15 P.M. that night out of Chicago.

Against the advice of everyone, Dan drove the ninety miles to Chicago. He missed the Chicago turnoff and didn't arrive at the bus station until almost midnight. Still, he felt compelled to stay in the vicinity. He went from one level to another at the huge bus depot, then ran two blocks to the other downtown Chicago bus station. Then he walked a three-block radius around the neighborhood, terrified to be in such a place at that time of night, but unable to leave. Something was telling him to stay, to keep looking.

At 2:30 A.M. he was on the escalator going up to the main lobby, ready to give up his search, when something made him turn his head. There, on the down escalator, he saw the back of his daughter's head.

Reunited, they hugged each other, then talked for a long time. The next day they began working on the problems Trina was having at school, and then started family counseling.

What kept Dan in that bus station for so long? He says, "The power of prayer, that's what."

I think there may have been a guardian angel or two on duty that night as well.

Lord, give me a sense of faith so strong that when my mind tells me one thing, I will still follow my heart. Give me confidence in the power of prayer.

If you had a hundred sheep and one of them strayed away and was lost in the wilderness, wouldn't you leave the ninety-nine others to go and search for the lost one until you found it?   LUKE 15:4

SEPTEMBER 21

Today, September 21, is the feast of St. Matthew the Apostle. When our parish was celebrating the feast day of our patron saint, a letter from a neighboring Lutheran church was published in our Sunday bulletin: "On this, the feast day of St. Matthew, Apostle and Evangelist, we your sisters and brothers at All Saints Lutheran Church are remembering you in prayer. We pray too, that on the celebration of All Saints Day, that you will be remembering us in prayer as well. It is not only good, but necessary, that we pray for one another and that we publicly acknowledge those prayers for the good of all the Church."

Many of us at St. Matthew's felt our faith renewed by the ecumenical spirit of love and sharing from the people at All Saints Lutheran.

Why don't you ask your pastor if your church could become praying partners with a church of a different denomination? Who knows what miracles might take place! Just think what a great way that would be to teach your children about the spirit of Christian unity.

Of course, this idea can extend to relationships with ex-husbands (and ex-wives) as well. If we could cast away past bitterness and resentment and focus on the good two parents can accomplish if we just pool our efforts, single parenthood wouldn't be nearly so scary.

Father, let all of us come together in a spirit of love. Let us pray for one another and grow together as your children.

We who have been made holy by Jesus, now have the same Father he has.   HEBREWS 2:11

SEPTEMBER 22

Happy birthday, ice cream cone! Some people believe that in 1295 Marco Polo returned to Italy from the Far East with a recipe for a frozen dessert that included milk.

In 1851 ice cream became a full-fledged industry in the United States when Jacob Fussell, a Baltimore milk dealer, found himself oversupplied with cream and began producing ice cream in quantity.

The cone came much later: On September 22, 1903, Italian emigrant Italo Marchiony applied for a U.S. patent on the pastry mold he invented to hold his luscious lemon ices.

Ice cream is a make-you-feel-good-all-over confection. So today, why don't you make everyone in your family happy with an ice cream treat? The birthday of the ice cream cone is the perfect day to buy a couple gallons of ice cream in different flavors, plus some toppings and bananas. Invite your friends over for a banana split feast. Remember, events like this are the fabric of our children's childhood memories. It may cost $20 for the ingredients, but you'll be rewarded a hundredfold with ear-to-ear, banana-size grins from your children and from those you invite.

Heavenly Father, thank you for parties, spontaneous or otherwise, and for good friends to invite to them. Thanks also, for chocolate malt ice cream covered with pecans.

God's laws are pure, eternal, just. They are more desirable than gold. They are sweeter than honey dripping from a honeycomb. PSALMS 19:9-10

SEPTEMBER 23

In 1987 I taught a class in advertising copywriting at Milwaukee Area Technical College. The second week of class, after drastically failing the first quiz, a young man slammed down his textbook and roared, "I don't like the way you're teaching this class! I want to know right now ... are we going to be graded in here on what's in this book or on what you talk about in class?"

I felt as if I'd been hit with a shotgun at close range. I wanted to quit teaching right then and there.

I thought about my class preparations. I'd shared ideas from the text in class, spent hours gathering interesting materials, kept the atmosphere relaxed with roundtable discussions, and as a working copywriter, had plenty of firsthand experience and anecdotes to share.

I knew I was doing a good job, so I swallowed hard and explained, for the second time, that each week I'd quiz them on the chapter of the week. It was his responsibility to read that chapter. But our classroom discussion would center on practical ideas and theories I had learned "on the job."

The young man eventually became a good student. But his frustration reminded me of what the apostles must have felt when Jesus taught them a whole new way of thinking and living. Sometimes they balked at his methods. Sometimes they were paralyzed with fear, like the night the fierce storm rose up when they were out in the boat with Jesus.

My experience with my students also reminded me of the way I felt when I first became a single parent. I had to find new ways to do everything and believe me, I was scared silly at times!

Have you ever felt frustrated, either as a student or as a teacher? Do what Jesus did with his followers ... and what I had to do with my class ... just make sure you're prepared, pray for patience, and never give up!

Lord, help me to be a better teacher and a better parent.

> But when the Father sends the Holy Spirit—he will teach you much, as well as remind you of everything I myself have told you.　　　　JOHN 14:26

One year, as my two daughters and I watched the *Miss America Pageant* on TV, I noticed that the television cameras panned the audience while Miss Tennessee took her famous runway walk. Suddenly someone in the audience held up a large sign that simply said in bold letters, *JOHN 3:16.*

Like most people, I don't have many Bible verses committed to memory. So that night I looked up the verse.

The more I thought about that verse and the person who cleverly shared it with millions of prime-time viewers, the more I realized that in that one sentence rests the entire message of the New Testament. If we believe those twenty-seven words, we have learned the bulk of what Christianity is all about.

There's also a powerful message for single parents in that particular verse. It speaks of the amazing relationship between child and parent. If we truly want what is best for our children, we must understand that our chief role is to teach them not to need us so they can grow up strong and confident and become productive, capable citizens. It may be hard to let your children go, as it was for God the Father to let his only son go, but it's absolutely necessary.

Lord, help me to be such a good parent that I can let go when the time is right, so my child can soar.

For God loved the world so much that he gave his only Son so that anyone who believes in him shall not perish but have eternal life.　　　JOHN 3:16

SEPTEMBER 25

Did you know that the fourth Sunday in September is Good Neighbor Day? When I was a child, the first of May was Good Neighbor Day. We'd make dainty little May baskets out of paper or buy fancy ruffly ones and fill them with mints, nuts, and little wrapped candies. Then came the real fun ... delivering them to our neighbors' front doors, ringing the doorbell, and then running away before they could see who brought the little gift basket.

I've been blessed with good neighbors my entire life, in a dozen homes in four states. I've had cookie-baking neighbors who always shared their bounty. One neighbor mowed our lawn when we were away. Other neighbors watched my children, told great stories, and brought in my mail. Neighbors with grills invited us for cookouts. Neighbors with pools let us take a dip.

We've been in the same house in Wisconsin since 1980 and our next-door neighbors, Cary and Linda and their children Mandy and Brandon, should be nominated for Neighbor of the Decade award. In those dozen years we've never had a cross word. Cary snowblows our driveway. Their children play in our front yard and cut through our backyard to visit their friends. Cary gives me advice on repairs or fixes things when they break. Mandy and Brandon are well-behaved, delightful kids who fill our lives with fun, interesting conversations. Cary and Linda are a happily married couple who have been wonderful role models for my children. Perfect next-door neighbors. Every single-parent family should be so lucky.

This week, Lord, help me make a special effort to show my neighbors how much I appreciate them. We single parents need our neighbors, Lord. Help me to be friendly everyday.

All ten [commandments] are wrapped up in this one,
to love your neighbor as you love yourself.
ROMANS 13:9

SEPTEMBER 26

When Andrew was eleven years old he was talking on the phone to his sister Jeanne, an art student in California. I kept talking to him in the background. "Be sure to thank Jeanne for the hat she sent you." Then, "Wish her a happy birthday." Then, "Ask how her classes are."

Finally Andrew said, "Mom keeps talking and interrupting me and I can't hear you, so I might as well hang up." He handed me the phone and stomped off to bed.

I felt as if I'd been slapped. I certainly hadn't meant to ruin his phone conversation.

Half an hour later I went to his bedroom to see if he was asleep. As I pulled the covers up to his chin, he opened his eyes and said, "I'm sorry, Mom. I didn't mean to hurt your feelings." He was saying "I'm sorry" to a mother who hardly ever said those words. I apologized to him for interrupting his conversation.

A few days later I was upset at a friend for being late when she picked me up for a meeting. I remembered how easy it was to say "I'm sorry" to Andrew after he had apologized first. So I said, "You know, sometimes I forget how busy you are. I'm sorry for not offering to drive more often." She apologized for being late, and the issue was closed. We *both* felt better and had a great evening together.

Lord, whether I'm holding myself rigidly right, or I need to break the ice, help me to bend with a heartfelt "I'm sorry."

If we confess our sins to him, he can be depended on to forgive us.   1 JOHN 1:9

The table is set. The food is on. Grace has been said. Whammo! We're off to the races. Everyone talks at once. Julia interrupts Michael. Michael reaches across the table for the bread.

"Will someone please pass him the bread?" I suggest. Michael laughs, "OK, Mom, can you pass the butter?"

I correct him, "Will you please pass the butter?" Michael says, "I can't, it's right in front of you!"

Jeanne stuffs lima beans discreetly into her socks.

Andrew cries out, "Michael won't let me talk!"

Julia, arms outstretched in a cheerleading pose, quiets the whole table with an announcement, "Attention, everyone. I need money for new cheerleading shoes, and Michael, will you please stop kicking me under the table?"

Jeanne jumps up, "I have to be excused for a minute."

I learn later, years later, it was to dump the lima beans into the toilet.

I try to find out what went on in school that day … in four different schools, actually. The answers are anything but enlightening. "Same old thing." "I don't know." "Nothing much." "Really, Mom, I'd rather forget about school while I'm eating, if you don't mind."

Mealtimes in our single-parent household can be chaotic … so much giggling, silliness, and bickering. Sometimes I even hated mealtimes … until I had dinner one night with a couple who had no children.

Lord, you have blessed me with four children. When they're noisy, boisterous, demanding, argumentative, and full of the dickens, remind me that life without them would be no life at all.

Let the cornets and trumpets shout! Make a joyful symphony before the Lord, the King!   PSALMS 98:6

SEPTEMBER 28

September's cool days reminded me that Wisconsin's long, cold winter wasn't far behind. Suddenly I'd be withdrawn, tired, and irritable just thinking about winter. I'd feed my depression with chocolate and other sweets, gain weight, and feel even worse.

One day I noticed my daughter Jeanne's 4-H Club folder on the kitchen table with the words *Health, Head, Hand and Heart* printed on the front. I thought, *Why can't I adopt the 4-H plan and try making small changes in my life to help me out of this depression?*

Health. Instead of trying to lose twenty pounds I replaced my mid-afternoon candy bar with a fresh orange or an apple and my usual late-night buttered popcorn with a diet soda and some crisp vegetables. I wasn't on a "diet" as such but I lost weight slowly. I also started jumping on a mini-trampoline and taking walks. As my energy increased, my depression vanished.

Head. I used my head to find a better job and discovered that as my self-esteem improved, so did my disposition.

Hand. Helping others is a surefire way to ease depression. I remember months spent correcting essays for an inmate who needed help on his writing and reading skills. Think about volunteering or giving a young harried mother a couple hours off each week by watching her children.

Heart. Let God into your heart and soul. Mealtime and bedtime prayers with your children bring the Lord into your home on a daily basis. Attending weekly church services as a family helps get the whole week jump-started.

God, thank you for the 4-Hs. Help me use them daily to blast away depression and keep my family on an even keel.

"Why so sad? You aren't sick, are you? You look like a man with deep troubles."   NEHEMIAH 2:1

SEPTEMBER 29

Why do we let our youngsters provoke us into raising our voices three decibels above normal, just to make a simple statement?

"Clean up that room or you're grounded for a week!"

"You can't go until you practice your piano! We're paying eight dollars a week for your lessons, you know!"

"Get these toys out of the living room, or I'm going to scream!" (I'm already screaming, of course.)

One day something happened that started me on the road to less yelling and more understanding. I was in the laundry room, up to my eyeballs in dirty clothes. I said to my five-year-old son, "Andrew, please go to the back bathroom and bring me all the towels."

Five minutes later Andrew still hadn't appeared, so I stomped down the back hallway, ready to yell. But when I saw him I couldn't even open my mouth.

There was Andrew, in the middle of the bathroom floor, surrounded by towels. First he'd pulled all the clean towels out of the cupboard, two shelves worth. Then he'd gathered all the dirty towels and tossed them on top of his pile. Now he was trying to lift the entire mountain.

Something told me that *this* was not the time to yell at my child. He was doing *exactly* what I'd told him.

Today, let's give those kids of ours a little more understanding, even when we're stressed. Count to ten. Then speak in a kinder, softer, more gentle manner and see what happens.

Lord, let my childrens' personalities and characters grow strong because I have the softness and patience to realize that they deserve the benefit of the doubt.

A word fitly spoken is like apples of gold in settings of silver. PROVERBS 25:11

SEPTEMBER 30

Teenage logic got you in a tizzy? Permit me to share a few sentences uttered by my beautiful daughter Jeanne.

Age three: "Mommy, can I wear your lipstick? And will you paint my fingernails?"

Age eight: "Oh gross, how can you stand to curl your hair with that hot thing? I'm never wearing makeup. It's just for boys to look at. It's dumb."

Age thirteen: "What do you mean I'm wearing too much eye makeup? And I like my hair permed and fuzzy like this. It's my hair and it's the style."

Age eighteen: "Mother, how can you possibly put that tar resin on your eyes? It's so phony! I'm *never* going to wear makeup, shave my legs, or perm my hair."

Age twenty-three: "Hi, Mom! Guess what? I shaved my head! Lots of women in California do it! It's elegant. With a little pressed powder and bright red lipstick, I look marvelous! I'll never have a bad hair day again!"

Age twenty-seven: "Thanks for the compliment, Mom. It must be my new lipstick. Or maybe the haircut. It's a good length, don't you think? I found this great stylist...."

Our daughters go full circle on many of life's little issues. The comforting thing is that they usually end up fairly sensible, paying taxes, and worrying about the cost of living like the rest of us. In the meantime, we only have to love them with all our hearts and get them through life as gently as possible.

Heavenly Father, as my children seesaw through life, help me to see the big picture ... the warm, wonderful adults they'll be if I just love and guide them with patience.

It's like this: when I was a child I spoke and thought and reasoned as a child does. But when I became a man my thoughts grew far beyond those of my childhood, and now I have put away the childish things.

1 CORINTHIANS 13:11-12

Prayer for October

Heavenly Father, help me
To be more careful
Of this land
That you created
And Columbus discovered
Over 500 years ago.

Remind me, Father,
Not to clutter up
My America.
Help me teach my children
To treasure and protect
These mountains, rivers, lakes
Plains, prairies, and forests.
Help me respect your creation.
To cherish it, love it,
And maintain it
For all the generations
After mine.

OCTOBER 1

The first Sunday in October is Grandparent's Day. I don't expect cards or flowers … just the chance to spend time with my two granddaughters, Hailey and Hannah. Hailey was born in 1993 to my daughter Julia and her husband Tim. Hannah came along three years later to my son Michael and his wife Amy. Those granddaughters of mine are a couple of charmers!

Before Hailey was born I wasn't sure if I was ready to be a grandma. I was in my forties and more concerned about buying new in-line skates and planning travel adventures than sitting in a rocker, letting my hair go gray.

But when Hailey was born I jumped into the role the minute I saw her. Joy came bounding into my heart as I held my first grandchild close and rocked her gently in the hospital room. The first time I took care of her for a whole day, I spent every second with her, even watching her sleep.

When Hannah was born, a month early, she weighed barely five pounds, and her full head of red hair made her the talk of the neonatal intensive care nursery. In the hospital I held her in one hand against my chest and rocked her.

Pure delight, unabashed joy, intense love, and powerful protection oozed out of every pore. I loved being a grandma.

This week, why not honor the parents of your ex-spouse? If they're like most grandparents, they would love nothing better than to be able to spend time with your children. Write them a note and have the children draw pictures to include in the letter. Believe me, the relationship between a child and a grandparent is magical. Let it bloom, *on both sides of the family!*

Lord, help me to be a loving grandma and role model to the children of my children and to cherish every moment with them. Help me to encourage a warm relationship between the parents of my ex-spouse and my children.

An old man's grandchildren are his crowning glory. A child's glory is his father.   PROVERBS 17:6

OCTOBER 2

October is officially National Pasta Month as well as National Pizza Month. I'd venture to say that pasta and pizza are the two most-served meals in the homes of single parents. Both are easy and quick, relatively inexpensive, and kids love them.

But too often as we eat these, fresh fruits and vegetables become distant memories, extra pounds begin to creep on us.

Once, when I was feeling particularly flabby, my uncle Ralph recited a poem he remembered from his childhood.

> "As a beauty I'm not a great star,
> Others are handsomer by far.
> But my face, I don't mind it
> because I'm behind it.
> It's the folks in the front that I jar."

I laughed, wrote the poem down, and made up a second verse.

> As a picture of fitness I have failed.
> When it comes to exercising I've paled.
> My flab, I don't mind it
> It warms me inside it.
> It's my heart that I hope will be hailed.

We may joke about our lack of exercise and our bad eating habits, but one of the most important things we can do is take the time to prepare nutritious meals and teach our children the value of daily exercise by doing it ourselves.

Let's serve generous helpings of fresh fruits and vegetables with our pasta and pizza meals. While we're at it, when we're making our own pizzas let's use nonfat cheeses and load them up with plenty of veggies.

Lord, thank you for your bounty of good-for-us foods.

> You open wide your hand to feed them and they are satisfied with all your bountiful provision.
>
> PSALMS 104:28

OCTOBER 3

One Sunday I had the whole day to myself. The older three children were all away at college, and Andrew was visiting a friend all day, so it was just me, a glorious sunshiny October day, and all the time in the world to do whatever I wanted.

I could have driven to downtown Milwaukee to the Festival of Performing Arts. Or invited a friend to join me at the Harvest Zoobilee Art Fair at Milwaukee's spectacular 194-acre zoo. I could have visited the Public Museum, taken a nature hike, or a bike ride in one of the many parks in our county. The list of "beautiful" things to do was endless.

What did I do? I turned on a football game on TV and fell asleep on the couch. And I don't even like TV football. When I woke up, feeling guilty that I wasn't doing *something* productive, I moped around the house. I wasted the entire afternoon.

The next morning, I noticed a plaque on an office wall: "Man shall be called to account for every permitted pleasure he failed to enjoy."

Next time I have a whole afternoon to myself, I'm going to find one of God's "permitted pleasures" and enjoy myself with abandon. And if I have to go alone, I will. We single parents need to learn that time alone is a treasure to be enjoyed.

Lord, you meant for us to have fun in this world, or you wouldn't have created such beauty and so many fun things to see and do. Get me off the couch so I can enjoy your world.

Come now, be merry; enjoy yourself to the full.

ECCLESIASTES 2:1

OCTOBER 4

This is the time of year when, depending on how our favorite baseball team did all season long, we either get very excited about the World Series or we brush off another year and think, "Well, maybe next year."

Columnist George F. Will once reported that there were 3,180 home runs hit during the 1988 professional baseball season. Seems like a lot, doesn't it? But that same year, 25,838 singles were hit! Eight times more singles than home runs. It makes sense, then, that more games are won by singles than homers.

Most of us, especially single parents, aren't what you'd call "home run hitters." We approach life ninety feet at a time (the distance between home plate and first base). We accomplish little things here and there, eventually learning that a winning lifestyle comes from adding up those deliberate, steady, not-so-grand-but-nonetheless-forward-moving strides. Day after day, week after week, we take care of our children, go to work, clean the house, make time for our friends, and sometimes even find time for ourselves.

Sometimes, as we plod along trying to raise children, we get depressed, but other times we hit a double or a home run and, wow, life as a single parent seems rich, rewarding, and wonderful. But mostly, we plod along, hitting singles, doing the job, yesterday, today, and tomorrow.

When our children are grown and we see them as happy, well-adjusted adults, we'll know that every little stride really paid off. Lots of little things put together win the big game.

Lord, give me courage to go on, in baby steps if necessary, when I'm discouraged. Help me to keep my eyes on the ultimate goal ... raising happy, healthy children into adults.

Forgetting the past and looking forward to what lies ahead, I strain to reach the end of the race and receive the prize for which God is calling us up to heaven because of what Christ Jesus did for us.

PHILIPPIANS 3:13-14

OCTOBER 5

Hanging on the wall in my bedroom is one of my most treasured possessions. It's the large, colorful, ornate wedding certificate that states: "Mr. William Barclay and Miss Mary E. Moore, both of Scotland Township, Illinois, were united in Holy Matrimony on the thirty-first day of October in the year of Our Lord, One Thousand Eight Hundred Seventy-Seven."

William and Mary were my great-grandparents. Both died many years before I was born. Their daughter, Minta Pearl Barclay, who was my grandmother, died when my mother was eleven years old. But in Minta Pearl's short life she carved a legacy of learning that has become an important part of my life and my children's.

In the early 1900s, few women finished grammar school, let alone college. But Minta earned her master's degree and became a professor of physics and mathematics at Ellsworth College in Iowa Falls, Iowa. I wonder what my great-grandparents thought of their maverick daughter as she climbed higher and higher up the educational ladder. No doubt they had to sacrifice greatly—both financially and emotionally—to help her accomplish her dream.

I like having a woman of Minta Pearl's determination and love of learning for my grandmother. But her parents, whose sacrifice stretched for generations, really impress me. Her father, born in Edinburgh, Scotland came to this country in the mid - 1800s to carve out a life as a farmer in a land that gave him the opportunity to educate his children clear through the university level.

It's important to support the dreams of our children. Our job as parents is to give our children roots and wings.

Lord, help me to learn all I can about my ancestors, as well as the ancestors of my children's other parent. Help me give my children the same values that my great-grandparents gave to my grandmother and that she gave to my mother.

You cleared the ground and tilled the soil and we took root and filled the land.   PSALMS 80:9

OCTOBER 6

"Hi, Mom, bad news."

Oh, how I hated phone calls from my college students that started that way! "What is it, Julia?"

"The check I wrote for my tuition bounced!"

The rest of the conversation was one-sided ... me, telling her in rather gruff tones that she simply *had* to start balancing her checkbook every month. She ended up in tears.

The next morning I was tempted to call her, apologize for my gruffness, and offer to send a new tuition check from my account. I fussed and fumed. *Do I bail her out or let her learn from her mistake?* I was so tormented that I drove the two miles to Lake Michigan to try to think it out in the majestic solitude I knew I would find there.

Two- to three-foot waves crashed loudly against the sand under immense white clouds. I walked close to the water, skittering back each time a wave rolled up close to my sneakers. Suddenly, a large wave caught me off guard and soaked my shoe, sock, and pant leg, making me quite uncomfortable in the fifty-degree weather. From then on I walked farther away from the shoreline—I'd learned my lesson!

That was the answer I'd been looking for! Julia had also been caught off guard. Perhaps if she had to "walk with wet feet" for a month at college by living without spending money, she'd learn a lot more about financial responsibility. She could use the money from her part-time job to make good on her tuition check. It would be uncomfortable—but sometimes that's the only way we learn.

Dear Julia, I thought as I made my way back to my car. *I love you. Try to understand.*

Lord, give me the courage and the knowledge to know when to "back off" and let my children do for themselves. Thank you, too, for calming places of majesty that help put the smaller problems of life back into perspective.

Teach a child to choose the right path, and when he is older he will remain upon it.   PROVERBS 22:6

OCTOBER 7

Happy birthday, Confucius! The great Chinese philosopher and teacher lived 500 years before the birth of Christ (551-479 B.C.), and established a religious system in China that emphasized the goodness of human nature. He extolled the virtues of benevolence, righteousness, propriety, wisdom, and faith.

Confucianism worked well in China except during A.D. 220-907, a period of political disunion and dynasty. Confucianism retreated during the social chaos.

I learned about this when my uncle, Major General James Knapp, a retired air force officer, gave me a hand-carved wooden statue of General Ulchi Moon Duk, known as the "Shield of Seoul." In A.D. 612 General Moon Duk's troops defeated 300,000 Chinese soldiers who had crossed the Yalu River, intent on attacking Pyongyang. The general's defense was so thorough that only 2,700 of the original Chinese troops made it home again.

I treasure this gift and keep it on top of my desk as a daily reminder that throughout history, the ideas of good people, like Confucius, have gone awry and for hundreds of years entire countries have been at war.

If you've gone through a divorce you may still be at war with your ex-spouse and his or her relatives. How long will you let it last?

Just remember that something very good came from the union of you and your ex-spouse ... your children. Don't let the war continue. Instead, focus on peace so that your children can enjoy the goodness of humanity, not the bitter recriminations of a war-torn divorce.

Lord, help me to forgive and to create peace with the family of my children's "other" parent.

Come, see the glorious things that our God does, how he brings ruin upon the world, and causes wars to end throughout the earth, breaking and burning every weapon.   PSALMS 46:8-9

OCTOBER 8

Have you ever been to the southernmost tip of the United States? It's not in Florida or Texas, but down a twelve-mile stretch of a winding, bumpy, one-lane blacktop road in great need of repair ... at the very southern tip of the island of Hawaii.

The day my daughter Jeanne, her boyfriend Canyon, my son Andrew, and I drove down that bumpy road to see South Point we saw the most amazing tree. Picture a beautiful, full-leafed tree about thirty feet tall, bent over about three feet from the ground and growing out straight and perfectly parallel to the ground. The winds on South Point are so strong that they caused this tree to grow across instead of up.

As we drove down that road we also saw two dozen huge, modern-looking windmills spinning wildly, producing massive amounts of electricity for towns all over the island. Those wind-mills made me realize that God certainly provides all we need—in this case, the strong winds—to make our lives complete.

In our lives as single parents, God provides everything we need: friends, family, faith, strength of character, and even the financial means to get the job done. Oh, sure, sometimes we blow it and let our self-esteem sink to the basement and worry about money. But if we step back and look at how God has provided for every creature on earth, with enough wind, rain, air, sun, and food to accomplish everything we need to survive ... then surely we should have enough faith to know that God has also given us the emotional, physical, and psychological strength to be good parents. We may not all do the job the same way, just like that bent-over tree, but we have within us whatever it takes to accomplish our goals and responsibilities. God, who does not create junk, has seen to it.

Heavenly Father, thank you for giving me everything I need to raise my children. Be there for me every day.

When I pray, you answer me, and encourage me by giving me the strength I need.   PSALMS 138:3

OCTOBER 9

At the radio station, one of my co-workers was an announcer who had a deep, rich voice. When I complimented Tom on his voice, I asked if he'd ever considered acting. With his deep, clear, powerful voice, coupled with his flawless diction and delivery, I imagined him as a great Shakespearean actor.

Tom smiled and said that as a kid everyone he met told him he should go into broadcasting. "Even today, it's amazing how many strangers tell me I should be in radio, TV, or on the stage because of my voice."

A few weeks later Tom stopped me in the hallway, laughing. He'd just gone to the drive-through window at a fast food restaurant. He placed his order at the electronic intercom then drove ahead to pick up his food. When he reached for his change, the restaurant employee commented, "You sure do have a nice voice. You know what you should be?"

Undaunted, Tom nodded understandingly.

Then the woman blurted out her answer, "A bingo caller! You'd be perfect."

God sometimes encourages us by the people we meet and their offhand comments. I can't count the times fellow workers or friends have made casual suggestions that made changes in my life.

"Have you ever considered teaching Sunday school? You'd be a good teacher."

"You ought to do more writing. Why don't you try to get your work published?"

If we remember that Jesus has no other voice but ours, we might listen more carefully when our friends, co-workers, and family members make suggestions. You never know when it's the voice of God speaking on your behalf.

God, help me to hear your voice in all those I meet. Keep me from being such a talker and instead, help me to listen more carefully.

Listen to the dream I had from God last night.

JEREMIAH 23:25

OCTOBER 10

One year for my birthday, my dear friend Betsy gave me a calendar that contained quotes about friendship. One quote really impressed me: "True friendship comes when the silence between two people is comfortable."

It's easy for husbands and wives, or parents and children to have many hours of silence. We know these people so well we don't *have* to talk all the time. When you're traveling in a car for hours, nobody has to speak if they don't want to, and the silence is not only comfortable, it's often refreshing.

Years ago my pastor told about a friend who lost his voice box to cancer. When Father was visiting the man he stood next to the hospital bed chatting about the operation, the weather, the man's family. The man could only nod his head, and Father soon ran out of things to talk about. So he pulled up a chair and just sat. Every once in a while they'd nod at each other and smile.

Father said the experience was actually more meaningful than if they'd been conversing. He discovered the form of communication called "presence."

Each time you experience communication by presence, remember that the presence of God in our midst makes the silence blossom into a form of exquisite communication.

Lord, help me to appreciate just being with a friend or loved one, even if we're together in silence. Help me to remember that your presence makes the silence blossom.

But the Lord is in his holy Temple; let all the earth be silent before him.   HABAKKUK 2:20

OCTOBER 11

My cousin, Marta, lives in a lovely old brick home with solid oak appointments in every room. There's even an oak panel between the kitchen sink and the window right over the sink.

One day when Marta was washing dishes, she noticed something green poking up through the small crack between the sink and the oak panel under the window. She opened the doors under the sink, moved the box that held her potatoes, and discovered a lone potato had rolled back to the outside wall. A sprout on that potato had grown straight up along that cold, dark wall, almost four feet, to reach the light.

When I saw Marta's vine I was amazed at the energy and determination that that little potato demonstrated in the face of all odds.

Sometimes I think we single parents feel like that little potato. When our marriages end we feel alone and cold in the dark. We get bogged down with problems, loneliness, bitterness, worries, and stress. But if we can just keep looking for that one little warm ray of sunshine and keep moving toward it, eventually we'll become whole again. The trick, of course, is to discover that ray of sunshine … a dear friend, perhaps, who is always available to listen? Some time outdoors in the fresh air? An hour alone inside a small, quiet church or chapel? Some time with an older relative who loves us no matter what? The light of God is all around us. We just have to look … and stretch a bit sometimes to get closer to it.

Lord, when I get discouraged remind me of Marta's potato and nudge me to keep reaching, stretching, and growing toward your light.

Jesus told him, "I am the Way—yes, and the Truth and the Life. No one can get to the Father except by means of me."   JOHN 14:6

OCTOBER 12

Today is Columbus Day. It's also my birthday. In 1987 my seven-year-old son, Andrew, and I celebrated both events by watching the sun rise over Lake Michigan.

6:30 A.M. We arrive at the deserted lakefront with our jug of hot chocolate and spread a blanket in the sand. Andrew and I snuggle close in the 40-degree weather as the cold lake wind slaps our faces.

6:40 A.M. We wait, shiver, snuggle closer, talk, sip our cocoa, and watch the clouds change color over the massive expanse of icy blue water. I wonder if Christopher Columbus was discouraged when the weather turned colder during the end of his voyage across the ocean. In the dusky haze of almost light I feel a sense of melancholy at being another year older.

6:50 A.M. More light escapes over the thick clouds lying flat against the horizon. We talk about how flat the world looks from here. No wonder the early explorers were confused.

7:01 A.M. Suddenly we both see an incredibly bright concentrated speck of orange light. In seconds the speck becomes an arc the size of a crescent moon and hops up on the horizon like the top of a neon pumpkin. Andrew jumps up and starts dancing in the sand. "Mom! We did it! We saw the sun rise!"

Suddenly I feel a sense of timelessness. I feel a kinship with Christopher Columbus, who must have felt the same elation as he watched land appear on the horizon. In one shining moment the chance for a better life becomes a reality ... a new opportunity to start over.

Sometime soon, why don't you take in this free spectacle and see if some of your problems don't diminish by the sheer beauty of it all?

Lord, help me get that "here it comes!" feeling each morning and to start each day and each birthday with the amazing grace of a sunrise.

The sun rises and sets and hurries around to rise again.   ECCLESIASTES 1:5

OCTOBER 13

Someone once said that life is made up of:

> The tender teens,
> The teachable twenties,
> The tireless thirties,
> The fiery forties,
> The fretful fifties,
> The serious sixties,
> The sacred seventies,
> The aching eighties.
> Shortening breath.
> Death, Sod, God.

When I first heard this little version of the stages of life I was in my late thirties … which hadn't been "tireless" at all. As a single parent with four young children and various part-time jobs, I'd been exhausted most of the time.

When I was in my "fiery" forties, most days I didn't feel fiery. Going through a divorce and then the death of my ex made me fretful, serious, and teachable.

What's "fretful" about the fifties? When I stepped into that threshhold, I didn't feel a bit fretful. "Tireless," perhaps, and other times "aching" with exhaustion from working and playing so hard.

A dear friend, in her seventies, is quite "teachable" as she takes one college course after another in her spare time.

A young mother in her twenties is certainly "sacred" as she searches for answers in Bible study classes and marriage enrichment programs.

We can all be exactly what we want to be at *any* stage in life. It's a fact!

Lord, help me not to stereotype myself or others according to age.

Moses was 120 years old when he died, yet his eyesight was perfect and he was as strong as a young man.   DEUTERONOMY 34:7

Mothers of teenage daughters know that shopping for clothes together is a test of patience, physical endurance, restraint, and basic human kindness.

"Mother, give it up! These pants are way too baggy!"

"They're skin tight!"

"Well, these shoes look and fit OK, but they don't have the little snail on the label, and everybody will know. I'll pay the $20 difference myself for the name-brand ones, OK?"

"When donkeys fly, you will."

O Lord, give me patience. Direct me out of this store and over to the place where they sell warm chocolate chip cookies. Quickly, Lord!

Then one day, a few years later, it happened.

"Mom," Julia asked sweetly, "may I borrow your yellow blouse and brown print skirt to wear to school tomorrow?"

"Could I try on your plaid skirt and one of your scarves?" Jeanne added.

"Sure, help yourselves!" At last my daughters were growing up. Our taste in clothes was starting to meld. I felt ten years younger.

When the girls emerged from my bedroom they were dressed practically head-to-toe in fashions from my wardrobe, including jewelry and accessories.

"Thanks, Mom! These are great!" they bubbled.

I wasn't so sure about the combinations they'd chosen, but I wasn't about to criticize. After all, I didn't want to ruin this tender passage from teendom to adulthood.

"Ya, they're perfect, Mom." Jeanne nodded. "It's nerd day at school tomorrow ... you know, everybody dresses up like the fifties, real dorkylike. These things are perfect."

Dear Lord, I need more patience. Lots more. And Lord, keep my sense of humor intact while you're at it, will you?

Dear brothers, is your life full of difficulties and temptations? Then be happy, for when the way is rough, your patience has a chance to grow.   JAMES 1:2-3

OCTOBER 15

On a glorious week-long vacation to Galveston Island, my brother and his family, my son Andrew, and I basked in the warm seventy-degree sun. We played in the pool at our rented condo, walked along the Gulf of Mexico's shore, and visited the local tourist places. One evening we drove out onto a wide pier that sticks out over the Gulf of Mexico a few blocks. The pier was wide enough for a large hotel and a driveway on either side.

When we reached the end and were circling back to the main road, I turned my head toward the gulf. At the end of the concrete pier a flowered wreath hung on a temporary fencelike barricade. A few feet past that I noticed a bouquet of roses tucked into the fence. Finally, the thing that caused my heart to stop … two framed photos, a young man and a woman, both smiling, both very young.

We saw a policeman on the pier and asked him what had happened. Two weeks earlier a car with the two young people inside plunged through the barricade at the end of the pier and into the gulf. It was a double suicide.

That experience jolted me into realizing that we parents must give our children a sense of hope for their futures by making sure they know we love them unconditionally. No matter what problems they have, they need to hear from us that we will always be there to guide them and to love them. Teenagers, especially, whose lives often seem to be on an emotional roller coaster, need to hear this message directly from us. A daily hug with a heartfelt "I love you" is a good way to begin.

Today Lord, if I know someone who is severely depressed, give me the grace and courage to reach out and get that person some help before a picture, a wreath, and a bouquet of flowers is all we have left of that life.

Oh, why should light and life be given to those in misery and bitterness, who long for death, and it won't come; who search for death as others search for food or money?   JOB 3:20-21

OCTOBER 16

Today is National Boss' Day, one of those goofy little holidays that is no doubt orchestrated by the candy and flower companies. We've all had good, bad, and mediocre bosses.

A dear friend sent me a copy of her husband's performance report from his boss. As I read, it occurred to me that the report said as much about her husband's supervisor as it did her husband.

> Superior performance by one of the company's best professionals. He has been instrumental to the success achieved by his division. His knowledge and experience are unmatched. He is the epitome of a quiet professional and displays those qualities found only in our best leaders. He is one of my most trusted advisors, who is universally respected by his peers and subordinates. He understands our employees and ensures they are always supported. Smart, articulate, and with exceptional good judgment, he has done a superb job in orchestrating the staff. In summary he is the best of the best. I would fight to secure his services in any future assignment.

As an employee I would walk on hot coals for such a boss. It's simply human nature to try to work harder for those who appreciate our efforts.

Today, why don't you write out a praise-filled "child performance rating sheet" for each of your children. After all, high praise is the polish that shines their hearts and souls. And to see it in writing makes it all the more wonderful.

Lord, remind me to praise my children often, so that their hearts and souls will be filled with a sense of pride in their hard work and good deeds.

> Let everyone be sure that he is doing his very best, for then he will have the personal satisfaction of work well done, and won't need to compare himself with someone else.　　　GALATIANS 6:4

In my family, reading glasses happen at age forty-two. When my dad turned forty-two he got them. Two years later, at age forty-two, my Mom got them. And when I turned forty-two, I was off to the eye doctor, complaining that I couldn't read the newspaper or the phone book. He smiled that knowing smile reserved only for those approaching "middle age" and wrote out a prescription for reading glasses.

Before I turned forty-three I noticed my knees started cracking every time I walked upstairs. Then my left shoulder ached whenever the humidity rose. Not long after that my young son announced, "You sure do have a lot of gray hairs on top, Mom."

My mother said it best when she recited the following poem shortly after she got her first pair of reading glasses. "I can see through my bifocals, my dentures fit me fine. My hearing aid does wonders, but Lord, I miss my mind!"

I laughed with her when she said it years ago ... and now that I'm into middle age myself I've decided to keep my mother's sense of humor about it. I've also added this to my favorite quotes about aging: "Age is a matter of mind. If you don't mind, it doesn't matter."

So whether we're thirty, fifty, or ninety ... if we just look for the positives and don't dwell on the "reading glasses" issues of life, we'll be a lot better off. To help me keep my perspective about it, whenever I reach for my reading glasses I try to remember to say one of my "aging" prayers:

Thanks Lord, that I only need glasses for reading ... and that my knees only crack when I walk upstairs ... that my back only bothers me when I overdo it with yard work ... that my gray hairs aren't that noticeable unless I'm standing in sunlight.

White hair is a crown of glory and is seen most among the godly.　　　　　PROVERBS 17:31

OCTOBER 18

At a workshop in 1982 I sat next to Marjorie Holmes, magazine writer, columnist, and author of numerous inspirational books. I was just starting to write in my spare time, and I complained, "I'd love to be a real writer but I've got four children at home. With all their activities and my part-time jobs, I just can't find time to write."

Marjorie looked me square in the eye and said, "Pat, the greatest thing that ever happened to my writing career was having four children at home. I learned to write in twenty-minute time blocks, and the children provided me with endless ideas for my articles."

I decided right then that I would never give up, ever. People who succeed *never* think of giving up. They keep at it, even if it's in little chunks of time here and there.

When I returned home, I started writing every day during *Sesame Street* while Andrew was glued to the educational antics of Big Bird and Cookie Monster. I wrote in the car while waiting to pick up Michael from basketball practice. I wrote at the kitchen counter while the roast was cooking and I was in-between homework questions with Julia. I wrote in the convent library for forty-five minutes every Monday while Jeanne took piano lessons.

If there's something you'd like to do with your life but think you don't have the time, think again. Instead of having two whole afternoons a week, perhaps you can find three twenty-minute time blocks each day. If you really want to, you *can* find the time. Even if you're a busy, busy single parent.

Lord, thank you for the gifts of persistence and determination. Help me to use my time productively.

Don't be fools; be wise: make the most of every opportunity you have for doing good.

EPHESIANS 5:16

OCTOBER 19

When I was a young girl, my grandmother, Effie Maude Knapp, was in her eighties. Every time we visited my grandparents, Grandma and I would sit on her squeaky porch swing and check to see how old we were by pinching up the skin on the back of our hands, just over the middle knuckle. Grandma said that years before, slave buyers used that method to tell how old slaves were.

When I pulled the skin up on my hand it flattened out smooth the second I released it. But when Grandma pulled the skin up on her hand it stayed that way, sometimes for a minute or two.

When I was in my late twenties, I certainly didn't have the energy I had in my teens. I thought I was getting old. In my thirties I discovered my first gray hairs. My forties brought on a touch of arthritis here and there, reading glasses, and a few extra pounds.

But now that I've reached my fifties it seems that I spend more time thinking up ways to keep my body and mind fit and full of energy. I'm determined to be roller-skating, biking, hiking, swimming, snorkeling, and skiing well into my seventies, maybe my eighties.

But most important, I want to grow older with the same grace that Grandma Knapp had. She never seemed to mind getting older. I'm sure that's because she had such strong faith in God and in the afterlife. I remember thinking that Grandma's skin got loose and lost its elasticity because it had to stretch over a heart that grew bigger every year.

Lord, let my heart and my faith in the hereafter grow bigger and bigger. Help me to show my children by example that aging isn't something to fear ... but to cherish.

You shall give due honor and respect to the elderly, in the fear of God. I am Jehovah.　　　LEVITICUS 19:32

"Andrew," I asked my four-year-old, "how would you like to help me make some chocolate chip cookies?"

"All right!" My little helper scurried into the kitchen.

As soon as I had the dry ingredients in the bowl, Andrew dumped in the eggs and the softened butter.

"Now can I stir, Mamma?" he asked with the confidence of Julia Child.

I handed him a large wooden spoon. "All right, but be careful. Hold the handle on the bowl because the batter is really stiff. It'll be hard to stir at first."

As soon as those words left my mouth, Andrew dug that spoon into the batter, tried to force a stirring motion, and the spoon exploded out of the bowl. Batter went everywhere ... on the counter, the floor, all over the fruit in the fruit bowl, under the microwave, in my hair ... everywhere.

I exploded too. "Andrew! I told you to hold onto the handle of the bowl! Why weren't you more careful?" As soon as I said those words I regretted them, but all I could see was red ... and an hour's cleaning job ahead of me.

Andrew's face registered surprise, guilt, then total defeat. He started crying, ran off to his room, slamming his bedroom door behind him.

I started cleaning. It only took ten minutes. I walked back to Andrew's room to tell him we could finish the cookies.

My child was sound asleep. So I finished baking the cookies alone, missing him and feeling guilty for not being more understanding.

I had turned a nice memory into a bitter afternoon, and somehow those cookies weren't any fun at all.

Lord, help me to be understanding and forgiving and to laugh at the little messes in life.

But you are a God of forgiveness, always ready to pardon, gracious and merciful, slow to become angry, and full of love and mercy. NEHEMIAH 9:17

"A kid called me 'Baldy' today at school," complained eight-year-old Matt to his twin brother, Nick.

Matt held the hand mirror behind his head and started to cry when he saw the bald patches on the back and top. "Look, Nick, I *am* getting bald!"

"I know what we can do." Nick smiled. "Let's both shave our heads so nobody'll be able to tell us apart again."

Matt, who was suffering from leukemia and undergoing chemotherapy, agreed, and the boys giggled as they shaved each other's heads. After that, things were back to normal at school, except for the three days every month when Matt checked into the hospital for treatment.

Because Nick shaved his head, Matt's attitude soared, and he eventually recovered from the leukemia.

Doctors know that mental attitude is extremely important in curing disease. A good mental attitude is also extremely important for single parents. It's easy to be upset, depressed, fearful, and give in to frustration and bitterness. But there are lots of us out here living the same kind of life you are. We're in this together! Join a singles group, go to singles dances and other get-togethers, or volunteer to host a singles Bible study or social group in your home.

Divided we fall, united we conquer. Sticking together in times of pain and sorrow, like Matt and Nick, can turn adversity into joy.

Lord, help me work on my attitude until it sparkles and shines. Help me to be a beacon of light and hope to other single parents who haven't yet turned their sad attitudes into positive ones.

And all the believers met together constantly and shared everything with each other, selling their possessions and dividing with those in need.

ACTS 2:44-45

We all get those pesky phone calls from telephone salespeople trying to sell us new siding, magazines, or what have you. I usually handle sales calls in one of four ways:

1. Hang up on them mid-sentence.
2. Let them finish their spiel and then politely decline.
3. Buy something I really don't want because I don't feel comfortable turning them down.
4. Purchase the product joyfully because it's a good idea or a nice value.

It's funny, but sometimes those are the four ways I find myself listening to homilies at church:

1. Some Sundays I "hang up" completely. My mind wanders and I think of other things.
2. Sometimes I listen, but at the end I decline politely by ignoring the message—and the Word of God.
3. Still other times I accept the words and their meaning, but once I get home I never quite figure out what to do with them.
4. Or I am a joyful listener who absorbs the word of God and happily puts it to good use in my daily life.

This Sunday I'm going to try harder to listen more carefully, joyfully, and with more acceptance of God's Word. And I'm going to put those words to good use. Will you join me?

Lord God, teach me to listen and to act on Your Word.

But if anyone keeps looking steadily into God's law for free men, he will not only remember it but he will do what it says, and God will greatly bless him in everything he does.   JAMES 1:25

OCTOBER 23

I love movies. I've seen hundreds upon hundreds of movies in my lifetime, everything from the Shirley Temple Saturday matinees in the 1950s, to the latest films that we rent to watch at home with a bowl of popcorn and a frosty root beer on a Saturday night.

But of all the movies I've seen, there are only two that I'm sure I will never ever forget. The first was when I took my oldest child, Jeanne, age three and a half, to see Walt Disney's *Fantasia*. It was Jeanne's first movie ever, and she was completely engrossed by the magnificent music, amazing cinematography, and the wide-screen antics of the Disney characters.

The second movie that I'll always remember was when I took my oldest grandchild, beautiful brown-eyed, blond-haired Hailey (who was also three and a half at the time), to her very first movie, *101 Dalmatians* on Christmas Day, 1996.

Hailey, whose parents were going through a divorce, was living in a town with her mother (my daughter Julia) which was, unfortunately, over two hours away from where her Daddy lived. Hailey missed her Daddy between her once-a-month visit. My heart ached for this innocent child. As I watched my little granddaughter escape momentarily from the hurtful world of divorce I knew that our snuggling was more than the result of a big-screen villain. It was the innocence of a child seeking safety in her world of confusion and little-girl fears.

Jesus, help me to be there for my children and grandchildren when they experience the pain of separation and divorce. Help me to give them moments of joy and special memories that will sustain them during the hard times.

But if any of you causes one of these little ones who trust in me to lose his faith, it would be better for you to have a rock tied to your neck and be thrown into the sea.   MATTHEW 18:6

OCTOBER 24

Today we celebrate the founding of the United Nations on October 24, 1945. The United Nations, located on the East River in Manhattan, in New York City, is a fascinating place. When you enter the gates of the United Nations Headquarters, you step into international territory. The UN Plaza is only about one block square, but the organization spans the world.

The purpose of the United Nations is twofold: to draw attention to world problems and to strengthen international cooperation to solve those problems. The UN uses six official languages ... Arabic, Chinese, English, French, Russian, and Spanish. Communication with all peoples of the world is one of the strengths and goals of the UN.

When Andrew (age eleven at the time) and I visited the United Nations in 1991, a pervading feeling of "goodwill toward mankind" seemed to bounce off the walls in every corner of the UN Plaza. For example, one huge, brightly colored mosaic created by Norman Rockwell depicts twenty-seven people of all nationalities, colors, and ages gathered together in a tight-knit group. The mosaic, titled "The Golden Rule" has eleven words written in large gold letters across the bottom third, "Do unto others as you would have them do unto you."

As I looked at the faces in the mosaic, I realized how important it is to teach our children the value of cultural diversity. We need to encourage our children to have friends of other nationalities.

Let's talk to our children about the importance of getting along with people of all colors, religions and beliefs. Let's teach our children to treat others the way they want to be treated.

Lord, help me to erase racism and bigotry from my family and to teach the Golden Rule instead.

The Lord will settle international disputes; all the nations will convert their weapons of war into implements of peace.   ISAIAH 2:4

OCTOBER 25

I saw a list of "Twelve Things to Remember" in a church bulletin years ago. They capture everything we need to have a happy, successful life. With only two months till Christmas, we may need to keep them in mind.

Here's the list and what I'm going to do to make them a part of my life.

1. *The value of time.* Stop watching so much TV.
2. *The success of perseverance.* Read the Bible every night.
3. *The pleasure of working.* Tell my children one good thing about my job every day.
4. *The dignity of simplicity.* Stop buying clothes and accessories. Wear what I have for three years.
5. *The worth of character.* Refuse to lie, cheat, steal, or tolerate those who do.
6. *The power of kindness.* Invite an elderly friend to dinner.
7. *The influence of example.* Be a careful, rule-abiding driver.
8. *The obligation of duty.* Never miss a chance to vote.
9. *The wisdom of economy.* Stop shopping, start saving.
10. *The virtue of practice.* Learn new computer functions daily.
11. *The improvement of talent.* Play the piano every day.
12. *The joy of originating.* Watercolor paint or bake with my kids.

Why not copy the twelve things and list ways you can accomplish them in your life?

Lord, help me to teach my children life's most important priorities by my own example.

Let me tell you how happy God has made me! For he has clothed me with garments of salvation and draped about me the robe of righteousness.

ISAIAH 61:10

Last May 9 we made up a new holiday, "Singlehood Day," and listed ten fun reasons to appreciate our singleness. I think it's a good idea to make up a new list of reasons every couple months of why it's nice to be single. Here are ten more reasons I thought of in just a few minutes:

1. There's nobody at home telling you what to do, how to do it, when to do it, or how much money you can spend doing it.

2. You can cook what you want (as long as the kids will eat it. And if you've trained them right, they'll eat anything as long as they don't have to cook it).

3. You can cook three times a week and eat leftovers the rest of the time.

4. You can tear whatever you want out of the newspaper, even if you're the first person to read it. (Kids usually only read the comics and the sports section, so it won't bother them if you read and rip to your heart's content.)

5. Your friends can drop into your home anytime without an invitation, and nobody's going to get mad.

6. You never have to wait for your spouse to get out of the bathroom so you can get ready.

7. You can clean house as much or as little as you want.

8. No one will keep reminding you that you've put on a few pounds since last year.

9. No one is going to throw a fit if you put a little dent in the car.

10. You can eat cookies in bed and listen to the radio at 3:00 A.M. if you want to.

Why, I feel better already, don't you? Why don't you sit down and list ten more? It'll help you appreciate your lifestyle as a single parent.

Lord, help me to appreciate the happy, joyful, fun aspects of being single.

If your eye is pure, there will be sunshine in your soul.
MATTHEW 6:22

OCTOBER 27

When my daughter Jeanne was sixteen, she wasn't anything like me when I was her age. Jeanne was flamboyantly silly one minute, intense and overly serious the next. I was more even-keeled at her age—more boring, actually.

As a high school sophomore Jeanne was confident that she would spend her life in the fine arts. I was thirty-five years old before I figured out what I wanted to do when I grew up.

In the middle of the semester of her sophomore year, Jeanne uprooted herself from her cozy suburban high school and enrolled in the Milwaukee High School of the Arts in the inner city so she could receive more intense training in visual art, theater art, music, and dance. I stayed with the same friends from grade school through high school at our comfortable, cozy, small-town Catholic schools. I'd never have been able to leave my friends and transfer to another school.

In high school Jeanne had the poise and maturity to play the piano and sing before groups, to try out for and win parts in one dramatic production after another. When I entered high school I quit piano lessons for fear I'd have to play in front of someone.

Over the years as I've watched this daughter blossom into an exceptionally talented fine artist who still plays the piano and even the accordion in front of others, I am amazed at how different we are. The wonderful thing is that we've both grown to love each other's differences and to cherish every moment we can spend together.

Lord, give me the good sense to step back and let my child create a life of her own, in her own time, in her own way.

The sun has one kind of glory while the moon and stars have another kind. And the stars differ from each other in their beauty and brightness.

1 CORINTHIANS 15:41

OCTOBER 28

During a trip to New York City I had to wait an hour at the airport, so I wrote out some postcards. When I tried to buy stamps from a machine it gladly accepted my fifty cents but did not produce any stamps. I shook the machine and kicked the base. I put in two more quarters. Nothing happened.

I finally found an address printed on the side of the machine, copied it down and when I got home wrote a terse complaint letter demanding that my dollar be returned. I tacked the company's address on the bulletin board over my computer and continued to seethe.

Every time I saw that address I got angrier. I hated being taken advantage of!

Six months later I still hadn't heard a word. A year later I was reorganizing my bulletin board. There was the address of that company. Every time I'd looked at it I'd felt cheated all over again.

I grabbed the paper, ripped it to shreds and threw it in the wastebasket. Poof! No more angry, resentful feelings.

Is something that you see everyday reminding you of something you'd rather forget? Get rid of the reminder! Remember, for every minute you are angry, you lose sixty seconds of happiness.

Lord, help me get rid of objects in my home that remind me of something unpleasant. Help me to write letters of appreciation, instead of complaint letters. When I do get on the bandwagon, help me to know when to leave well enough alone.

Don't let the sun go down with you still angry—get over it quickly; for when you are angry you give a mighty foothold to the devil. EPHESIANS 4:26-27

OCTOBER 29

Did you ever notice how quickly people express intense feelings they have for others when something horrible happens?

A high school boy takes a bad dive in the backyard pool, breaks two vertebrae in his neck and ends up a quadriplegic. By week's end the walls in his hospital room are covered with cards, letters, and messages of friendship, love, and support.

A favorite neighborhood lady, a grandma to all the kids for blocks around, suddenly dies in her sleep. Friends, neighbors and the media descend on "Grandma's" house to tell her adult children about all the people who loved her.

A young teacher is suddenly taken ill with a life-threatening disease. Children in every grade write letters, draw pictures, and tell stories about how special and beloved the woman is to each of them.

Why should we wait until something horrible happens to those we love? Why don't we write to them or tell them what's in our hearts right now?

You might start the letter or the conversation by saying, "I read about a boy who received 300 get-well cards when he was hurt in an accident. I decided I don't ever want to wait until something bad happens to tell you how I feel about you."

Lord, help me to say or write a "living, loving, legacy" to someone I cherish every day. And Lord, help me to include my children as recipients of my verbal or written devotion at least once a week.

Soon it will be too late! Of what use are your miracles when I am in the grave? How can I praise you then?
PSALMS 88:10

OCTOBER 30

When a deadly tornado sliced through the homes and businesses of all the residents of Barneveld, Wisconsin, population 579, something amazing happened a few weeks later. As the town tried to recover from the storm that killed nine people, injured eighty, and damaged or destroyed 90 percent of the homes and businesses in town, people in another Barneveld came to their rescue. The other Barneveld, in New York, population 497, held a Barneveld-Adopts-Barneveld Day to raise money for the Wisconsin community.

The New York Barneveld residents sold potatoes and corn, fresh from their fall harvest. Local artists raffled off paintings. A cross-country race was organized so the younger people in the community could get into the spirit. The day-long event raised $4,652. Every penny was sent to the residents of Barneveld, Wisconsin.

When I read about this story, I thought how important it is for single parents to bond together in times of stress and devastation. If you're a single parent because of a separation or divorce, you understand firsthand the pains other parents are experiencing as they go through a divorce.

Because we have a tie that binds, shouldn't we give of ourselves to ease the pain of fellow single parents? We can baby-sit a stressed-out single parent's children so she can have some time to herself. Or we could talk to our pastor about starting a singles group in our own church if there is none.

"Divided we fall, united we conquer" is true. Why don't you make one phone call today to another single parent and get something started?

Lord, give me the grace to begin to help conquer loneliness, fear, anxiety, or depression that's eating away at another single parent.

God is our refuge and strength, a tested help in times of trouble. PSALMS 46:1

OCTOBER 31

When I was a kid, my favorite holiday was Halloween. It wasn't just the promise of all that candy, either. It was the fact that my dad made it such fun. He'd plan crazy parties for my friends and me. After blindfolding us and then placing our hands into a bowl of cold wet spaghetti, he'd say, "I dug these worms fresh this morning right out of the garden." Or he'd hide in the cemetery across the street when we were trick or treating and make ghost noises when we walked by. The thrill of being scared by my dad was as wonderful as seeing a spooky movie snuggled up next to grandma. It was giggly, safe scariness.

These days so many Christians are up in arms about Halloween. They don't like the witches, goblins, and ghosts dancing around in their children's heads.

But Halloween is one of the most delightful holidays we have. It gives all of us, young and old alike, a chance to dress up in costume and step into another role or personality. We can become anyone or anything we choose for the day, giggling and shrieking all the way.

To all those protesters who keep their children from enjoying the festivities, I say: lighten up and let your children be creative, have the fun of being amazed, entertained, even scared in a safe environment. And if you really need a good rebuttal for the protesters, perhaps they need to know that the word "Halloween" means "Hallowed Eve," the eve of All Saints' Day on November 1. One custom that developed over the years on the "Hallowed Eve" of All Saints' Day was to dress up as evil spirits to fool the real evil spirits so the bad guys would leave the good guys alone. The good spirits would also trick the bad ones into giving them treats. Hence, "trick or treat."

Lord, thank you for the chance to step out of myself, to be silly, and to have fun with my children, their friends, and my friends on Halloween.

I am talking to you because you have won your battle with Satan.   1 JOHN 3:13

A Prayer for November

Did you make a mistake, God,
When you created November?
The glorious October
Leaves are gone.
The August harvest
Is but a tasty memory,
November's icy winds
And sunless sky depress me.

Did you make a mistake, God?
Or haven't I learned
To appreciate your genius?
Perhaps November is
A time for being indoors.
Relighting the fireplace.
Planning holiday parties.
Doing my spring housecleaning.
Reading to the children.
Perhaps November is
The perfect time
For saying "Thanks"
For all those other marvelous months
And for all the blessings
You've bestowed on us, heavenly Father.

NOVEMBER 1

Since the year 835 A.D., the Roman Catholic church has observed November 1st as All Saints' Day, a day to honor all the saintly people who have gone before us, especially those who have no special feast day.

I believe there are many saints among us today, blessed, holy people who think more of others than do they of themselves. People who look for the good in all that they see and do. People who truly practice the Golden Rule: "do unto others as you would have them do unto you." Here are some of the saintly people in my life.

Sharon ... who has never spoken ill of another person and whose quiet kindness and thoughtfulness stretches far beyond her own friends and family.

Gail ... a nurse who self-studied holistic medicine, helps many, even strangers, learn to treat themselves naturally, without drugs, and she does it without monetary reward.

Sister Guiseppa ... who taught full-time for over sixty years, well into her eighties. The thousands of children whose lives she touched do, indeed, call her blessed.

Katie ... who struggles with her own poverty, yet finds the resources to run the "Rainbow Dream House," a center for children with AIDS.

Linda and David ... happily married Bible scholars whose inner glow and happiness rubs off on every guest who enters their home and every young couple who takes their premarriage classes.

Today why don't you make a list of the blessed people you know? Perhaps a friendly phone call to tell them what an impact they have on your life would cheer them on.

Lord, bless, protect, and encourage your holy people, your saints. Help me to be more like them.

He has made his people strong, honoring his godly ones—the people of Israel, the people closest to him.
PSALMS 148:14

NOVEMBER 2

The first week in November is a hubbub of election activity. On Election Day, whether it comes on the first of November or the tenth, "we, the people" are able to decide how our government will run.

Though I'm not a very political person publicly, I do try to read up about the issues. I talk about them at home and discuss them with friends whose opinions I value. Then I make my decision. And I always vote.

When my youngest child, Andrew, was in grade and middle school, I'd take him with me to the polls. (My other three were all over eighteen, in college, and voting on their own.) Those days Andrew would go right into the voting booth with me, pull the red lever to close the curtain and then watch intently to see whom I was going to help put in office. The next day he'd be as anxious as I was to see which of "our" candidates had won.

Our children can only learn how democracy works from us. So it's important that we teach them about freedom of choice and the democratic process not only by what we say, but also by what we do. This election week, talk about the issues and candidates with your children. Take them with you when you vote. And make sure you do get out and vote!

Heavenly Father, bless the voters and the candidates. Help us all to make intelligent choices. And bless the children of this country. Help us to let them experience firsthand the importance of voting in a country where freedom is truly put into action on Election Day.

You must think constantly about these commandments ... teach them to your children and talk about them....   DEUTERONOMY 6:6-7

NOVEMBER 3

Sometimes I step outside during November, look at the lifeless barren trees, feel the knife-in-the-back cold wind, and wince sadly. November is a pretty dreary month in Wisconsin. That's why I've learned to keep my mind on a few good projects during November. Here are a few of my favorite:

- Lose eight to ten pounds. We all know losing weight is simple if you reduce fat and calorie consumption ... and exercise every day. A brisk thirty-minute walk every day may change your attitude about a lot of things. Exercise *always* makes both your body *and* your mind feel better.

- Plan shopping trips with each of your children, one-on-one. Make it a whole-day adventure, including lunch out and maybe even a movie. The kids will never forget their day alone with Mom, and you'll get all your Christmas shopping done before December.

- Take the children and drive to a distant relative's or friend's house for the weekend. An inexpensive mini-vacation is just what the doctor ordered.

- Pick one closet or section of the basement, garage, attic, or family room each weekend this month and *clean it!*

- Write one letter to a distant friend or relative every Sunday night. Get the kids to join you and stick their notes in your envelope. Before long, the mailman is bringing *you* letters! And suddenly, there's a *lot* to smile about in November.

Lord, help me to lighten up our lives this month with family projects. And don't let me give up on them until the job is complete.

For though once your heart was full of darkness, now it is full of light from the Lord and your behavior should show it!   EPHESIANS 5:8

NOVEMBER 4

A woman who filed for divorce from her husband spent almost three years battling with him in court over division of property and child custody. She spent that time trying to convince their daughter what a terrible, evil person her father is. The thing is, he's a good father who truly loves his daughter and has demonstrated that he has her best interests at heart. After many court-ordered counseling sessions, he was awarded physical custody of the child. The mother was given visitation rights. Still she persisted in bad-mouthing her daughter's father. Each time the young girl returned from visiting her mother it would take the dad a couple of days of teeth-gritting patience and love to get her to stop being rude, mean, and disrespectful.

Divorced parents, don't make your children victims of your failed marriage. Instead, give them the gift of knowing that *both* of their parents love them.

Concentrate only on what kind of parent *you* are, and learn how to be the best one-parent family you can be.

Lord, help me to accept my share of the blame for my failed marriage, then give me the wisdom to bury the pains of yesterday, create the joy of today, and to plan for the excitement of tomorrow. Help me to think and act kindly toward my child's "other" parent.

Do you want a long, good life? Then watch your tongue! Keep your lips from lying. Turn from all known sin and spend your time in doing good. Try to live in peace with everyone; work hard at it.

PSALMS 34:12-14

NOVEMBER 5

The scene: 5:30 P.M. on a night in November. The odor of one of my "which leftover is it this time" casseroles wafts through the kitchen and into the living room, drawing the entire family into a flurry of pre-meal activity ... all within twenty feet of me.

I'm fixing a salad. Jeanne is practicing the piano just a few feet away. She's now on page two of "Für Elise" for the eighth time. Julia is setting the table at breakneck speed, listening to her favorite station on a small portable radio strapped to her waist. ("It helps drown out the noise from the piano, Mom.")

Michael answers the phone for the third time in ten minutes, relays the message, and goes on with his riddle onslaught. (Will the person who gave ten-year-old boys the right to read riddle books please stand up?)

Andrew knocks over his tower of blocks that he has stacked up chimney-high in the middle of the kitchen. ("It's the only place that isn't carpeted, Mom.") Then he starts beating through my end-of-the-day headache on his new drum, and hollers in his loudest three-year-old voice, "I'm hungry! I want a drink. Can I have an apple?"

I flip on the garbage disposal, which at that moment seems a sensible addition to the cacophony at hand. Somewhere in my head I hear a little voice saying "Why me, Lord?"

Then I remember. In one hour, Jeanne will be baby-sitting at the neighbor's. Julia and Michael will be in their rooms doing homework. Andrew will be engrossed in puzzles or Play Doh. And me? In my favorite rocker reading the newspaper, finishing the novel I started months ago or watching TV. So for now, at least, I go with the flow.

Heavenly Father, help me to step outside the circle of pandemonium and see my 5:30 kitchen for what it really is: a place for my family to huddle back together after a busy day apart.

I am in deep trouble. Rush to my aid, for only you can help and save me. O Lord, don't delay.

PSALMS 70:5

NOVEMBER 6

Do you ever get the blues during the holidays? Over the years as the children grew and each holiday season seemed to be a little different, I adopted the six-part-plan for holiday happiness. Since all six became part of my life, I haven't had a bad Thanksgiving, Christmas, or New Year's.

1. *Be thankful.* Instead of concentrating on what you don't have or what you can't afford to buy your kids, concentrate instead on what you do have.

2. *Live in the moment.* Don't set yourself up for depression. Be flexible. If plans don't go off as you expected, don't worry about it. Just enjoy each moment as it happens.

3. *Start a new tradition.* Instead of trying to recapture all the Christmases past and the two-parent-family traditions that went with them, do things differently. Be creative!

4. *Do something for someone else during the holidays.* It's a known fact that if you spend your time trying to make someone else happy, your own happiness will just naturally follow.

5. *Stop self-induced physical abuse.* Nothing causes depression to attack faster than a holiday diet laden with sugar, fat, and alcohol. Take a fast walk every morning during the holiday season. Laugh a lot to stimulate those good-for-you endorphins.

6. *Be more childlike.* It's OK to make a mess when you bake cookies. It's OK to lie in the snow and make snow angels. Be silly … carefree … spontaneous. Before you know it, you will have discovered the childlike wonder of this glorious time of year.

Dear Lord, be with me every day during this hustle-bustle holiday season. Help me to keep it simple and to keep my expectations in line with my ability to make these holidays special.

I am very sad and I was pouring out my heart to the Lord.   1 SAMUEL 1:15

NOVEMBER 7

For eight years after my mom died, my dad, who retired from his job when she became ill, kept busy puttering in his barn, traveling with Bev, my wonderful step-mom, and doing basic repairs and improvements on his house. He also took a lot of naps, especially in the winter.

The winter before his sixty-ninth birthday, he and his old friend Fritz decided to clear away the trees and brush along the Hennepin Canal, just a few blocks from Dad's home in Rock Falls, Illinois.

Every winter morning, as long as the ice on the canal was thick enough to stand on, Dad and Fritz bundled up and, with their gas-powered chainsaws, blasted away the unsightly tangled overgrowth on the slope next to the water. By springtime they'd cleared a mile stretch, six to eight feet wide. The next winter they did 1.2 miles, completing the project.

The Rock River Development Authority, impressed with the new look, widened and resurfaced the old tow path along the canal for bikers, walkers, and joggers ... and in July organized raft and canoe races. Next, the Department of Conservation did some landscaping and even added park benches and a concrete handicapped ramp to the tow path.

Because of the initiative of two retirees, a beautiful new state parkway was created for the whole town to enjoy.

Is there a project that might improve your town that you and your children could do together? Cleaning up debris along a river or creek? Painting old park benches? Raking leaves for an elderly neighbor? All it takes is one person to get the project started. Could it be you?

Lord, get me started; keep me busy; and thanks for helping me teach my children about the joy that comes from doing for others.

Even in old age they will still produce fruit and be
vital and green.   PSALMS 92:14

Years ago in Ann Landers' column I read a letter from a woman who had been wandering around an art exhibit amidst hundreds of strangers. Suddenly a young woman approached her and said, "You are a beautiful lady." The older woman was thunderstruck, saying in her letter, "I am eighty-eight years old and never considered myself anything special to look at. But I'm healthy and happy and grateful to the good Lord for all His blessings. Maybe this is what comes through in my face. What a delight to be told that I am beautiful by a stranger. Every day this week I have been cheered by that lovely compliment."

After I read that, I asked myself, "Why shouldn't we compliment strangers?" I often see someone in a crowd who is inspiring … an older man with a wonderful smile, or a harried young mother who treats her children with respect in a difficult situation in a department store. But to compliment a stranger out loud? I didn't know if I could do it.

A few weeks later when I was at the beauty shop, I took a deep breath and said to the woman next to me, "You have such beautiful hair. That style looks great on you."

The woman beamed. We started talking and before long discovered we were practically neighbors and knew some people in common. Now, whenever I see her around town we smile and exchange greetings. We're no longer strangers.

Lord, give me the courage to brighten someone's day by giving them a compliment. When I feel shy, remind me that you have no voice but mine.

Love each other with brotherly affection and take delight in honoring each other. ROMANS 12:10

NOVEMBER 9

One day when I was taking my morning walk, I noticed a sheep in someone's yard. I thought it was real, but upon closer inspection I saw that it was only a piece of plywood cut out in the shape of a sheep with a face painted on it and real sheep wool attached to the wood.

As I continued, I noticed a two-dimensional wooden girl in a swing in the next block. Before I got home, I saw flat cut-outs of birds, painted red and blue and placed in the trees of a house on the corner.

When I got home I saw my teenage son totally engrossed in the two-dimensional images of his computer. Later that night I sat staring at the TV set, being entertained by flat two-dimensional images.

Are we becoming a nation of zombielike creatures who are entertained, informed and educated by flat, single-sided images? Are we becoming *watchers* instead of *doers*?

We don't have to let that happen. Instead of flat, fake pets we can make sure our children grow up with *real* pets. Instead of *watching* life whiz by on TV, we can make sure our children have lots of opportunity for outdoor adventures and travel. Instead of being *captured* by the computer, we can limit the time we spend in front of the computer screen and encourage our children to live life in 3-D instead.

Lord, help me to guide my children away from the machines and into the great outdoors where real animals live and real adventures are waiting just around the corner.

I am expecting the Lord to rescue me again, so that once again I will see his goodness to me here in the land of the living. PSALMS 27:13

When my son Andrew was in eighth grade, he suddenly came out of the funk that had weighed him down after the death of his father four years earlier. During those years he'd been wonderful at home but had "acted out" at school, and his grades were poor. But that first quarter in eighth grade Andrew made the honor roll! I was thrilled, but Andrew was despondent.

"Mom, the kids all think I'm a nerd now that I'm making good grades. They liked me better when I was goofing off all the time. It's not worth it!"

I talked, pleaded, praised, and coaxed my son, but it was as if he couldn't hear me. So I made copies of Andrew's report card and a letter explaining the situation and sent them to Andrew's big brother in college, to his grandfather in Illinois, to my uncle Jim in Omaha, and to my brother in Louisville. I called in the troops.

Every one of them called or wrote letters of encouragement to Andrew, and gradually I noticed that he stopped talking about hating school. His good grades continued.

As single parents there's no way we can do the job all by ourselves. These days I'm still "calling in the troops," including some of my friends' husbands, to help raise this fatherless young man. And it's working! Just ask anyone who knows Andrew.

Lord, don't let me think for a minute that I can do this parenting thing alone. Give me courage to ask for help. Thank you, Lord, for the dedicated people who can take some of the credit for the raising of my son.

But anyone who won't care for his own relatives when they need help, especially those living in his own family, has no right to say he is a Christian. Such a person is worse than the heathen.   1 TIMOTHY 5:8

NOVEMBER 11

Today, November 11, is Veteran's Day. I've always been intrigued with the ways people face fear. I can't imagine what it must have felt like for my Dad, a World War II fighter pilot in the South Pacific, flying mile after mile over the ocean, trying not to think about the enemy aircraft that could attack at any minute.

Another time I was impressed with the way people faced fear was when my daughter Julia and her husband rode their bikes over a long spillway to get to a small island near their home in La Crosse, Wisconsin. Julia said the cement spillway was only about five feet wide. The lake was flush with the top of the cement on one side and there was a two-foot vertical drop on the other side. The water on the concrete embankment where they had to ride was two to three inches deep, and since it was early March, patches of ice along the route made it especially dangerous.

"Weren't you scared?" I asked.

"Terrified," Julia answers. "But I kept my eyes in front of me and kept on pedaling. I knew if I lost my concentration I could slip and fall into that icy lake, so I just kept pedaling, eyes forward, one push after another."

Whether we're facing an enemy in war, an icy-cold wet disaster just feet away from our bike tires, or struggling to make it through the next paycheck with four kids underfoot, if we just have faith in the hand of Jesus to guide us, we'll make it across safely.

Lord, help my faith to grow so that I can reach out to you and find comfort no matter how dangerous the waters are.

Peter went over the side of the boat and walked on the water toward Jesus. But when he looked around at the high waves, he was terrified and began to sink. "Save me, Lord!" he shouted. Instantly Jesus reached out his hand and rescued him. "O man of little faith," Jesus said. "Why did you doubt me?"

MATTHEW 14:29-31

At a conference for single people, a psychotherapist told of a study that asked a large number of people who earned $20,000 if that was enough money. Eighty percent said "No." Then they asked people who earned $40,000 if that was enough money. Again, eighty percent said, "No." Those who earned $60,000 a year were asked the same question. Same response. Eighty percent said, "No, it wasn't enough." And so it went. No matter *how much* money people earned, at least eighty percent said it wasn't enough.

The instructor asked us, "How much money *is* enough, do you think?"

I shot up my hand. "I think the answer is $10,000 a year." I'd just sent in my income tax form for the previous year in which my adjusted gross income was $8,673. Of course my house was paid for, and that income didn't include the Social Security I'd received for my son, but nonetheless, my earned income was below poverty level, and I was blissfully happy. Still am.

It's a solid-gold fact: Money does *not* bring happiness. Usually the opposite is true. Money brings greed and the need for more money, a bigger lifestyle, fancy cars, houses, clothes, and with that comes stress.

I'm still in the poverty-level range incomewise, but I count my riches in glistening friendships, happy relationships, and the freedom to spend my life exactly the way I want. If a long walk in the morning with a friend is part of my days I don't feel guilty that I'm not at my computer. I treasure those moments because they're more valuable than cash in the bank. Life is for living, not for earning money.

Lord, thank you for my riches ... family, friends, faith, enough food, clothing, and shelter to survive and especially for the good health with which to enjoy it all.

It is easier for a camel to go through the eye of a needle than for a rich man to enter the Kingdom of God. MARK 10:25

NOVEMBER 13

Even though my father worked as a rural mail carrier for over thirty years, most of his ancestors were farmers. When Dad was seventy-six years old he began to research his family tree. With help from the Mormon library in Salt Lake City he learned that his great-grandparents, Bernard and Maria Kobbemann, who were born in the mid 1700s, owned a farm in Ottmarsbocholt, Germany. They had nine children, the youngest of whom was my dad's grandfather.

A few months later, while visiting Germany, my brother Joe visited the tiny village. The parish priest told him exactly where the Kobbemann farm was located. Joe drove out and was delighted to see a beautiful, modern farm with neat buildings, a nice home and a couple in their seventies who greeted Joe and invited him inside. With their mix of broken English and German, Joe was able to learn that the farm had been in the Kobbemann name since the 1400s!

Dad and Joe's discovery about our family heritage gives me roots that are deep and strong, and a sense of pride that I am a part of a large family that is still working the land in our home country.

It's been said that giving our children roots and wings are the two most important things we can do for them. Today, why don't you do research to help your child learn more about his or her roots?

Don't forget, your children have *two* parents, two sets of grandparents, great-grandparents, and so on. Be sure to include *both* sides in your research.

Lord, bless my family ... then, now, and those who will live in the future.

For their sakes I will remember my promises to their ancestors, to be their God.   Leviticus 26:45

NOVEMBER 14

The words appeared in our church bulletin:

Hugs are not only nice, they're needed. Hugs relieve pain and depression. They make the healthy healthier and the happy happier, and the most secure among us even more so. Hugging feels good ... overcomes fears ... eases tension ... provides stretching exercises if you're short, provides stooping exercises if you're tall. Hugging also does not upset the environment ... saves heat ... is portable ... requires no special equipment ... makes days happier and makes impossible days possible.

I taped that to the wall of my desk at the radio station. Tony, a big bear of a young man, read it and said, "Yeah! Hugs *are* great therapy. They take away the blues and make you feel good from the inside out." Then he smiled, put his arms out, and gave me a big bear hug. Next he hugged Debbie, across the aisle.

After that, whenever anyone seemed down in the dumps, Tony was always there with a soothing, bigger-than-life bear hug.

What about you? Do you give and receive enough hugs with people outside your home? Of course some people aren't receptive to public hugging. If you open up your arms and the person doesn't step forward to receive the hug and extend one to you, just drop your left arm and shake that person's hand instead. But if he or she hugs you back, you've set a wonderful precedent.

Why not start some hug therapy today?

Lord, help me to reach out to others, embrace them with open arms, and squeeze them with love.

Greet one another with a holy kiss.

1 CORINTHIANS 13:12

NOVEMBER 15

When Andrew was sixteen, he experienced the tragic traffic accident death of one of his classmates. According to the two passengers, the sixteen-year-old driver was listening to loud music, laughing, and looking at his friend in the front passenger seat when the accident occurred. None of the boys were wearing seat belts.

Andrew and all his classmates were forced to realize that life is a gift that can be taken away at any moment. They were also forced to accept the fact that inexperienced teenage drivers who think they're going to live forever, may not.

As a single parent who believes in tough love, I didn't allow my children to buy or own a car while they were in school and living at home. I tried to make sure my kids were never "cruising" in their friends' cars. They were taught that riding in cars was for one purpose only ... to get from one place to another, preferably from home to a school-sponsored event. And seat belts? I was fanatical about them.

Tough love isn't easy, especially when teens answer back, "Everybody else does it, why can't I?" Tough love means when you say no, you mean no. But sometimes even tough love isn't enough. Sometimes you still have to go to the funeral of a sixteen-year-old who never gave a serious thought to the possibility that he might die before the end of his sophomore year.

Lord, for the gift of life you've given me today, thank you. Help me to be a responsible parent who isn't afraid to say no to my children.

For you have saved me from death and my feet from slipping, so that I can walk before the Lord in the land of the living. PSALM 56:13

NOVEMBER 16

One day at my job as copywriter for a radio station in Milwaukee, I was asked to write an ad for the Freedom From Smoking Center. Some of the copy information included a list of things every smoker gets absolutely free with every pack of cigarettes: "dirty ashtrays, sore throats, smelly fingers, possible heart attack, chronic headaches, tobacco in your pockets, raspy voice, high blood pressure, yellowed windows, chest pain, stained teeth, coughs, holes in your clothing, bad breath, emphysema, burning eyes, fatigue, shortness of breath, gum disease, bronchitis, and lung cancer."

What a devastating list! Although I'm not a smoker, my smoking friends, acquaintances, and co-workers have to fight those things. Sometimes I run into people who want to smoke in my home. I say no. I've also had a number of men who smoke ask me out on a date. I've always said, "No, thanks." I won't date a smoker because I know that putting up with the above side-effects is more than I could stand. I choose to be healthy, and sidestream smoke is not a part of that equation for me.

This month, as our country once again promotes the Great American Smokeout, let's pray that all smokers will have the courage, determination, and persistence to stop practicing slow motion suicide.

Lord, help me encourage people who are trying to give up smoking. I also need your help, Lord, to be kinder and more understanding of those so addicted to nicotine that they blow smoke in my face.

He gives power to the tired and worn out, and strength to the weak. ISAIAH 40:29

NOVEMBER 17

Larry the Legend, a flamboyant radio announcer who worked in Milwaukee during the seventies and eighties, would invite his listeners to call in and "speak their onions ... tell it like it is."

Larry and his radio listeners heard tragic personal stories: an old woman robbed for the fifth time in a year; a young widow with three small children who lost her paycheck; or a fire or crime victim who could barely face another day.

Periodically Larry started a radio Love Fund so his listeners could help those people.

I started my own Love Fund. I simply put a large cardboard box in a closet where I put usable clothing, toys, bedding, housewares, and canned goods. Whenever I found a Bible at the local Goodwill store or at a neighborhood rummage sale, I'd stick that in the box as well.

My children even got into the act, adding to the "stuff to give away" from their own collection of outgrown clothing or underage toys. They always felt better about having to clean out their closets or desks when they knew another boy or girl might enjoy some of their things.

Whenever we heard of another family who had suffered a tragedy, we'd pack up suitable items from the box and donate it to an agency that would direct the package to the proper place.

Today, why don't you start a Love Fund box in your family?

Lord, help us turn our good thoughts into action.

> And I the King will tell them, "When you did it to these my brothers you were doing it to me!"
> MATTHEW 25:40

I've lived in the Midwest most of my life and have learned to enjoy the four distinct seasons. Summer is as hot and sweaty as winter is cold and snowy. Spring's balmy days are as welcome as the magnificent colors of autumn's falling leaves.

November's weather is often a mystery. One minute it's fifty degrees and blowing like a spring storm. The next minute it's twenty degrees with snow flurries in the forecast.

But what I miss most in November is the sun. It's as if all these gray November days are telling us, "Beware, old man winter is going to get you, and this is just the preview!"

If only I could appreciate November more. If only I could stop missing the sun so much, stop dreaming about the great bike rides and walks along the lake last summer. If only I could erase this overwhelming feeling that all the big holidays are imminent, and that my house is a mess, and that I'm going to have a ton of houseguests.

Life is not about "if only's." I'm going to enjoy life a lot more if I concentrate on the positives instead of the gloomies. Tonight I'll build a fire in the wood burner, pop some popcorn, and make a list of things to do in the coming months. I *will* get through November, no matter what!

Lord, thank you for letting me get more sleep at night and more accomplished during the day. Now, at last, I can get my spring house-cleaning done. Now I can figure out new ways to make the coming holidays more meaningful for my loved ones. Yes, Lord, thank you for November.

I know you well—you are neither hot nor cold; I wish you were one or the other! But since you are merely lukewarm, I will spit you out of my mouth!

REVELATION 3:15

NOVEMBER 19

Every November I lapsed into a sort of depressed state of mind. No energy, no ambition. I often had to prod myself to do even the simplest chores ... and then only after I promised myself a nap afterwards. By January I'd have gained ten pounds from nibbling out of boredom.

Then I read about "seasonal affective disorder" or SAD ... a form of depression resulting from a decrease in light during the fall and winter. Those affected by SAD slow down, oversleep, feel fatigued, crave carbohydrates, overeat, experience difficulties with work and relationships, and become pessimistic. That was me, all right.

Scientifically, a hormone in the brain, called "melatonin," controls mood. Darkness produces more melatonin, causing depression, and light decreases it. Some people drastically affected by seasonal affective disorder move to the south, where there is more light during the winter months. Sitting under artificial light also helps certain people.

Now, every time those gray drizzly November days give me a case of SAD, I say to myself, "look for the light, look for the light." I make sure there are plenty of lights on in every room where I'm working. I take walks whenever the sun is shining. On particularly gloomy days I light a fire in the wood burner, turn on the bright fluorescent lights in the family room (plus a lamp near my chair), curl up with the book of Psalms, and fill my soul with the light of God. You'd be surprised what twenty minutes of that therapy can do!

Heavenly Father, when the skies are gloomy help me to remember this prayer: "The Light of God surrounds me. The Love of God enfolds me. The Power of God protects me. The Presence of God watches over me. Wherever I am God is!"

But while I am still here in the world, I give it my light.   JOHN 9:5

Marybeth, a member of our church, had spent the days before Thanksgiving filling and distributing food baskets for the poor and unemployed in our town. Late Wednesday afternoon, the day before Thanksgiving, she went home, exhausted, to prepare her own family's Thanksgiving meal.

She was elbow-deep in salads and turkey dressing for her big family when the phone rang. A man pleaded. "My brother is out of work. He and his wife and three kids don't have anything for Thanksgiving. I'd help, but I don't have enough for my own family. Is there any way you could get them a basket of food?"

There wasn't any food left, but the words, "Meet me at the Human Concerns building in one hour," tumbled out of Marybeth's mouth before she could stop them.

Two minutes after she hung up the phone it rang again. It was Fr. Bill, our parish priest. "Marybeth, someone just donated an entire Thanksgiving dinner: turkey, vegetables, salads, beverage, desserts, everything from soup to nuts, and it's sitting here in the hall at the rectory. Do you know anybody who needs a whole dinner?"

Bless us all, oh Lord we pray ... the needy, the givers, the workers ... each day!

Ask and you will be given what you ask for. Seek and you will find. Knock and the door will be opened.

MATTHEW 7:7

I believe that true happiness comes from three sources: our relationships with those we love; whether or not our career is directly related to our God-given talents; and how much stress-free time we have to enjoy life.

One of my favorite examples of someone who understands true happiness comes from a woman I've never met. I heard about her during a class I took at a singles' convention. This single woman was a powerful advertising executive. She earned $85,000 a year and lived the so-called good life. Fancy apartment on Michigan Avenue in Chicago, big car, expensive wardrobe, power lunches, and hectic social life.

But the woman was not happy. The more money she earned, the more her bosses made her feel compelled to earn more. The stress made her depressed. The harder she worked, the less time she had to be outdoors with her dogs, something that made her truly happy. So, after much soul-searching, she decided to give up her career and become a professional dog walker. Every day she walks dozens of dogs for people too busy to do it themselves. She walks with energy, smiling at everyone she sees. The woman is happy, free, and doing what she truly loves. Instead of wearing expensive business suits and carrying a briefcase, she wears jeans and holds dogs on leashes as she saunters down Michigan Avenue enjoying the great outdoors.

Lord, remind me that money does not bring happiness. Help me to adjust my life and my "wants" so that I have more time with my children and loved ones. Also, help me find work that uses the talents you gave me.

The man who knows right from wrong and has good judgment and common sense is happier than the man who is immensely rich! For such wisdom is far more valuable than precious jewels. Nothing else compares with it. Wisdom gives a long, good life, riches, honor, pleasure, peace.   PROVERBS 3:13-17

NOVEMBER 22

I love to browse in libraries and bookstores. Depending on my mood I can choose adventure, history, self-improvement, travel, health, romance, or mystery books and read to my heart's content.

Have you ever wondered why they call the Bible "the Good Book"? I think it's because it *is* a good book ... interesting, entertaining, and filled with adventure, history, self-improvement, travel, health, romance, and mystery.

Thanksgiving week is National Bible Week ... a good time to find those seven special-interest categories in the Bible and to read the "good book" each day from a different perspective.

Sunday—Adventure: The book of Tobit tells the adventures of Tobit and his family, and the angel sent by God to solve their problems. Or read Jonah. What could be more adventurous than being swallowed up by a whale?

Monday—History: The Bible is packed with family history. Read First and Second Samuel, First and Second Kings, First and Second Chronicles, First and Second Maccabees, Ezra, Nehemiah, Joshua, and Judges.

Tuesday—Self-improvement: Read Proverbs and you'll be completely "new and improved."

Wednesday—Travel: Try the Acts of the Apostles ... and make sure you have an atlas handy.

Thursday—Health: Read Proverbs such as 17:22, 22:4, and 25:20. For advice on drinking read Jeremiah 35. For some great exercise tips read 1 Timothy 4:7-10.

Friday—Romance: The Song of Solomon is very romantic. And the book of Ruth begins with sadness and ends with romance.

Saturday—Mystery: Read Revelation and try "decoding" the meanings of the numbers and colors.

Father, help me to begin today to enjoy the Good Book in all its many different ways and to share what I learn with my children.

In the beginning ...   GENESIS 1:1, KJV

On the day of the funeral of assassinated Jewish Prime Minister Yitzhak Rabin in 1995, the daughter of Egypt's Anwar Sadat, whose father had also been assassinated a few years before, talked about the deaths of both leaders and the long quest for peace in the Mideast. She said, "We must remember that a clock will never reverse. It may slow down and stop, but it will never reverse. It will only go forward."

I think she was trying to tell the world that neither Israel nor the Arab countries can relive those awful years of fighting. They should forget the bitter past and look for peace.

The woman's words struck me as being very powerful for someone who is involved in the breakup of a marriage. Sometimes there are huge battles and daily fights. The pain can continue for years. But no matter how hard we try, we can't get the clock to reverse itself or to stop. We can never have those days of fighting back again. They are lost forever, wasted.

We need to take those days, hours, and minutes and move forward, just like the ticking clock. We need to divide the property as fairly as possible, treat each other with as much dignity as possible, solve family problems, and get counseling if necessary. In short, life is simply too precious to waste fighting.

Lord, set me on a forward-moving path toward peace and harmony with everyone who is a part of my life. Help me to live this moment as if it were my only.

But don't forget this, dear friends, that a day or a thousand years from now is like tomorrow to the Lord. 2 PETER 3:8

They're here ... Thanksgiving, St. Nicholas Day, Christmas, Hannukah, New Year's. And along with the holidays come parties, presents, pandemonium, pressure, and pounds, right? The worry season.

Are you worried that all your children think about, from the moment the Christmas catalogs arrive in September, is what *they* want for Christmas? So *change* things. Call the director of a nursing home and ask for a list of the names and room numbers of the residents. Buy a big box of Christmas cards and let the children write notes on each. Just before Christmas, take the whole family and deliver the cards in person.

Worried about surviving the cookies, candy, hot toddies, and six-course dinners that the season brings without adding a spare tire to your middle? Center your entertaining on events. Organize a Christmas caroling party in the name of your favorite charity. Or pay a farmer to take you and your friends on a moonlight hayride on star-filled country roads.

The holidays don't have to be filled with dreary old family traditions. Start some new ones. Single parents have it made this time of year. We can do anything we want. Talk to the kids. See what they expect from the holidays, then add some of your own ideas. Most of all, *enjoy* the season!

Lord, keep me from growing weary during the next few weeks by keeping a joyful, creative spirit within my heart.

So don't let anyone criticize you for what you eat or drink, or for not celebrating Jewish holidays and feasts or new moon ceremonies or Sabbaths. For these were only temporary rules that ended when Christ came. They were only shadows of the real thing—of Christ himself. COLOSSIANS 2:16-17

NOVEMBER 25

Does your family bond together in mirth and merriment as you gather to celebrate Thanksgiving? Or are you all in the family room watching TV before the day is over?

This year, I'm going to tell my family how Christmas Day was celebrated during the reign of King Henry VIII. Christmas was the only day each year he allowed his subjects to play games. Snap Dragon was a favorite. Brandy was poured on a dish of dried fruits then set on fire. The object was to snatch a piece of fruit without burning your fingers. If the fruit was too hot, the players shouted "Snap Dragon!" The dragon, of course, was the fire ... vicious and dangerous.

Other games included Hunt the Slipper, Hoop and Hide (an early version of our Hide and Seek), and Blindman's Bluff. The last holiday game was Yawning for a Cheshire Cheese. Toward midnight everyone sat in a circle. Whoever yawned the widest, longest, loudest, and produced the greatest number of yawns from the other players, was given a Cheshire cheese.

This holiday season, as I gather friends and family, I'm "turning off" the TV, videos, and computer games. Instead, we'll be "turning on" to family games and "live" activities, like board games and charades. Who knows, we may even end the day with a yawning contest!

Jesus, instead of watching life happen on a screen, help me to encourage my family to be active participants. Help us to be with each other in activity and conversation, not just next to each other in front of a screen.

For people will come from all over the world to take their places there.   LUKE 13:29

The week before Advent, I asked nine-year-old Andrew to set up the manger scene on the chest in the entry way of our home. He carefully unwrapped the delicate, hand-painted animals, shepherds, wisemen, Mary, Joseph, and Baby Jesus and placed them in the wooden manger. The next day I noticed Baby Jesus was missing. *Andrew's playing a joke on me,* I thought.

When I started fixing supper, I opened the breadbox on the kitchen counter and there was Baby Jesus next to the bread! I laughed and asked Andrew why he'd hidden Baby Jesus in the breadbox. His explanation was simple. "In religion class, Mrs. Hatzenbeller said Jesus is the Bread of Life, Mom. Besides, he shouldn't be in the manger until Christmas."

Ever since Andrew put Jesus in the breadbox, it has become a family tradition. Now, from the first day of Advent until Christmas Eve, Jesus sits on top of or in the breadbox to remind us that he is the Bread of Life. Each time I reach for the bread I'm reminded to say a quick prayer of thanksgiving for our daily blessings, including our daily bread. On Christmas Eve, Andrew ceremoniously places the baby in the manger between Mary and Joseph.

After Epiphany, on January 6, we put the manger away for the year. All except for Baby Jesus; he goes back in the breadbox as a daily reminder that just like our daily bread, the spirit of Christmas is an everyday, yearlong event.

Father, as we prepare our homes for the birth of your son, help us create family traditions that will remind us each day to carry the spirit of Jesus Christ to all our loved ones throughout the season ... and the year.

No matter how many of us there are, we all eat from the same loaf, showing that we are all parts of the one body of Christ.   1 CORINTHIANS 10:17

Have you ever made an Advent wreath for your family? It's easy. Our Advent wreath begins with a large, flat woven basket my mother and father bought in the Caribbean as a special remembrance of their twenty-fifth anniversary trip.

Next, I place large pinecones into the basket, pinecones I scooped up from our front yard when we lived at the foot of the Rocky Mountains years ago. Then the candles: three purple, one pink. The pink one, the symbol of hope, is for the third week of Advent ... the halfway point between the darker, more somber violet candles of preparation and the white candle of Christmas joy.

Finally, I add a few sprigs of holly and four silk poinsettia flowers given to me years ago by my godmother, Aunt Bernadine. At last, the Advent wreath, created with memories and love, is ready. Each night before we eat, the children take turns lighting one candle before supper the first week, two candles the second and so on until Christmas. Then they read one of the special advent prayers that I typed on index cards. Here are a few examples:

"Father, bless this wreath and help us prepare our hearts for your Son. Help us to be worthy of the bountiful blessings that your Son's coming will bring."

"Jesus come to us. Dwell in our hearts and fill us with your love. Give us the gifts of faith, hope, and charity so we may enter your kingdom as your holy people."

> Prepare a road for the Lord to travel on! Widen the pathway before him! Level the mountains! Fill up the valleys! Straighten the curves! Smooth out the ruts! And then all mankind shall see the Savior sent from God. LUKE 3:4-6

NOVEMBER 28

Our family calendar was such a jumble of activities that I couldn't keep it all straight. One winter day, while I was at work, I called home around 5:30 P.M. to tell my older son, Michael, that I'd be late.

I knew my teenage daughters had after-school drama rehearsals and wouldn't be home till after 6:00 P.M. But when I called home the phone rang and rang and rang. My heart raced. *Oh no, did Michael leave for basketball practice before the girls got home? Where is Andrew?* After ten or twelve rings, someone answered the phone but didn't say anything.

"Andrew? Is that you?"

"Hi, Mama," he squeaked in a tiny little mouse voice.

"What's wrong, honey? You're not alone, are you? Is Michael still home? You sound sick. What's the matter, Andrew?" I couldn't stop asking questions.

"Well," his little voice barely whispered, "Michael's outside snowblowing the driveway. I'm inside by myself."

My arms longed to reach out and hug my frail and fearful son.

"Tell you what, Andrew. How about if I just talk to you on the phone until Michael comes in? I'll finish my typing while we talk. Tell me what you did today in kindergarten."

Andrew talked in broken sentences ... slowly, sadly, weakly. Ten minutes later Andrew suddenly came back to life, practically shouting, "Mommy! Michael's coming in the house! I'm gonna watch cartoons now. See you, Mom!"

Loneliness had whipped the spirit out of my child. But as soon as he knew his big brother was with him all was well.

Dear Jesus, thank you for a busy kind of life that keeps me from being lonely. But if my children are lonely, Lord, because I'm at work too much, help me to fix that ... today.

At that point, all the disciples deserted him and fled.
MATTHEW 26:56

I remember feeling angry when my mother died. Angry that she was just fifty-seven years old. Angry that I'd lost my best friend. Angry that she'd suffered with Lou Gehrig's disease. Angry that she died, not in my arms, but while my family and I were on vacation. Angry that she died when I was pregnant and that she would never get to know and love her grandson. The day of her funeral I went out behind the barn at home, plopped my pregnant self on a stack of lumber, and proceeded to wail.

The Greek philosopher, Aristotle, said, "We praise a man who feels angry on the right grounds and against the right persons and also in the right manner at the right moment and for the right length of time."

Next time you're angry, consider Aristotle's five anger qualifications. Make sure your anger is for the right reason and person and that it's delivered correctly at the right time for an appropriate length of time.

Heavenly Father, I know anger is normal. After all, Jesus was angry when he threw the money changers out of the temple. But when anger grabs hold of me, help me to get over it quickly. Touch my heart with love, compassion, forgiveness, and understanding.

Stop being mean, bad-tempered and angry.... Instead, be kind to each other, tenderhearted, forgiving one another, just as God has forgiven you because you belong to Christ.   EPHESIANS 4:31-32

NOVEMBER 30

We parents are our childrens' biggest fans. But sometimes we simply get caught up in our own lives and forget to think of creative ways to build up their self-esteem. That's why it's important that we encourage other adults to become part of our kids' cheerleading squad.

At the beginning of his junior year in high school, my son Andrew received a letter. Dad and Bev (my wonderful step-mom) had just visited us. Dad wrote:

Dear Andrew,

Years ago, Yogi Berra said, "You can observe a lot by watching."

I see how you have become a fantastic young adult with high ideals and goals to achieve. I just want you to know that we are very proud of you and hope and pray that you will keep your high ideals, think of the future, trust and respect the judgment and decisions your mother makes for you because what she decides is strictly for your good.... I'm stopping here before you get the feeling this is a lecture. It's only intended to be a fan letter. We love you.

Grandpa and Grandma

I can't tell you how much that letter meant to Andrew. I'm sure it'll be kept right alongside the treasured notes and cards he received from his dad.

Today, call or write to a special friend or relative and ask that person to write a note of encouragement to your child. Hearing words of praise from another adult besides mom or dad can mean more to a child than we'll ever know.

Lord, help me to build self-esteem in someone else's child today by sending him or her a "you're special ... way to go!" note. Remind me to ask them to do the same for my child.

Encourage him as he prepares to take over the leadership. I will give the land to the children they said would die in the wilderness.   DEUTERONOMY 1:38-39

A Prayer for December

Oh, yes, Heavenly Father,
Christmastime, for me, is
Advent wreath glowing.
Christmas tree sparkling.
Wide-eyed children.
Eager friends.
Devoted relatives.
Cookies, carols, gifts,
And love sharing.
Christmastime, for me, is
Exquisite!

But Father, for others,
This season is no different
From any other.
The same dirty, paint-chipped
Prison walls.
The same sterile, fearful
Hospital bed.
The same day-in, day-out
Nursing home.
Help me, heavenly Father
To find the sad, lonely people.
Help me to give them
Some of *my* Christmas.

DECEMBER 1

One cold December day in Milwaukee, Frank, a fourteen-year-old high school freshman, hopped on the number ten city bus for the ride to his home in the suburbs. Next, a woman boarded at the county medical complex grounds, even though the bus was going the opposite direction of where she was headed. The woman, about thirty-five years old, pregnant with her ninth child, was wearing a tattered gray coat, thin, torn socks, and no shoes ... even though the temperature was a bitter ten degrees.

As the woman stepped inside, John, a veteran city bus driver, said, "This is the wrong direction, Maggie. You want to go downtown, right?"

The woman pulled the old coat around her thin frame and sat down in the front seat. "I'll get on anyway and make the round trip. It's too cold to wait for the east-bound bus."

In the back of the bus a handful of rowdy high school boys started snickering. "Hey, nice coat, lady. Is that a Saks Fifth Avenue special? Doesn't she know we don't serve patrons without shoes?"

Maggie leaned over and spoke to John. "I had just enough to buy shoes for the kids, but not for me." The bus driver and the lady spoke of poverty and how folks had to cope with it.

Frank listened intently. Finally it was his turn to get off. He walked up the aisle slowly and paused in front of Maggie.

"Here lady, you need these more than me." And with that Frank handed her his week-old, name-brand athletic shoes for which he'd saved his allowance for months. Then he walked off the bus and into the ten-degree day in his stocking feet.

If you believe in angels, as I do, you'll understand why those shoes fit Maggie perfectly.

Lord, give me a nudge when I see someone hungry, tattered, torn, battered by the ravages of poverty or in need of a friend. Help me to do something right then and there.

"Humble men are very fortunate!" he told them, "for the Kingdom of Heaven is given to them."

MATTHEW 5:3

DECEMBER 2

When I was a young mother, I would panic when my folks or other relatives or friends would come for overnight visits. I insisted that the house be cleaned to white-glove perfection, extra-fancy food prepared, and makeshift beds assembled with clean, fresh towels folded in cute designs on top of each bed. Before the houseguests arrived, I'd work myself into a short-tempered, exhausted frenzy. By the time they arrived, I was often too tired and too crabby to enjoy them.

That was years ago, during my "trying to be perfect" stage of life. Since then, I've learned that a perfectly clean house is simply not a necessary ingredient for a pleasant visit. Slaving over elaborate meals doesn't make sense. Now, I go with the flow. If guests ask if there's something they can do to help I say, "Sure!" then rattle off a few suggestions. They're usually delighted to be useful, and I'm thrilled with the help.

When Jesus moved from village to village, preaching his message of love, he must have been one of the all-time-great houseguests. People invited him into their homes for meals and a place to sleep. And I'm sure Jesus was right there in the kitchen, lending a helping hand.

This holiday season, if you've got guests coming, don't panic. Let them help with the work. After all, if they feel like they're not a huge burden to you, they'll want to come back ... and because you had help, you'll be thrilled to have them back. It's a win-win situation.

Lord, help me to enjoy all my guests during the holidays. Help me not to worry about being a perfect hostess, rather help me to be a more perfect friend or relative.

They must enjoy having guests in their homes and must love all that is good.   TITUS 1:8

DECEMBER 3

Like it or not, Christmas has been evident in the stores since September, if not before. That's because Christmas is big business. Some companies do more business during the pre-Christmas season than they do all the rest of the year.

For over twenty centuries people from every Christian country celebrated the birth of one little baby in the tiny town of Bethlehem. Twenty centuries worth of glittering pageantry, parties, knightly tournaments, miracle plays, peacock pies, plum puddings, carols, cards, cookies, trees, traditions, toasts, mysteries, magic, and merriment.

Isn't it amazing that one baby could cause all that commotion? Just imagine everything that goes on at Christmastime and to think it all started because of one little baby.

One little baby caused millions of people to shower gifts on each other. One little baby caused untold millions of people to get together to make merry for weeks. One little baby brought hope for a better life to millions of people all over the world. One little baby. Amazing.

Isn't it wonderful that that one little baby is still able to nudge such warm feelings of love closer to the surface of our hearts and souls and prove that faith, hope, and charity are still alive and well in the world?

A huge neon sign at a car care center in a Milwaukee suburb dazzles drivers with its message, "It's a boy! Congratulations Mary and Joseph!"

Heavenly Father, thank you for giving us your Son, one little baby ... Jesus ... the reason for the season.

And there was the baby, lying in the manger.

LUKE 2:16

DECEMBER 4

Three weeks before Christmas, my cousin Mary Beth sent us an absolutely charming gingerbread house that quickly became the center of attention on the dining room table. The children and I and all our holiday visitors were charmed by the little house with its real gingerbread siding, candy doors and windows, and colorful icing trim.

Two days after Christmas, the house was the main attraction at Andrew's seventh birthday party. When we visited my family in Illinois over New Year's weekend, it went with us so we could all nibble at the cookie and candy exterior.

When we returned home, I placed what was left on our deck for the squirrels. All during January and February they perched on the little roof and chewed that house down to the cardboard.

That gift delighted everyone for a full three months. But I'd spent more time talking about the gingerbread house than I had about the real meaning of Christmas. I thought about the other "house" we'd had on display during the holidays, the manger scene, and had to admit that I hadn't given it much prominence.

The next year, I placed the manger in the center of the dining room table for over a month. During January I moved it up to the fireplace mantle, where it was a daily reminder.

This Christmas season why don't you make the manger scene the center attraction in your home?

Gentle Jesus, come to us and reside in the most prominent place in our home and then stay within our hearts all year long.

Thanks be to God! For through what Christ has done, he has triumphed over us so that now wherever we go he uses us to tell others about the Lord and to spread the Gospel like a sweet perfume.

2 CORINTHIANS 2:14

DECEMBER 5

When I was a radio copywriter, I often started writing Christmas commercials in September. Some even aired in September with words like "order now for the coming holiday season" or "just in time for your holiday gift giving...."

By November I'd often find myself muttering "bah humbug." Bitterly, I'd think, *Why does Christmas have to be such a long, drawn-out mega-merchandising affair? Why can't it just be a simple celebration on one day, proclaiming the fact that Jesus was born to save the world?*

Then I read something by Dr. Earl Count, an American scholar, who defined Christmas as: "A spontaneous drama of the common folk, a prayer, a hymn. All the while that Raphael was painting the Sistine Madonna, Frenchmen were building the Chartres Cathedral, English Bishops composing *The Book of Common Prayer,* Handel his *Messiah,* Bach his *B-Minor Mass* ... the common people, out of whom these geniuses sprang, were composing Christmas."

And what a composition it turned out to be! From the lighting of the first candle on the Advent wreath four weeks before Christmas to the Epiphany celebration, the Christmas season really is the most amazing time of year.

If Christmas starts to get you down, help create it for others: Fill a food basket and give it to your pastor to present to a needy family. Take two or three nursing home residents out to lunch. Fill little stockings with holiday treats and toys and hand them out in the children's wing of the hospital. Offer to take the children of a single parent shopping so they can buy a gift for their mom or dad.

Lord, this year, help me turn the holiday commercialism into holiday spirituality by creating Christmas for others.

And how does a man benefit if he gains the whole world and loses his soul in the process?   MARK 8:36

DECEMBER 6

Today, December 6, is the feast of Saint Nicholas, a fourth-century bishop of Myra, in Asia Minor, who was known for his kindness to the poor. One legend tells of the time Nicholas helped a poor merchant provide dowry money for his three unmarried daughters by dropping gold bags down the merchant's chimney. One of the girls had her stockings hanging in the fireplace to dry, and when the gold fell down the chimney, it landed in one of the stockings. Since that day, children have hung stockings near fireplaces or on doorknobs, hoping for another visit from St. Nicholas. In our family we place one shoe outside our bedroom doors on the eve of St. Nicholas' feast day, and in the morning a piece of fruit, candy and perhaps one small gift appear in each shoe.

In the seventeenth century, the Dutch people who settled in New Amsterdam called Saint Nicholas "Sinter Klaas." From this Dutch name we derived our own name for him—"Santa Claus."

In the twentieth century we see Santa Claus arriving in helicopters, space craft, race cars, and on trains and elephants. But in spite of the modern touch, it's nice to know that Santa Claus really did evolve from the beloved fourth century bishop, Saint Nicholas, to the jolly gent up on our roof top. No matter what he looks like or what we call him, Santa Claus has emerged, thanks to Saint Nicholas, as a champion of good, a gentle giver, and the patron saint of the true spirit of Christmas.

This Christmas, Lord, let me be a champion of good and a friend to the poor.

Remind each other of God's goodness and be thankful.
EPHESIANS 5:4

DECEMBER 7

In 1995 I celebrated my fiftieth birthday by taking a trip to Hawaii with two of my children. One of the most memorable days was the day we visited Pearl Harbor.

The National Park Service and the United States Department of the Interior have created a magnificent visitors' center dedicated to the memory of the lives lost in the historic attack on Pearl Harbor on December 7, 1941. The battleship *USS Arizona*, destroyed by the Japanese during the attack, still rests just below the surface of the water at the bottom of the harbor. Of the men assigned to that ship, 1,177 were killed or are missing in action. Most of them remain entombed in the hull of the ship. Visitors take navy boats across the water to the ship's memorial, where the American flag is ceremoniously raised and lowered every hour.

The *USS Arizona* Memorial is a somber place. Photos of the harbor and the city before, during, and after the attack line the walls. A movie describes the events of the day and the state of the world during the second big war. People from all over the world, including many Japanese, sit elbow to elbow next to Americans as they watch the film. The mood is quiet and respectful. The name of every man who gave his life that day in December is inscribed on a huge marble wall at the memorial. They are the names of real people: fathers, sons, brothers, uncles ... entombed forever in a bowels of a ship.

Heavenly Father, protect my children from war. Let them grow up learning how to be peacemakers instead of warriors. Bless all who have died in wars all over the world. Bless their families.

What is causing the quarrels and fights among you? Isn't it because there is a whole army of evil desires within you? You want what you don't have, so you kill to get it. You long for what others have, and can't afford it, so you start a fight to take it away from them. And yet the reason you don't have what you want is that you don't ask God for it.   JAMES 4:1-2

Some friends and I, overwhelmed by the demands of our holiday preparations, were griping one day over tea. One friend shared that she had never received a Christmas gift from her husband. His parents never exchanged gifts, so he felt that giving his own wife a gift wasn't necessary. She was hurt. She *wanted* a gift from him.

Another woman said, "My husband buys me too many gifts. Some years he's got ten things for me under the tree. It's embarrassing."

One thing was perfectly clear. Few of us were satisfied with our gift-giving customs. One woman suggested that we ignore the customs of our growing-up years and focus instead on *new* ways to show our love for those around us.

Teens might offer to do yard work or shovel snow for the old couple down the street. Dad may suggest that fast-food meals once a week might help him with the busy hustle-bustle weeks ahead. Mom might make a date with each one of her children for a one-on-one Christmas-cookie baking night. The younger children might offer to do one extra chore each day during Advent.

Perhaps it's time to change some of our Christmas customs, especially if we've only been single for a year or two. Remember, change is good.

Lord, help me to give good gifts … my time and my talent being two of the best.

Some of us have been given special ability as apostles; to others he has given the gift of being able to preach well; some have special ability in winning people to Christ, helping them to trust him as their Savior; still others have a gift for caring for God's people as a shepherd does his sheep, leading and teaching them in the ways of God.   EPHESIANS 4:11

DECEMBER 9

One December Saturday, I was invited to a Christmas luncheon at a women's church group. During lunch, Ellen, the group's moderator, agonized, "It's bad enough when I have to speak at our regular meetings of twenty people, but today I have to speak to 100 members and guests! I'm terrified!"

As Ellen walked nervously to the stage, the program chairwoman who was about to introduce her suddenly stopped. Her face brightened, and she said, "Before Ellen begins, you simply *must* see her shoes!" All eyes fell on Ellen's shoes.

As Ellen held up one foot the group oohed and aahed, then applauded at the sight of her stunning black velvet flats with lots of shiny red, green, and gold Christmas designs embroidered all over them. Ellen blushed, then laughed and joined the applause. "Isn't she lovely to get us all into the Christmas spirit?" the chairwoman said. With that, the ice was broken and Ellen delivered a talk that was both relaxed and inspired.

Now whenever I feel anxious around strangers, I try to be more spontaneous and down-to-earth. Not long after that Christmas luncheon, I was asked to speak to my son's English class about what it was like to write articles for magazines and newspapers. I told the students about one article I'd written about an old baggy yellow shirt my mother and I traded back and forth as a joke for seventeen years. Just before class I pulled that old, torn, faded shirt out of my bag and wore it during the class. The eighth graders loved it and made me feel very welcome. Their many interesting questions after my talk reminded me once again that when we humble ourselves the way Jesus often did, we shall, indeed, be exalted.

Lord, keep me aware of all the times I can be more spontaneous and humble in the way I reach out to people.

Therefore anyone who humbles himself as this little child, is the greatest in the Kingdom of Heaven.

MATTHEW 18:4

DECEMBER 10

Are bells a part of your holiday decorations? On Christmas Eve in medieval England, Scotland, and Ireland, the village church bells tolled mournfully for an hour before midnight. It was the annual celebration of the devil's funeral. Then, just at the stroke of midnight, the bells rang out jubilantly because it was believed that the devil died when Jesus was born.

Today, church bells and carillons still call the faithful to church. The church across the street and down the block a bit from my house plays a beautiful electronic carillon every day all year for six minutes at 1:00 P.M. and again at 6:00 P.M. I love being outdoors when those bells begin to play.

But the best bells of all are the ones we hear on Christmas Eve and morning ... church bells proclaiming that the Savior is born.

This year when the church bells toll, let's add to those beautiful sounds of Christmas, a few sounds of our own.

"God bless you!"

"May I help?"

"Praise God!"

"Welcome home!"

"I forgive you."

"I love you!"

Let's see how many beautiful sounds of Christmas we can say everyday during this busy holiday season ... and beyond.

Lord, thank you for the gift of being able to hear the bells and other sounds of this holiday season. Help me to appreciate, especially, the Salvation Army bells and to be generous in spirit and donation so that the goodness of this season lasts for the other eleven months as well.

Yes, sing your highest praises to our King, the King of all the earth. Sing thoughtful praises!   PSALMS 47:7

Imagine this conversation between two shepherds in the cold, rainy hills outside Bethlehem:

First shepherd: We must think of a present to take the baby.

Second shepherd: Why not give him your crook?

First shepherd: No! How could I tend my sheep without my crook? Besides, what would a baby do with that?

Second shepherd: How about a basket of chestnuts or bread and cheese?

First shepherd: For the baby's parents, perhaps, but the baby is being fed by his mother and cannot eat such things.

Second shepherd: Why not your fife? He would enjoy the music.

First shepherd: No, the child is too young to play on it. I know! We'll take this gourd with dry seeds inside. It rattles and the baby's tiny hand will just fit around its small end.

Second shepherd: Perfect: You're a smart man. A gourd shaker. Yes, the baby will be pleased.

Christmas gift giving started when the Magi brought regal gifts of gold, frankincense, and myrrh. But don't you imagine the shepherds and the townspeople who came to see the baby also brought gifts ... small gifts, perhaps even more thoughtful and more practical than the exotic ones presented by the three kings?

How often do we really try to find something that will please the receiver of a gift? Or do we, instead, give something more expensive and more elaborate to make ourselves look good?

Lord, help me to remember that a simple gift, given in love, is infinitely better than one given to impress or to ease the guilt of a bruised friendship.

Some of us ... have a gift for caring for God's people as a shepherd does his sheep, leading and teaching them in the ways of God.　　　EPHESIANS 4:5

DECEMBER 12

Even though our backyards backed up against each other, I hadn't seen Patty for a couple-months. The frigid November and December Wisconsin weather and a myriad of preholiday activities kept us both indoors. When she called to tell me she'd been sick for three weeks I was shocked.

I offered to help with whatever she needed, but after we hung up I wondered if Patty would feel comfortable telling me what she needed in the way of help. So often we say the words, "If you need anything, let me know," but does the person who hears those words *know* that we really mean it?

That afternoon I got busy and made a list of specific things I could do for my neighbor during her illness. Andrew delivered it to her front door. My list of specific ways I could help included:

1. Take care of Sara and Steven (Patty's youngsters).
2. Double my supper recipes and give her half.
3. Run errands for her.
4. Rent movies for her to watch during her recuperation.
5. Help wrap her Christmas presents.
6. Help get her house in order for the holidays.

When she received my list, Patty called right away and accepted my offer for child care, supper the next night, and help with her Christmas wrapping. Suddenly I felt closer to my neighbor than ever before. I felt "needed"! Thanks to Patty, our Christmas season was one of the most joyous ever as the word "giving" took on a whole new meaning.

'Tis the season for giving and sharing, Lord. Help me to find specific ways to give myself to others ... and to you.

When I come, although I can't do much to help your faith, for it is strong already, I want to be able to do something about your joy: I want to make you happy, not sad.   2 CORINTHIANS 1:24

DECEMBER 13

Ever wonder whose bright idea it was to send Christmas cards to every living soul we ever met during this, the most hectic time of year? Even though I do send Christmas cards, with letters included, to dozens of people each year, I also feel sorry for the poor overworked postal workers. That's probably because my dad was one of them.

The custom of sending cards during the holiday season, instead of writing letters, began in England in 1843. Sir Henry Cole had just become director of the Victoria and Albert Museum in London, and he was so busy that year that he had no time to write letters to all his friends, as was the custom at Christmastime. So Sir Henry commissioned artist John Horsley to paint a scene that was both merry and charitable. The scene was reproduced on cards and sent out to Sir Henry's friends, who undoubtedly thought it was quite unusual.

Three decades later, after the installation of mail delivery in the United States, a German immigrant, Louis Prang, founded the American Christmas-card industry. His lavish printing process, using Bavarian limestone, could reproduce seventeen colors in a single picture.

Christmas cards in America are such a tradition that they're often displayed on fireplace mantles, taped to doorways or walls, and actually become part of the holiday decorations.

Lord, as my children and I try to stay in touch with friends and loved ones near and far, help me to make each Christmas card a personal expression of my love and devotion ... and not just a tedious obligation.

Then you send your Spirit, and new life is born to replenish all the living of the earth.   PSALMS 104:30

"Mommy, come here a minute," six-year-old Andrew giggles.

I walk toward him, noticing how coy he's trying to be as he stands on a chair under the mistletoe in the hallway.

Suddenly this golden-haired child of mine throws his arms around my neck and plants a kiss on my cheek. "I love you, Mommy!" He squeals with delight over the fact that he has "caught" me under the mistletoe.

In many homes, delicate green mistletoe branches with tiny white or yellow berries hang gracefully in doorways, beckoning those who meet underneath to enjoy a kiss or a hug.

Where did we get this custom? Some say during Roman times, enemy soldiers who met under the mistletoe plant would put down their arms, stop fighting, and embrace.

Early Christians were sure it was the forbidden fruit from the Garden of Eden. Another legend says mistletoe was once a tall forest tree, but shriveled with humiliation into a dwarf-size shrub after one was cut down to make the cross of Christ.

There's probably a different legend and custom in every country where mistletoe grows. But I like ours the best.

In America at Christmastime mistletoe opens the way for a bit of human warmth in the form of a simple kiss or a hug. And we all know that reaching out to each other in the spirit of love is exactly what Christmas is all about.

Mistletoe is the perfect excuse for giving those teenagers, tots, and toddlers lots of kisses and hugs during this busy, busy, high-stress season. And when you hug someone, you'll be amazed how much it suddenly feels like Christmas.

Lord, bless this house and the people in it. Help us to capture some of the nicest holiday customs and hang on to them all year long.

Greet one another with a holy kiss.

1 CORINTHIANS 16:20

DECEMBER 15

One song that will no doubt stay on the charts forever is the old Yuletide favorite "Joy to the World." The lyrics to this song were written by Isaac Watts, who is often called the founder of English hymn writing.

Many old English hymns were originally set to the music of time-honored classical artists. The music for "Joy to the World" was borrowed from a classical work composed by George Frederick Handel, who also wrote the *Messiah* in 1742.

Songs come and go off the "Top 40" charts like lightning bugs popping in and out of the darkness. But our old Christmas hymns have endured and filled our hearts with joy every Christmas for hundreds of years. Could it be that the subject of so many of these songs, the birth of one little baby boy, is of such epic proportions that these songs will survive for time eternal? I'd bet a Grammy on it!

One simple thing we single parents can do to create Christmas in our homes is to fill those rooms and our children's hearts with holiday music. Buy some Christmas carols on tape or CD and play them at meal times or anytime the children are home. Music makes the heart merry ... you can count on it.

Father, fill my heart and the hearts of my children with the joy of Christmas music ... and keep those words and notes echoing in our heads all year long.

You love him even though you have never seen him; though not seeing him, you trust him; and even now you are happy with the inexpressible joy that comes from heaven itself.   1 PETER 1:8

I love the fragrances of Christmas. Cookies baking, fresh-cut pine trees, gingerbread, cinnamon, nutmeg, peppermint candies, marshmallow-topped cocoa, those wonderful bayberry candles.

Legend tells us that the bayberry tree gave shelter to the Holy Family during a storm on their way back from Bethlehem after Jesus was born. Because of this, it is said that lightning never strikes the bayberry tree.

Another legend says that sweethearts who light bayberry candles when they are separated at Christmas will supposedly be reunited to each other by way of the gentle scent of the bayberry.

What scents permeate your home during the holiday season? Fresh-cut Christmas trees? Turkey and dressing? Peppermint? Scented oil from an oil-burning lamp? Fresh-baked bread? Floral arrangements made with pine and eucalyptus plants? Smoky logs burning in the fireplace or wood burner? Fresh-baked gingerbread, hot apple pie or strudel? Marshmallows and chocolate for s'mores melting on a winter campfire?

The scents of the holiday season ... aren't they wonderful? Today, why don't you make sure there's a special holiday fragrance welcoming your loved ones home.

Like the legend of the bayberry candle, may the gentle fragrances of your Christmas draw all your loved ones into your home to help you enjoy this glorious, many-scented reason.

Lord, thank you for making me feel so alive with my five senses. Thank you, especially, for my sense of smell at this glorious time of year.

Then Mary took a jar of costly perfume made from essence of nard, and anointed Jesus' feet with it and wiped them with her hair. And the house was filled with fragrance.   JOHN 12:3

DECEMBER 17

When Dad retired, many of his elderly mail route patrons spoke about the times Dad would walk up their long country lanes, sometimes through two or three feet of snow, to deliver the mail right to their door, rather than leave it in the mailbox at the end of the lane.

Sometimes he would trudge up those lanes on foot to hand deliver an eagerly awaited Christmas letter from a son or daughter stationed overseas in the military. Or he would leave a large package inside a front porch rather than propped up against the mailbox in the snow.

Extra services, completed with a smile and a positive attitude … that was the way Dad delivered the mail during those hectic holiday weeks.

Today, let's take time to thank someone whose job is particularly difficult, stressful, or more time consuming this time of year because of the holiday season: the factory workers who create the billions of gifts we give; the people in the transportation industry who take us home for the holidays; the telephone operators who let us visit with our loved ones over the phone; the mail carriers who deliver our holiday mail; the store clerks who wait on us with a smile; the pastors who with outstretched arms welcome multitudes of us into church.

Lord, bless all those who help make our Christmas a little brighter because of their hard work. Give them extra energy, patience, and kindness, especially when dealing with those of us who may be a little cranky because of the stress of the season.

And I am sure that God who began the good work within you will keep right on helping you grow in his grace until his task within you is finally finished on that day when Jesus Christ returns.   PHILIPPIANS 1:6

DECEMBER 18

Christmas week of '87 looked like a real bummer. My divorce had just become final, and my ex-husband was already remarried. For the first time ever, one of my children wouldn't be with me on Christmas: Jeanne, my oldest, was a foreign exchange student in Yugoslavia. The annual New Year's Eve get-together in Illinois with my relatives had been cancelled. And it was my turn to host the huge neighborhood Christmas bash.

But here's what happened that week: On Christmas Eve my other three children made it clear that they wanted us to attend the traditional family service at our church. Later, they continued another family tradition: reading the Christmas story from the Bible before we opened presents. At midnight my friends Bob and Betsy whisked me off to the candlelight service at their church. Two days later they offered to cohost the neighborhood party, and all the neighbors pitched in with food and beverages. On New Year's weekend my out-of-town family came to my home, ending the holiday week with loads of laughter and love.

Because I gave in to the gentle nudgings and invitations of friends and family, that Christmas week became a memory that I treasure. Sometimes it's hard to get through the Christmas season when you're a single parent. But if you reach out just a little, you may be surprised what happens during Christmas week.

God bless you … and know that someone in Oak Creek, Wisconsin, who understands how you feel, wishes you a very Merry Christmas.

Thank you, Lord, for family, friends, neighbors … and for Christmas. Happy birthday, Jesus!

You have sorrow now, but I will see you again and then you will rejoice; and no one can rob you of that joy.   JOHN 16:22

DECEMBER 19

Who would think that broken crockery and radishes would provide the means for a Christmas celebration? In the city of Oaxaca, 340 miles southeast of Mexico City, a three-day festival honoring the mother of Jesus begins on December 19 each year.

During the three-day event, when vendors sell their wares in the streets, each purchase includes a free crockery saucer, which is then hurled into the air to smash into bits on the ground below ... a custom which is supposed to bring good luck in the coming year. By the end of the evening the crockery shards are almost ankle deep.

On December 23, the plaza stalls display gaily decorated, enormous radishes. The radishes are carved into religious scenes, landscapes, replicas of bullfights, men riding horses, elephants, and burros. No one eats these radishes, they're much too strong. Instead, the radish figures are judged, awarded prizes, then sold to be used as home decorations for the Christmas celebration.

Is there an unusual ethnic holiday custom in your family? Perhaps this year is the year to find one. Ask grandpa, great-grandma, aunts, uncles, or cousins how Christmas was celebrated in the "old" country or in Christmases past in your family.

Start your own family holiday tradition. Something as simple as a family night when you all string popcorn for the tree while you listen to Christmas carols might become a custom that you and your children will cherish every year from now on. Creating new traditions is fun.

Lord, thank you for the diversity of our ethnic cultures. Help me create a few new events in our family holiday celebration that will become traditions.

God's Man is here! ... Bless him, Lord! ... Praise God
in highest Heaven!   MATTHEW 21:9

One of our most beloved carols comes to us from a little church in Arnsdorf, Austria. The song was written because mice had eaten holes in the bellows of the church organ, and there would be no music for Christmas. The saddened parish priest sat down the day before Christmas Eve and wrote the words to "Silent Night." When the organist, Franz Gruber, heard the words he set them to music and sang them to the congregation on Christmas Eve in 1818. Just think, if it weren't for those mice, "Silent Night" might never have been written!

These days the Christmas season is such a big production that it's easy to forget exactly why we celebrate in the first place. The holidays aren't just an excuse to spend more than we can afford or entertain more than we should or to give lavish presents to make up for the time we don't spend with loved ones. No, this is the time of year when a magnificent song can be written because mice ate holes in the church organ. A time when an hour spent with a little child can provide a better memory than the most expensive toy in the world. A time when a tiny baby born in a stable was able to change the world.

Lord, during this hectic Christmas week, help me to find you in small, everyday things. Help me to make time to take a walk with each of my children, one-on-one, at least once this week. Help me not to get so bogged down and exhausted from spending so much time buying unnecessary gifts for people. Instead, help me to find more time to spend with my children this week and every week, just enjoying each other's company.

The Lord protects the simple and the childlike; I was facing death and then he saved me.   PSALMS 116:6

DECEMBER 21

An American child would shudder at the thought of Christmas without Santa Claus. But in most other countries, Santa either doesn't exist at all, or he has a different name, background, physical characteristics, means of transportation, and method of gift giving.

In Brazil Santa is called "Papa Noel," and he comes in through the window instead of down the chimney. In Denmark, there is no Santa. Instead, Juenisse, a little dwarf who lives in attics and barns, brings gifts to Danish children. In England, Santa is called Father Christmas. In Holland, Santa is called Sinter Klaas and children stuff wooden shoes with hay and carrots for his horse. In Italy, it's a woman, La Befana, who brings gifts on Epiphany instead of Christmas Day. In Spain, the three wise men leave gifts for the children. In France, "Le Pere Noel" is the festive toy giver. In Syria, there's no Santa Claus, but a camel who delivers gifts. In Ethiopia, children dress up and go to the royal palace to receive presents from the emperor.

Santa Claus may not be part of the Christmas celebration in every country, but Baby Jesus certainly is. Jesus is the one person who unites Christians in every country in the world on Christmas Day in the spirit of love and giving.

This year, let's each share this universal Christmas message of Jesus with one little child by pointing out that in every country in the world, it isn't Santa Claus, but Jesus who is the real gift giver. It is Jesus who brought us the greatest gift of all ... the love of God.

Gentle Jesus, thank you for bringing us your Father's love this Christmas season. Help us to cherish it, nourish it and spread it all year long.

Trust should be in the living God who always richly gives us all we need for our enjoyment.

1 TIMOTHY 6:17

DECEMBER 22

The weekend before Christmas 1996, my oldest, Jeanne, and her boyfriend, Canyon, were flying standby to get home to Wisconsin from New York. To pass the time, Jeanne and Canyon talked to a middle-aged couple and their twenty-year-old daughter. Just before that family's plane departed, they gave up their seats on the over-booked plane in exchange for an extra ticket voucher per person, plus tickets on another flight early the next morning.

Then something amazing happened. The man, a psychologist, and his wife, invited Jeanne and Canyon to spend the night with them in their Manhattan apartment!

The Caffreys took Jeanne and Canyon out for dinner, then drove them to their elegant Manhattan apartment for a good night's sleep. Mrs. Caffrey even phoned me in Milwaukee to assure me that she was taking good care of my daughter, and then insisted that I speak to Jeanne myself. The following morning when the family had to depart earlier than Jeanne and Canyon, they simply asked them to leave the key with the doorman when they left.

When that Christmas season was over and I'd survived the madcap merriment and mayhem of having seventeen houseguests in and out for fifteen days straight, I found myself wondering, if, during all the commotion of the holidays, I'd even found Christ in Christmas that year. Then I remembered Mr. and Mrs. Caffrey and how they gave two strangers shelter during the cold Christmas season. Thanks to their generous, unbelievably trusting hearts, I most definitely did find Christ in my Christmas.

Jesus, when I think my house is full and there's no more room at the inn, give me a generous heart and let me take in strangers, if necessary.

And while they were there, the time came for her baby to be born; and she gave birth to her first child, a son. She wrapped him in a blanket and laid him in a manger, because there was no room for them in the village inn.

LUKE 2:6-7

One of my favorite things about decorating for the holidays is placing Christmas candles on the tables, window sills, on top of the TV, and, of course, on the fireplace mantle. Saint Jerome said candles were a way to express Christian joy, a symbol of the enlightenment Christ brought to earth. I guess that's why I like candles so much.

In Norway, there is a legend that says candles must never burn out on Christmas Eve or the family will have bad luck all year long. In Germany, tiny candles placed on the branches of Christmas trees represent the stars in the heavens. In Ireland and eastern Europe, one big candle is lit in homes every night during the twelve days of Christmas to symbolize God's presence on earth.

As dusk falls and my family or friends arrive from their busy days at work or school, I light my own holiday candles. As the lights flicker and glow, I am comforted by the fact that God's love truly enfolds me protectively. Isn't it a wonderful thing to know that wherever we are, God is there also?

Tonight, as your loved ones gather, light a candle in your home to remind yourself and your family that God is present in your household.

Welcome home, my children.

Heavenly Father, during this holiest of seasons as night falls quicker and weather becomes colder, may these candles remind me that your light surrounds and your love enfolds all who enter my home. Help me to welcome everyone as you would with infinite kindness.

You are the world's light—a city on a hill, glowing in the night for all to see. Don't hide your light! Let it shine for all; let your good deeds glow for all to see, so that they will praise your heavenly Father.

MATTHEW 5:14-16

The parking lot at the movie theater was nearly empty. My friend, Dianne, another single parent, was waiting inside the door.

"Hi. Doesn't look too crowded, does it?" Dianne sounded as glum as I felt.

Inside the theater there were four other people waiting for the movie to begin. After the show, around 5:00 P.M., Dianne and I said good-bye and returned to our homes.

The house was pitch dark and empty. The children were spending the day with their father. It was "his" turn. I'd forgotten to fill the wood burner before I left, and the family room downstairs was cold. I sat in that dark, cold room and simply gave in to a monstrous wave of loneliness and despair on that Christmas Day of 1987.

Since then, I've avoided the "Christmas Day miseries" by planning ahead … inviting friends over or making sure they know I'm going to be alone so they'll invite me to their homes. When I hear of other single parents whose children must "take turns" with the ex-spouse on Christmas Day … I invite them to my house, light the wood burner, turn on all the Christmas lights and holiday music, and we make "merry" together.

With nearly half of our country's marriages ending in divorce, you won't have to look far to find adults who might be spending Christmas day alone. Reach out! Invite them over. Insist on it. That lonely Christmas afternoon and evening when I was so steeped in misery, I'm sure it would have taken a forceful invitation to pry me out of the house.

Lord, during this hectic, busy, wonderful "family" season, remind me to include my single friends as part of "my" family.

I have not joined the people in their merry feasts. I sit alone beneath the hand of God.   JEREMIAH 15:17

DECEMBER 25

Merry Christmas! I wish you all the joy and happiness that comes from sharing the joy of Christ's birth with those you love and who love you.

I have a gift for you. One thing that I truly enjoy making is homemade granola. Whenever I make it (always a little different from the last time) the children and I call it "My Best Batch Ever." And so, dear friends, today, on Christmas, I give you a special hug ... my very own homemade granola recipe.

"Best Batch Ever" Homemade Granola

2   42-oz. boxes of "old fashioned" oats (not the "quick cooking" kind)
1   14-oz. cereal box of high fiber All-Bran or Bran Buds
1   12-oz. jar wheat germ
2 c. chopped nuts and/or sunflower seeds
1 c. packed brown sugar *or* one cup honey
1-1/2 c. of corn, canola, or olive oil
2 tbsp. of cinnamon
1-2 c. coconut
1 c. raisins
1 c. dried cranberries or dried cherries

Combine oats, bran, wheat germ, nuts, seeds, brown sugar, and oil in a huge stainless steel or metal bowl or turkey roaster. Stir thoroughly and bake at 275° for 30 minutes. Stir. Bake for another 30 minutes. Stir. Add the coconut. Bake another 30 minutes and remove from oven. Stir in raisins and dried cranberries (or cherries). Allow mixture to cool for at least an hour, then place in sealed containers.

Lord, help me to fill my children's stomachs, but most of all their hearts, minds, and souls with all the love and goodness you brought to our world.

Thank God for his Son—his Gift too wonderful for words.   2 CORINTHIANS 9:15

DECEMBER 26

During one Christmas vacation when I was a little girl, my family and I awoke to the sight of ice hanging heavy on the trees in glorious snowflake patterns. The ice hung on the power lines so heavily that a few of them had snapped.

Silence greeted us that morning. No radio. No furnace sounds coming from the utility room. Not even the hum of the electric clock in the living room. Without electricity we couldn't heat the house, cook, or even get water back into the toilet after it was flushed.

But those few days were the most special of my life, because we were forced to depend on each other for survival and for entertainment. Dad hauled water in buckets from a neighbor's house down the road that had a well and a hand pump. He kept the fireplace going and the wood pile stocked. Mother created fascinating meals, cooked over the open fire.

In the evening, after Dad lit antique kerosene lamps so we could recognize each other in the dark, we read, played games ,and popped popcorn. Mom and Dad told stories about their childhood that we'd never heard before ... stories about a time when electricity in a home had been a luxury, not a necessity.

Today after I start the dishwasher, fix a snack in the microwave, load the clothes washer, turn on the lights, turn up the heat, turn off my computer, turn on the TV, and sit back to relax, I'm going to remember those three wonderful days, forty years ago, when we depended on each other for our warmth.

Maybe I won't turn on the TV after all. Maybe the children and I will play Scrabble or Monopoly instead. Or I could tell them about the time ... .

Lord, during this holiday season as we gather with loved ones help us to capture the warmth and togetherness of days gone by.

Your words are a flashlight to light the path ahead of me, and keep me from stumbling.   PSALMS 119:105

New Year's Eve will be here soon. As a single parent, why not plan a special evening at home with your children, your friends, and some of your children's friends? It could be a "bundling party," which is a sort of old-fashioned slumber party.

In eighteenth and nineteenth century rural New England and northern Europe, "bundling" was simply two or more unrelated people sleeping in the same bed together with all of their clothes on. Some say the custom began because of the scarcity of beds and lack of heat in their homes. Husbands and parents frequently permitted travelers to bundle with themselves and their wives and daughters as a way to keep everyone warm.

Public inns permitted several unassociated guests to bundle and sleep together in one bed as long as everyone kept all their clothes on for the sake of warmth and modesty.

Bundling was even a part of the dating ritual in early America. After all the chores were done a young man might walk five miles to visit his intended. Instead of wasting candles and firewood, the young couple would bundle and get to know one another under the downy coverlet of a good featherbed, usually in the same room where the parents slept.

This New Year's Eve it could be fun. Just toss lots of pillows, sleeping bags, and covers on the floor of the family room, pop lots of popcorn, dim the lights, pop in a video or pull out the board games, and party till the wee hours. When the little ones tire, they can "bundle" together on the floor … and so can the older ones later on.

Who knows, the "bundling" party at your house could be the start of an annual New Year's Eve custom. Hugs to you all! Sleep well. Sleep warm.

Lord, thank you for cold winter nights, warm cocoa, downy comforters, and lots of loved ones to cuddle with.

Also, on a cold night, two under the same blanket gain warmth from each other, but how can one be warm alone? ECCLESIASTES 4:11

DECEMBER 28

Every winter, after every snowstorm, my neighbor Cary snow-blows my long, double-wide driveway after he does his own. Shortly after the second or third snow, I dash out to buy Cary a gift certificate at a nearby department store.

"Cary, you have no idea how I appreciate your snowblowing my driveway. It would take me all day to do it by hand!"

"But Pat," Cary objects, "you don't need to get me anything. I like doing it. It's good exercise." He grins.

A few days later Cary's wife or one of their children appears at my door with homemade cookies or another treasure wrapped in holiday paper.

"Linda," I say. "You don't have to get me anything!"

"Every winter you let our children sled down the hill in your yard. You don't have to let them do that," she says almost apologetically.

And so it goes, every winter, usually around the holidays. We're good neighbors to each other. But I know Cary would snowblow my driveway even if I didn't buy him anything. And I would certainly let the children play on my hill, even if I never received a gift from them.

It's sort of the way single parenthood works at Christmastime. Our children love us and need us. We love them and take care of them. But if, one year, your child doesn't give you a present wrapped in holiday paper, don't feel bad. Remember, it takes another adult to help a child get to the store, pick out a gift, pay for it, and get it wrapped. And if there's no adult around to help them, don't sweat it. That special love, gilded with daily actions, that you share with your child is the critical part, not silly presents wrapped in paper.

Lord, help me teach my children the real meaning of this season by encouraging them to "show" their love with actions rather than gifts.

Pride and trust should be in the living God who always richly gives us all we need for our enjoyment.
1 TIMOTHY 6:17

DECEMBER 29

It hadn't been a good week. I'd just spent the weekend in a distant city visiting my daughter and her husband, who were on the verge of separating for the second time in two years.

The next day one of my dearest friends, Gail, stopped by to tell me that both of her adult children, who had just graduated from college, were moving away to start their careers. Her daughter was moving to Italy! And perhaps because of the empty-nest feeling or the middle-age blues or whatever, Gail and her husband were having some marriage problems.

That afternoon, I had my first mammogram in four years, and the next day the radiologist's office called to say that they'd found masses in both breasts and could I come back in a week for additional X-rays and an ultrasound?

Then my friend, Ellen, called to tell me that a wonderful woman who'd been a founding member of our writer's group had died of cancer in Arizona the day before.

As I said, it was not a good week.

As I stormed heaven with prayers for my friends and tried to expel the nightmarish fear welling up inside me because of the bad mammogram, I got a call from my friend Linda, who simply told me to read Psalm 91. "Just read it carefully. Hold it close to your heart and stop worrying … completely."

I read Psalm 91, then immediately knelt down in the living room and simply said, "God I give it all to you. I will not worry anymore. I trust you completely to protect me and my friends and family. Thank you."

Today, I give you Psalm 91. You know what I did? I typed Psalm 91, then covered it with clear adhesive paper. I keep it in my purse so I can use it to provide comfort to anyone I meet who's not having a good day.

Lord, thank you for your words that are so very comforting, words that allow my faith to grow.

We live within the shadow of the Almighty, sheltered by the God who is above all gods.

This I declare, that he alone is my refuge, my place of safety; he is my God, and I am trusting him. For he rescues you from every trap, and protects you from the fatal plague. He will shield you with his wings! They will shelter you. His faithful promises are your armor. Now you don't need to be afraid of the dark any more, nor fear the dangers of the day; nor dread the plagues of darkness, nor disasters in the morning.

Though a thousand fall at my side, though ten thousand are dying around me, the evil will not touch me. I will see how the wicked are punished but I will not share it. For Jehovah is my refuge! I choose the God above all gods to shelter me. How then can evil overtake me or any plague come near? For he orders his angels to protect you wherever you go. They will steady you with their hands to keep you from stumbling against the rocks on the trail. You can safely meet a lion or step on poisonous snakes, yes, even trample them beneath your feet!

For the Lord says, "Because he loves me, I will rescue him; I will make him great because he trusts in my name. When he calls on me I will answer; I will be with him in trouble, and rescue him and honor him. I will satisfy him with a full life and give him my salvation."   PSALMS 91

DECEMBER 30

I'll never forget this conversation I had with five-year-old Andrew. Harold and I had separated a few months earlier and even though he saw his dad every weekend, Andrew missed him.

"Mom, Jesus really loves Daddy, doesn't he?"

"Of course he does, Andrew. Why do you ask?"

"I mean he really, really loves my daddy. First Jesus made that Christmas song for him, 'Hark, the *Harold* Angels Sing.' And then there's the 'Our Father' prayer. You know it, Mom. 'Our Father, who art in heaven, *Harold* be thy name.' That's why I know Jesus really loves my daddy."

That conversation pointed out the awesome responsibility we parents have. Our children, bless their hearts, elevate us to an amazing level. Andrew believed that his daddy was very special to Jesus. And he was absolutely right.

Most children think of their parents as being larger than life. In their little eyes we are the problem solvers of the world. A child's parents *should be* the two people that child can count on most to care for him and love him ... just the way God the Father cares for all of us.

You may be thinking about changes you want to make in your life for the new year. We all have days when we focus on our problems. But we really need to focus on being the best parents we can be for our children. We must care for them the way God cares for us.... unconditionally and without measure.

Heavenly Father, thank you for loving me so much and for being there for me 365 days a year. Help me to be a loving parent for my children every single day of this next year and for all the years to follow.

But when the time came for the kindness and love of God our Savior to appear, then he saved us—not because we were good enough to be saved, but because of his kindness and pity.   TITUS 3:4-5

DECEMBER 31

Well, we got through a whole year together—365 hugs. I hope each day has helped ease you through another year of single-parenting. We parents have so much to learn and so much to experience as we do this monumental job.

As this year ends and another begins, just know that on those days when you blow it … yell at the kids, fall into bed exhausted with dirty dishes on the table and unpaid bills covering your desk … tomorrow is another day, another year, another chance.

Most important, we need to remember that time does not stop, no matter how frustrated we are, how far behind we get, or how unhappy we let ourselves become. Tomorrow keeps happening, and before you know it, our children will be grown and gone, and we'll be missing them and wishing we could do it all over again … only this time we'd do it better, right? Well, there's no dress rehearsal for parenting. So make the most of every single day of the coming year.

I wish I could squeeze you in a big bear hug, partly to thank you for bearing with me all year and because I feel as if we've become friends. Because you've allowed me to share my ups and downs, I feel close to you. That's why I don't mind asking you to join me in making a few New Year's resolutions today.

Let's resolve to work less and play more; complain less and pray more; to compliment others more often and criticize less often; to get outdoors more and go shopping less; to be healthier, exercise every day, and take care of us. Let's give our children the gift of our time and stop worrying about giving them "things." Let's hug our children every day and make sure they know how much we love them.

God bless you.

Thank you, God, for the year that's ending and for the hope and promise of the new one beginning tomorrow. Help me to be a good parent, Lord.

I am the A and the Z, the Beginning and the End, the First and Last.   REVELATION 22:13